BOOKS BY JAMES F. FIXX

Games for the Superintelligent
More Games for the Superintelligent

THE COMPLETE BOOK of RUNNING

James F. Fixx

Random House
New York

THE COMPLETE BOOK of RUNNING

Published in the United States by Random House, Inc., New York, and simultaneously in Canada by Random House of Canada Limited, Toronto.

Library of Congress Cataloging in Publication Data

Fixx, James F
The complete book of running.

1. Running. 2. Jogging. 3. Sports—Psychological aspects. I. Title.
GV1061.F55 796.4'26 77–5984
ISBN 0–394–41159–5

Manufactured in the United States of America

123456789C

Illustrations by Robert Handville
Cartography by David Lindroth

Designed by Carole Lowenstein

This one,
at last,
is for my mother

It's a treat, being a long-distance runner . . .

—Alan Sillitoe,
The Loneliness of the Long-Distance Runner

Acknowledgments

I am particularly grateful for the long-suffering aid and counsel of Bob Anderson, Thomas J. Bassler, M.D., Hal Bowser, Ted Corbitt, David L. Costill, Ph.D., Leroy H. Getchell, Ph.D., Bob Glover, Joe Henderson, Nina L. Kuscsik, R.N., Kathryn Lance, John F. Moe, M.D., Jerry Nason, Stephen Richardson, Ph.D., Bill Rodgers, George A. Sheehan, M.D., and Charles Steinmetz, M.D., running aficionados all; for permission to quote a number of passages from *Runner's World, The Jogger,* and *The Physician and Sportsmedicine;* for the incalculable help of my wife, Alice; and, above all, for the indispensable assistance of all those running companions and competitors who, usually without knowing it, offered ideas and inspiration when I could not have taken another step without them.

J. F. F.

Contents

On the Subversive Nature of This Book

The purposes of this book are, first, to introduce you to the extraordinary world of running, and second, to change your life.

If you are not yet a runner, it will show you how to become healthier and happier than you have ever imagined you could be. It will do so no matter how out of shape or fat or old or ungraceful you are, and no matter how many times you have tried other exercise regimens and failed. With proper preparation and a few elementary precautions, practically anyone who can walk can run.

If, as I hope, you are already a runner—even if you are already a very good one—this book will help make you fitter, faster, more knowledgeable, and better able to enjoy your sport's special pleasures.

Whatever your skill or lack of it, this book will acquaint you with the many benefits of running and show you how to share in them. In these pages you will learn, among other phenomena, about:

- The remarkable adaptations the human body makes to training, even in old age.

- Running as a natural tranquilizer.
- Running as an enhancer of sexual pleasure.
- The nutritional secret that lets runners eat foods absolutely forbidden to most dieters—and lets them lose weight while doing it.
- Runners who, without strain, cover as much as 200 miles at a time.
- Heart-attack victims who, with their doctors' blessing, not only compete in twenty-six-mile races but feel better than they did before their attacks.

You will, in short, discover that running has a vast number of beneficial effects, some of which are only beginning to be understood.

I will not be surprised if the foregoing claims strike you as extravagant. You therefore have every right to ask who is making them and on what authority. The answers to those questions will emerge piece by piece throughout these pages, but a preliminary summary may be in order.

One day almost a decade ago I was playing tennis with a friend named Walter Guzzardi. Guzzardi and I were evenly matched, and we always played hard. I was in my mid-thirties and worked at a big magazine in Manhattan. One of my more pleasant duties was to entertain authors at lunches and dinners, and what with too many martinis and too little exercise my weight had climbed, ounce by flabby ounce, from the 170 it had been during my teens to a beefy 213¾. (This figure is absolutely precise. I still have in my files a sobering report, dated November 25, 1968, from a medical institution I went to for a physical.)

Nonetheless, by virtue of ancient reflexes and guile I still played a respectable if roly-poly game of tennis. Moreover—I confess it—I prided myself on my game. That is why I was so irrationally irritated when, as Guzzardi and I played that day, I felt a ripping sensation in my right calf. I had been running toward the left side of the court and Guzzardi, in order to catch me off balance, had hit the ball to the right, away from my direction of movement. His strategy worked. I tried to change direction too fast, and the effort pulled the muscle.

The injury was not serious, and even though I limped painfully for a week or two I never even bothered to see a doctor.

What was striking was the way I felt about the damage. My body had betrayed me, and I was angry. I still thought of myself—secretly, at least—as an athlete. Someone who all his life had played tennis, touch football and Saturday-afternoon softball shouldn't be thus laid low.

So I was not prepared to accept my fate. As soon as the pain had eased, I decided to do some running* to strengthen my legs. The only running I had ever done had been in Army basic training, and I had hated it. I can still hear the voice of a tall, dyspeptic sergeant from Texas as he shuffled alongside us puffing "Hut-two-three-four," just as I can still feel Virginia's summer sun tormenting me and my sweating fellow recruits as we tried to keep up. But because Army running was all I knew, I laced on a pair of heavy boots, went outdoors, and started shuffling slowly along the sidewalk.

I saw no sign that in doing so I had begun to change my life, yet this is exactly what was happening. Although my thighs ached and my lungs burned—it didn't help that I smoked two packs of cigarettes a day—I kept at my running. I very much wanted to avoid another pulled muscle. Three or four times a week I would shuffle a half-mile or so, seldom more. When the pressures of work became too great I would stop altogether, but sooner or later I always drifted back to it.

Eventually I moved from New York to suburban Connecticut, where running was pleasanter. There were country roads, streams and rivers, grassy parks and woods. I stopped smoking—the Surgeon General's report scared me—and I began to run somewhat more. Sometimes I ran with a young neighbor, Ned Tuthill, who had just been discharged from the Marines and was very fit. He ran faster than I really wanted to, but his ebullient spirit cheered me on, and if he didn't press too hard I could usually stay with him.

One day I read in our local newspaper that in two or three weeks, on Memorial Day, there was to be a five-mile race right in the town where I lived. Anyone could enter, even thirty-five-year-old overweight geriatrics cases like myself.

Next day I tried running five miles. My pace was snail-like, especially toward the end, but somehow I managed to finish. I mailed in an entry blank for the race and trained hard, running every morning before work.

The night before the race I slept badly, just as I had years earlier whenever I faced an important tennis match. At the starting line in front of City Hall, I looked around. There must have been two hundred runners, most of them young and lean. Their ribs showed; their cheeks were hollow. But there were also a good many men in

* We may as well dispose of a question of definition right now. Although some would argue the point, there is no particular speed at which jogging turns into running. If you feel that you're running, no matter how slow you're going, no one can say you're not. For purposes of the present discussion, therefore, it's all referred to as running, no matter what the speed.

their forties, fifties and even sixties, and a scattering of women and children. With luck, I might not do badly. The mayor was introduced, wished us well, and then fired the starting gun.

I couldn't believe the pace. The front runners had turned the first corner almost before I had taken a dozen steps. But at least I was not in last place. I kept moving—under a bridge and some railroad tracks, over another bridge that spanned a stream, into a park. Although my legs were getting heavy I pushed on. I looped through the park and started uphill, but now I was slowing badly. Women and children had begun to pass me. Soon I was dead last. Ahead of me those women and children were moving steadily away.

I was discouraged and mystified. Just why had I done so badly? I had tortured myself with all that training, and I was plainly not the fattest, oldest, or clumsiest runner in the race.

I went to the local library and hunted up some books on running. A friend loaned me some copies of a magazine called *Runner's World.** I began to learn what training was. I also learned why, if you did it right, not only would you get faster and healthier, but, in both the psychological and physiological senses, younger. I found myself thinking about running more and more. Not everyone likes it, but I did. I forced myself to lose weight in order to do better at it, and I began to run every day. Friends started to tell me I looked wonderful. No one had said *that* for a long time. Finally, two years after I had taken my first running steps, I even managed to win a minor championship—the Connecticut 10,000-meter title in my age category.

But what I found even more interesting were the changes that had begun to take place in my mind. I was calmer and less anxious. I could concentrate more easily and for longer periods. I felt more in control of my life. I was less easily rattled by unexpected frustrations. I had a sense of quiet power, and if at any time I felt this power slipping away I could instantly call it back by going out and running.

Every runner is familiar with these changes. Though they have been compared with those that occur in transcendental meditation, they are something more than that, perhaps because they are magnified by an unusual degree of physical fitness.

I am steadfastly suspicious when it comes to out-of-the-ordinary psychological states. But even my most hard-headed, skeptical self admits that running has produced some remarkable psychological

* For more about *Runner's World* and its peculiar role in runners' lives, see Chapter 21.

side effects in me.* When I first began to suspect that this was the case, I wondered whether mine was so uniquely private a view that it had no application to anyone else. So I began to ask other runners about their experiences. It turns out that a great many other runners have had experiences much like my own. There is, in fact, an almost invariable pattern of development. Typically, a person begins running in search of fitness—to lose weight and to look and feel better (although an occasional person takes up running in order to find an outlet for unused energies). After several months or years, he or she gradually begins to spend far more time running than the requirements of fitness alone would dictate. Finally, he or she realizes that something in running has a uniquely salutary effect on the human mind.

This aspect of running is what makes this book such an incongruous combination of elements. Who ever heard of a book that dealt with both transcendence and jockstraps? Yet running cannot be adequately or accurately described without giving equal attention to the physical and the psychological.

The main physical benefits (and hazards) of running have long been under scientific scrutiny, while the psychological effects are only in the earliest stages of exploration. Still, it would be misleading to slight running's physical benefits, for there are many of them and they are closely related to its psychological benefits.

The general plan of this book, therefore, is this:

In Part I we will look at the ways running changes you, physically, mentally, socially, and spiritually.

In Part II we will examine the various theories and techniques of running to find out how to search for—and find—the beneficial changes and the improvement that all runners experience.

Finally, in Part III, we will look into the world of running—its mystique, some of its significant people, and some of its odder aspects—to see what awaits you.

There is one final step, one necessarily beyond the compass of this book. That is the running itself, and it is up to you. It is also up to you to decide how long and how far you run—except that, at first, remember that long-distance running requires training. Re-

* One might even say they have been spiritual. The wife of a running friend of mine, asked how her husband reconciled his Methodist convictions with the fact that nearly all races are held on Sundays, replied, "Tom *used* to be a Methodist. Now he's a runner." The distinguished historian Johan Huizinga, author of *Homo Ludens: A Study of the Play Element in Culture,* probably gave as much thought to the meaning of recreation as anyone ever has. Citing the fact that Plato equated play with ritual, Huizinga wrote: "The Platonic identification of play and holiness does not defile the latter by calling it play; rather it exalts the concept of play to the highest regions of the spirit."

searchers who have studied running's physical effects agree that fifteen or twenty minutes as few as three days a week are enough to produce measurable benefits. (At first this may seem like a lot, but it doesn't take much training to be able to do that much.) On the other hand, many beginning runners find, as I did, that as they get stronger and fleeter they want to run more just because it's fun. Many cover eight to ten miles a day, and find the hour to hour and a half a stimulating interlude. But each of us is different, and each of us responds differently to running. You may feel just as refreshed after a mile as I do after ten, so listen carefully to your own body for its unique exultations and complaints. Run as much or as little as you want to. Perhaps, over a period of time, you will want to run more—or less. Whatever you decide, you should find yourself perfectly at home in this book; most of its principles are as applicable to a run around the block as to a marathon.

JAMES F. FIXX

Riverside, Connecticut
Mountain View, California
Sarasota, Florida
Patriots' Day, 1977

A good run makes you feel sort of holy.
—Nancy Gerstein, New York City

Part I
THE WHYS of RUNNING

1

Feeling Better Physically

Running as an Antidote to What Ails Us

One gray November morning I was running along the edge of a lake in Winchester, Massachusetts, a suburb north of Boston. On the path ahead of me was an old man shuffling along slowly, using a cane. As I ran by him I called out, "Good morning!" He returned my greeting and then unexpectedly called after me, "Say, what do you gain by running?" I hollered back: "It makes you feel good!"

What I said was true enough, but it was hardly the whole answer. This chapter is an attempt to do belated justice to the old man's question.

For convenience, running's benefits can be divided into the physical and the psychological, even though the demarcation between them is not really clear. (The psychological lift of running, for example, goes hand in hand with exercising for a certain length of time—forty-five minutes or so.) In this chapter, we will look briefly into some of the physical benefits of running.

Most Americans are in terrible shape. We smoke and drink too much, weigh too much, exercise too little and eat too many of the wrong things. A California pathologist, Thomas J. Bassler, says on the basis of autopsies he has performed that two out of every three deaths are premature; they are related to what he calls loafer's heart, smoker's lung and drinker's liver. Thomas K. Cureton, a professor at the University of Illinois Physical Fitness Laboratory, has said, "The average American young man has a middle-aged body. He can't run the length of a city block, he can't climb a flight of stairs without getting breathless. In his twenties, he has the capacity that a man is expected to have in his forties."

What about people who aren't so young? Cureton goes on: "The average middle-aged man in this country is close to death. He is only one emotional shock or one sudden exertion away from a serious heart attack." If that strikes you as overdramatic, for the next few days notice the ages in the obituary columns.

But isn't there a contradiction here? Participation in sports has been increasing since World War II: from 1946 to 1963 the numbers of participants doubled, and a glance at any tennis court or golf course is enough to suggest that the rate of growth since then has accelerated. Unfortunately, only a fraction of the population does most of the participating. The rest of us are spectators. Certainly more than half of all Americans do not exercise enough to do themselves any good, and fifty million adult Americans never exercise at all.

The experience of Neil Carver, a Philadelphia criminal lawyer, is typical. Carver is tall, rangy and sturdily built, but at thirty-three he was out of shape. "I was carrying my two kids upstairs one night to put them to bed," he told me. "I got so winded I could hardly breathe. I said to myself, I've got to do something about this." Carver started running. Today, seven or eight years later, he has not only competed in an eight-mile race but spends part of every summer climbing with his wife and children in New Hampshire's rugged Presidential Range.

Even American kids are out of shape. In one Massachusetts school only eight fifth-graders out of a class of fifty-two were fit enough to earn presidential physical fitness awards. In a class in Connecticut, only two students out of forty qualified. Not long ago a study at Massachusetts General Hospital showed that 15 percent of 1,900 seventh-graders had high cholesterol levels and 8 percent had high blood pressure. (Both conditions are associated with an increased likelihood of heart attacks and strokes.) Nor, despite our growing interest in sports, is our children's physical fitness getting any better. When 12,000,000 youngsters ten to seventeen years old were tested by the University of Michigan for the U.S. Office of

Education, strength, agility and speed showed no improvement over a ten-year period. (The one exception: Girls had slightly more endurance.)

The very people we might reasonably look to for guidance—physicians—are in no better shape than the rest of us. In Southern California not long ago, fifty-eight doctors were given physical exams. Most were found to be in poor physical condition. One out of five smoked; two out of three were overweight; one in four had high blood pressure; one in five had an abnormal electrocardiogram while exercising; more than half had high serum lipid levels.* Their condition may reflect the attitude of a young physician friend of mine who smokes heavily. "I don't worry about lung cancer," he told me. "By the time I get it they'll have a cure for it."

The fact that our doctors often don't offer the rest of us a very inspiring example may be because, as John F. Moe, a thoughtful Indianapolis physician, put it, "The problem of physician ignorance and physician apathy are closely tied together. To compound the situation, there has been a great lack of impetus from the medical schools. When I was in school ten years ago, very little (if any) time was devoted to the serious study of physical fitness in the sense that you and I know it. I strongly suspect that the situation has not changed much.

"The underexercised, coronary-prone physician sees himself as the authority on health matters. He tends to reflect to others his own life style and thinks he is giving good, sound advice. Because he views himself as an authority figure, he finds it difficult to accept ideas foreign to his own concepts, especially when they differ radically from what he believes to be sound, conservative practice."

Can the federal government help make us fit? It's not likely, despite the example of several European countries. Although the government undeniably takes an interest in our health—to the tune of about a billion and a quarter dollars a year—it doesn't in truth do much good. "Health problems today are an instructive paradigm of the limits of government . . . ," George F. Will wrote in *Newsweek*. "It is to be prayerfully hoped, but not reasonably expected, that some political leader will find the gumption to blurt out the melancholy truth: each additional dollar spent on medical care is producing a declining marginal benefit."

If neither our doctors nor the government can be expected to bring us good health, to whom can we look? The answer is plain: to ourselves. This conclusion received support not long ago from Dr. John H. Knowles, president of the Rockefeller Foundation. Noting

* Serum lipids include such substances as cholesterol and triglycerides. Both are strongly implicated in heart disease.

that many Americans regard "sloth, gluttony, alcoholic intemperance, reckless driving, sexual frenzy and smoking" as constitutional rights and expect government to pay for the consequences, Knowles argued that this attitude—and the kind of medical system it produces—will inevitably lead to higher costs. The next major breakthrough in medicine, he predicted, will come through changes in the way we live, not through anything doctors, hospitals or drugs can do for us.

An easy way to effect a favorable change in your way of living is by running. Running is one of the best exercises there is, and certainly the simplest. When, for example, workers in a Soviet factory took up running, they reduced the number of days lost annually through sickness from 436 to 42. Furthermore, studies have shown that practically everyone benefits from the sport. At the University of Michigan's Physical Performance Research Laboratory, Drs. Merle L. Foss, Richard M. Lampman and David Schteingart have demonstrated that even extremely overweight people can significantly improve their physical condition in as little as three weeks.

The most important single indicator of overall health is cardiovascular endurance, which is what running develops. Of course, there are other exercises that build such endurance—bicycling, swimming, and rowing among them. But only running can be done anywhere, requires practically no equipment and costs almost nothing.* You can go right out your front door and get started. You don't need a bicycle, a swimming pool, a boat or a court. You don't need a track, either; running can be done anywhere. I have run on paths, roads and highways, in parks and fields, and on the main streets of New York, London, Florence and Vienna. You can run at dawn, at midnight or whenever it suits your schedule and your fancy. I have run—and enjoyed it—in snow, sleet, wind and hail, and on the most forbiddingly hot days of Florida's summer. As Stan Gerstein, a runner from Melrose, Massachusetts, told me, "There's nothing quite like the feeling you get from knowing you're in good physical condition. I wake up alert and singing in the morning, ready to go."

Running's physiological values are attested to by the growing number of physicians who use running to practice preventive medicine, in the belief that it's better to keep someone well than to cure him after he gets sick. Dr. George A. Sheehan, a New Jersey cardiologist,† says running "is a physiologically perfect exercise.

* Running shoes, which are all you need aside from old clothes, cost about a penny a mile.

† And a distinguished runner and philosopher of the sport. For more about Sheehan, see Chapter 22.

Running uses large thigh and leg muscles in rhythmic fashion at a personally controlled rate. This is the requirement for safely developing maximum cardiopulmonary function." It is for this reason that Sheehan recently referred to "a new trend in medicine—prescribing sports instead of drugs." Nor is his merely a personal or idiosyncratic view of the matter. Writing in *Sport: A Philosophic Inquiry,* Yale philosopher Paul Weiss said: "Athletics, because it enables one to move from a poor to a better state of being, can be viewed as a branch of medicine, but one which fortunately finds room for the expression of spontaneity, ingenuity, and judgment."

Appendix B describes how our bodies change when we run and how those changes benefit us. For the moment, let us consider only the effect of running on the risk of developing heart trouble.

Dr. Robert Jones, a preventive-medicine specialist at the University of Rochester School of Medicine, cites fifteen factors that influence the likelihood of having a heart attack:

Blood pressure
Activity
Weight
Mood and coping style
Fasting blood sugar
Triglycerides
Fibrinolysins
Cigarette smoking
Diet
Electrocardiogram readings
Uric acid
Pulmonary function
Glucose tolerance
Heredity
*Cholesterol**

Of the fifteen, exercise may improve all except heredity. Although smoking and dietary habits, for example, are not directly altered by running, anyone who becomes a regular runner will probably stop smoking, eat less and eat a greater proportion of wholesome food. Running can therefore significantly reduce the risk of developing coronary heart disease, a fact that has long impressed me, since my own coronary heredity is not all it might be. It can also, as will be discussed in Chapter 20, help bring heart-

* Recent research suggests that cholesterol itself is probably not the chief culprit. Rather, the significant factor seems to be the ratio of high-density and low-density lipoproteins, the compounds that transport cholesterol.

attack victims back to full vigor, even allowing them to compete in grueling 26.2-mile marathons.

While not all the physical effects of running are so dramatic, most of them are equally welcome. William J. Fortner, a physician in Kaufman, Texas, told me that his chronic tension headaches go away when he runs. David M. Worthen, a La Jolla, California, opthalmologist, thinks the incidence of upper respiratory infections is reduced by running. And Barbara Orr, a Loma Linda, California, physician, said, "I love running because you feel so good. It keeps my tennis game in shape—I can get to the ball better—and my legs slim." Benefits like these have attracted to the sport such disparate devotees as Senator William Proxmire, Erich *(Love Story)* Segal, Joseph *(Catch-22)* Heller and Jacqueline Onassis.

Running does some other startling things. We live in an age when it is considered desirable to be young and unfortunate to be old, so if staying young is what you want, running can help. Dr. Fred W. Kasch, director of San Diego State University's Exercise Physiology Laboratory, studied forty-three middle-aged men for up to ten years, checking at intervals on their maximum heart rate, their oxygen-processing ability, the pumping power of their hearts, and what doctors call peripheral vascular resistance—all of them commonly accepted indicators of aging. Through previous studies it was known what would happen to a group of sedentary middle-aged men during a similar period. What Kasch was interested in finding out was what, if anything, would happen differently if the men exercised, so he put them on a program of either running or swimming. At the end of the decade none of the four indicators showed any signs of increasing age, and two of them—the body's oxygen-processing capacity and the amount of blood pumped in a single heartbeat—suggested a decrease in age. (As an incidental side benefit, blood pressure stayed below average, and in a number of cases even declined.)

These scientific findings are borne out by common-sense observations. In their sixties and seventies, runners move with an easy grace not often found in people even two or three decades younger. I have often seen what I took to be a young man or woman running toward me, then been startled to discover that he or she was in fact middle-aged.

Stephen Richardson is such a person. In his mid-fifties, he is tall and lean. When training for marathons he runs as much as twenty miles a day, and he has run them fast enough to be the envy of many twenty-year-olds. Richardson is almost always taken for a man in his forties. (For what it's worth, people usually think I am seven or eight years younger than I actually am. At any rate, they

Stephen Richardson

say that's what they think; it may just be that I look as if I could use a little flattery.) This sort of compliment can, however, have its grisly side effects. Richardson works at the Albert Einstein College of Medicine. Not long ago an anatomist colleague looked him up and down and remarked, "You'll make a fine cadaver—no fat to cut through."

Another benefit of getting into shape through running is that the pleasure of sex, for both men and women, is invariably heightened. The reason is not at all mysterious. Being in good physical condition involves not just muscles, the heart and the lungs but all the senses as well. Runners are more aware of themselves and of others and are able to participate more fully in all aspects of life, including the sexual.

Despite its proven effect on physical vigor and the aging process, however, running has not yet been shown to make people live longer,* though in all likelihood, as Chapter 4 suggests, it will one day be demonstrated that it does exactly that. After all, it has already been proved that physically active rats live 25 percent

* Says Robert Glover, one-time physical fitness director at the West Side YMCA in New York City and a tireless proselytizer of running: "We don't guarantee to add years to your life, but we will add life to your years."

longer than sedentary ones. If a longevity effect is someday demonstrated, it will not have to be a large one to pay a significant dividend. Suppose, for example, you run a half-hour a day from age twenty to age sixty-eight, a span of forty-eight years. You will then have spent a full year running. If as a result of running, your life lasts a year and a day longer, every minute of your running time will have been returned to you—along with a twenty-four-hour dividend!

Unlike many other physical activities, running qualifies as what the American Medical Association calls a lifetime sport—one that can be participated in long after contact sports have become too hazardous.

Running helps your entire body feel better—not just your legs and lungs. When you run regularly you feel lithe, springy and energetic. You have a sense of power obtainable from few other sources. Furthermore, an easy run of a few miles can cure minor indispositions—a headache, an upset stomach, a hangover. Once, when a friend told me he wasn't feeling well, I asked him whether he was going to see a doctor. "Running is my doctor," he replied.

This comment contains a profound truth. Dale O. Nelson, who teaches physical fitness at Utah State University, told me recently about a forty-five-year-old student of his named Quintin Snow. A former Army pilot, Snow had undergone surgical removal of one-third of his stomach. He weighed 221 pounds, could barely climb out of a swimming pool, and suffered from assorted medical problems. Snow joined Nelson's physical fitness class, started running, and within three and a half months had lost forty pounds and had recovered from many of his ailments. At last report he could run six miles without stopping.

The list of disorders that can be helped by running is a long one. A University of Oklahoma graduate student named Mike Levine has cerebral palsy. In spite of it, he completed the Artesia, New Mexico, marathon, taking first place in the college and university division and in the process giving his self-confidence an incomparable lift. His father, Jack Levine, a Brooklyn orthopedic surgeon, told me that "running has played a vital role in Mike's life. The change in his self-image permitted him to expand what had been an extremely circumscribed social life."

A Stanford University researcher, Peter D. Wood, argues that running helps prevent cancer, at least indirectly, because runners almost never smoke. "For reasons not entirely clear," says Wood, "smokers who become runners always quit smoking."

Most important, though, running is fun. Many of us have been brought up to feel that any physical effort must be made out of a sense of duty, not for the fun in it. The armed forces' conditioning programs certainly make us feel that way, as do most physical training programs in our schools and, in the opinion of many, Kenneth Cooper's forbidding and joyless aerobics charts: you run so far in so many minutes simply to earn aerobics points. But if you miss the pleasure in running you miss its essence. Imagine an autumn day. The air is crisp and filled with bright, swirling leaves. I head out my door, down a hill, through a park, and along a road that leads to wood-chip trails and broad beaches. I am stiff and creaky as I start, but within a few minutes I begin to sweat lightly and my stride smoothes out. Pheasants, rabbits and chipmunks scatter at the sound of my footsteps. I reach the halfway point, near a flower garden and an old brick wall. Running easily, I glide along the edge of the sea, through marsh grasses and then along a beach. Soon I am home again, breathing lightly and feeling both spent and exhilarated. (Exactly the same thing happens, by the way, to runners who must do their running in competition with exhaust smoke, smog and eighteen-wheelers.)

Any description of such an hour pales beside the experiencing of it. But the experience is—I guarantee it—very much there, waiting for you. This helps account for the growing popularity of running. It is why, for example, there are today twenty-five million runners in the United States (some 25,000 of whom run full-length 26-mile marathons), why at least one chapter of the Road Runners Club of America has quadrupled its membership in the past five years, and why Bob Glover, as charismatic a guru as any sport ever had, has recently started no fewer than 3,000 men and women on running programs.

But the physical benefits of running, as we shall see in the next chapter, are only the beginning.

2

What Happens to Your Mind

Exploring the Brain-Body Phenomenon

Few psychological frontiers are more fascinating than the changes that occur in your mind as a result of running. Profound and far-reaching, these changes provide clues to the intricate relationship between our minds and our bodies. For several months, as I did research for this book, I traveled a great deal, talking with all sorts of runners and other people whom I hoped could supply me with information about various aspects of running.

In almost every case I would start the discussion with a specific subject in mind—running following a heart attack, say, or racing tactics, or the types of muscle tissue involved in running—and for a while we would stick to that subject. But at some point the conversation would invariably slip off into a topic I had not even brought up: the psychology of running. Everyone, it seemed, was secretly interested in—in a surprising number of cases obsessed by—what goes on in runners' minds and how the sport changes people. I found this such a curious phenomenon that I finally asked Joe Henderson, the editor of *Runner's World* and a man who has thought as deeply as anyone alive about the running process, what he made of it. "I'm not surprised," he told me. "I think the mental aspects of running are going to be the next big field of investigation. That's where the breakthroughs will come."

I agree. Currently our society puts considerable emphasis on personal development and the maximizing of one's potential. Zen, transcendental meditation, assertiveness training, est and similar movements are all directed at making us fulfilled human beings. Sometimes, to judge by the testimony of their adherents, they work well. Sometimes, however, they do not, and I suspect the reason in many cases is that they fail to mesh with the inescapable peculiarities and idiosyncrasies of individual character. In constrast, while running often alters a person profoundly, the changes all come from within and are therefore tightly integrated with the total personality.

In this chapter I plan to discuss the psychological changes that result from running. First, we will examine some of the emotions runners report they feel as a result of running. Then we will look at the ways in which the psychological phenomena of running work to change lives.

Most of the people I talked with told me they felt they had benefited psychologically from running. This did not surprise me, for I myself have long known that I have. Some of the benefits, as already indicated, are easily described: a sense of enhanced mental energy and concentration, a feeling of heightened mental acuity. (You don't necessarily notice these things every day, or after every run. But most of the time they're there.) Because our everyday language is not often called upon to describe such phenomena, other benefits are more difficult to put into words. To cite only one example, the qualities and capacities that are important in running—such factors as will power, the ability to apply effort during extreme fatigue, and the acceptance of pain—have a radiating power that subtly influences one's life.

The people I spoke with described these phenomena in persuasive and even poetic terms. Their articulateness did not seem to depend on intelligence or vocabulary. As soon as the subject turned to the mental aspects of running, they all displayed an impressive eloquence.

Nancy Gerstein, for example, is a young editor who was working at *The New Yorker* when I spoke with her (she has since left to join George Plimpton's staff). Nancy runs six miles four or five times a week. She told me: "Running gives me a sense of controlling my own life. I feel I'm doing something for myself, not depending on anyone else to do it for me. I like the finiteness of my runs, the fact that they have a clear beginning and end: I set a goal and I achieve it. I like the fact, too, that there's real difficulty in running; when you have to push yourself to finish a run, you feel wonderful afterward. A good run makes you feel sort of holy."

Allan Ripp is in his early twenties. For years he was bothered by asthma. ("Every gasp was terrible," he told me. "I couldn't think about anything else.") Then he took up running. Although he is careful not to claim that running cured his asthma, he does say that it made it easier to tolerate the attacks when they come. Ripp said: "Running is the greatest thing that ever happened to me. It's the focus of my daily routine, the source of everything. It gives my life a sense of rhythm. It's not just a game or a sport, something *outside* of life; it's *part* of life. It's an adjective—something that defines me."

Ted Corbitt was a member of the 1952 Olympic marathon team, and two years later became marathon champion of the United States. He has competed in nearly 190 marathons, many longer races and innumerable shorter ones—enough, certainly, to have squashed any lingering romanticism about running. Yet when I talked with him he said in his soft-spoken, understated manner: "People get a relief of tension from running. It's like having your own psychiatrist. You have various feelings. Sometimes it's joyous. Everyone benefits from running, both in ways they recognize and in ways they don't. One thing that almost always happens is that your sense of self-worth improves. You accept yourself a little better."

Nina Kuscsik is another veteran runner who in 1972 won the women's division of the Boston Marathon. She told me: "There isn't much freedom in our lives any more. Running gives you freedom. When you run, you can go at your own speed. You can go where you want to go and think your own thoughts. Nobody has any claim on you." And Joe Henderson: "Running is a childish and a primitive thing to do. That's its appeal, I think. You're moving like a child again. You strip away all the chains of civilization. While you're running, you go way back in history."

No one, however, put the matter as simply or as briefly as a runner from Millburn, New Jersey, named Mark Hanson. "To run is to live," he told me. "Everything else is just waiting."

Hanson is not the only person who equates running with living fully. As I talked with people all over the country I discovered that many of them thought of their running hours as their happiest, partly because running is such a powerful antidote to anxiety, depression and other unpleasant mental states. A Brooklyn, New York, runner named Monte Davis told me: "Running long and hard is an ideal antidepressant, since it's hard to run and feel sorry for yourself at the same time. Also, there are those hours of clear-headedness that follow a long run." Beth Richardson, a Boston runner, said, "I feel less cranky and bitchy when I run." A witty Sarasota, Florida, newspaper columnist named Bill Copeland, whose bon mots are often quoted in *Reader's Digest* and elsewhere, spoke evocatively about running on the beach: "As you run, you sink your bare feet into the moistly yielding sand along the surf and invoke the known benefit of sole massage, the next best thing to soul massage for curing the uglies." Finally, another New Jersey runner, Russel Gallop, said, "Several years after college I was struck with both a failing marriage and a leg injury. I had to face a psychologically debilitating divorce and the physical limitations that come with knee surgery. I was in a physical and psychological rut. Running seemed a logical way to get my knee back to its normal function. The unexpected dividend was that I got my head together, too."

The feelings these runners describe have been scientifically documented. Richard Driscoll, a psychologist at Eastern State Psychiatric Hospital in Knoxville, Tennessee, found that running makes people less anxious, particularly if they think pleasant thoughts as they work out. Dr. Michael B. Mock of the National Heart, Lung and Blood Institute told me that "in a society where for many reasons there is a tendency for a large majority of people to have depression, exercise has been found to counter depressed feelings by increasing one's feeling of self-esteem and independence." I even came across one psychiatrist, Dr. John Greist of the University of Wisconsin, who, having assigned a group of abnormally depressed patients to either a ten-week running program or ten weeks of traditional psychotherapy, found the running to be more effective.

The sense of well-being that comes with running is corroborated by still other observers. Dr. Fredrick D. Harper of Howard University's School of Education reports on a semester-long research project designed to assess, among other things, the psychological changes that occurred when students worked their way up from a quarter-mile to several miles of running. Among the results reported by the participants were decreased anxiety, greater sexual appreciation and a better feeling about themselves—including, in Dr. Harper's words, "positive feelings about their body." He also reports on some side effects of the project: "By jogging on the athletic track, the students were subject to spectators, including the football team, which practiced around the same time. Some of the girls felt self-conscious in the beginning because of wisecracks from male bystanders. At the end of the jogging project, the girls

had gained respect for their ability and perseverance in getting up to a distance of four and five miles. Some of the football players even commented that the joggers inspired them to practice harder."

The same diminution of anxiety cited by Dr. Harper and others has also been reported in a study carried out by Dr. Herbert A. deVries of the University of Southern California's School of Medicine and Gene M. Adams of the same university's Gerontology Center. DeVries and Adams solicited volunteers from a retirement community, Leisure World, at Laguna Hills, California. The volunteers ranged in age from fifty-two to seventy, and all had such symptoms as nervous tension, sleeplessness, irritability, continual worry and feelings of panic in everyday situations. The researchers tested the volunteers after 400-milligram doses of meprobamate, a widely used tranquilizer; after taking an identical-looking placebo; and after exercising moderately for fifteen minutes. The exercise, it turned out, reduced the volunteers' tension more effectively than the tranquilizer did.* Dr. Terence Kavanagh, medical director of the Toronto Rehabilitation Center in Canada, asserts that most

* Even without the benefit of a formal study, most runners come to value the tranquilizing effect of their sport. Robert Gene Fineberg of Beaverton, Oregon, reports: "My vocation, market analysis, keeps me under extreme pressure each day, but nothing seems too big when I know that these miles after work will be as smooth as silk. Running gives the mind a boost worth all the tranquilizers in the world." Similarly, Dr. Stephen D. Storey, an orthopedic surgeon in Salinas, California, said: "I find that running allows me to escape from the numerous pressures of private practice. I usually do my running during the noon hour, and I feel much less hassled during the afternoon. I have been through a transcendental meditation program and for a period of time meditated regularly. Running has much the same effect on me as TM."

heart patients in his running program report "a great improvement in mood and morale." And Dr. Alan Clark of St. Joseph's Infirmary in Atlanta says, "It is well known that exercise is the best tranquilizer. I refuse to medicate patients with simple neurotic anxiety until they give aerobic exercises an adequate trial."

In a classic study at Purdue University, sixty middle-aged faculty and staff members, all of them in sedentary jobs, participated in a four-month exercise program consisting chiefly of running. Their personalities were evaluated, both before and after the program, by a standard test, the Cattell 16 Personality Factor Questionnaire. As they became more fit, the subjects were found to become more emotionally stable, more self-sufficient, more imaginative and more confident.

While I was looking into the mental dimensions of running, I noticed that many writers have in fact been circling the subject for some time. Roger Bannister, the first person ever to run a mile in less than four minutes, once wrote:

> I can still remember quite vividly a time when as a child I ran barefoot along damp, firm sand by the seashore. The air there had a special quality, as if it had a life of its own. The sound of breakers on the shore shut out all others, and I was startled and almost frightened by the tremendous excitement a few steps could create. It was an intense moment of discovery of a source of power and beauty that one previously hardly dreamt existed. . . . The sense of exercise is an extra sense, or perhaps a subtle combination of all the others.

Another runner, a woman, says: "My jogging is very symbolic of my active participation in my life." And still another woman runner, Annette McDaniels of Bethesda, Maryland: "I experience a complete unification of body and mind."

Finally, a runner named David Bradley, writing in New York's *Village Voice,* describes one of his runs in these words:

> I am producing alpha brain waves. I am hurting far more than most people ever do unless they are sick or injured, yet feel relaxed, almost happy. I am deeply inside myself and yet totally aware of my surroundings. . . . I no longer touch the ground: I am moving through the air, floating. The incline is not a hill, it is just air that is a little thicker, and I can breathe deeply and draw myself up without effort. My body is producing draughts of a hormone called epinephrine, which researchers have linked with feelings of euphoria. This, combined with the alpha waves and the repetitive motion of running which acts as a sort of mantra, makes me higher than is legally possible in any other way.

Many of the states these people describe are, of course, much like those that occur occasionally in the lives of all of us, whether we run or not. The important difference is that running makes them more predictable; if you are a runner, you can summon them whenever you want to.

Some runners even argue that running brings about mental states so remote from those of everyday life as to be unimaginable to most of us. The founder of Esalen, Michael Murphy, says many athletes are "closet mystics," people who have had paranormal experiences during competition.* And Mike Spino, Esalen's sports director, has written: "Running . . . can be a way of discovering our larger selves. I am finding that average people as well as superstars touch spiritual elements when they least expect it."

New Zealand's John Walker, who as I write this is history's fastest miler (3:49.4), has in these remarkable words described his victory in an Olympic 1,500-meter race: "When I hit the front I got a flash of compelling certainty. I didn't look over my shoulder, but I sensed someone coming up on me fast. And I knew it was Rick Wohlhuter of the United States, even though I couldn't see who it was. I just knew it. I was already at full stretch. But I went into a sort of mental overdrive, and my subconscious mind took over completely. I've experienced it in races before, and I can't explain it. I burned Wohlhuter off."

In rereading William James's *Varieties of Religious Experience* not long ago, I was struck by how similar runners' language was to that of many of the mystics whose minds James explores. And is it pure accident that, as mentioned earlier, more races are held on Sunday mornings than at any other time? Probably so. Yet it is not difficult to find explicit references to the religious qualities of running. A thirty-year-old runner in Arizona, Coreen Nasenbeny, told me of having become a "true convert" to running in 1976. Then she added: "And I don't think I'm far off in equating my experience with a conversion."

Significantly, no one has yet undertaken a comprehensive investigation of the mental changes that occur as a result of running. Although several writers—Roger Bannister, Joe Henderson, George Sheehan and the psychiatrist Thaddeus Kostrubala prominent among them—have touched upon the subject, no one has yet attempted a full-scale description of the mental phenomena associated with running. In *The Madness in Sports,* Arnold R. Beisser suggests a reason for the neglect: "The reluctance to penetrate into comprehending the meaning of sports is understandable. We prefer not to know too much about what we treasure. . . . The lover of a beautiful woman protects his cherished concept of her from any-

* A professional football player, for example, has described a game in which all the players were inexplicably surrounded by "auras." By looking at a player's aura, he reported, he could tell which way the man was planning to move.

thing which may detract from her beauty. 'Better let well enough alone,' he feels. This is the prevailing attitude of Americans toward their love affair with sports."

Nonetheless, a few adventurous thinkers have tried to figure out what it is about sports that tugs at us so strongly. Let us see how much light their thoughts shed on the running experience.

Any decently thorough inquiry into the meaning of sport will eventually bring us to the source of much of present-day thinking on the matter: Johan Huizinga's profound *Homo Ludens: A Study of the Play Element in Culture,* mentioned earlier. Published in 1949, the book argues that man is not best defined as *Homo sapiens* (man the wise) or *Homo faber* (man the maker) but as *Homo ludens* (man the game player). This is so, Huizinga says, because we have a propensity for turning all aspects of life, no matter how serious, into games. Beethoven, writing his Fifth Symphony, was playing a game. Faulkner, writing his complex Yoknapatawpha County novels, was playing a different game. Whether corporation president, general or surgeon, when we are at work we are playing games.

If we accept the idea that our lives are games, might not it also be true that what we call our games are in fact a deeper part of our lives than we may hitherto have suspected? This would help explain the frenzied intensity of the hockey fan, the monklike concentration of the chess player, the scholarly zeal with which some people devote themselves to batting averages.

However, none of this would explain why sport penetrates our lives so deeply. For that, we need to turn to another clue in another book, Paul Weiss's *Sport: A Philosophic Inquiry.* Weiss holds that champion athletes are more than merely themselves; they are excellence in human form. We like to watch a Rosewall backhand not just for what it is but for what it represents: pure, idealized, platonic perfection.* So it is with running, both the running of champions and our own. The champion—Bill Rodgers or Filbert Bayi, let us say—is excellence in human form, and we just as surely are our own excellence. When you next watch a race, notice the expressions of ecstasy on the faces of those who cross the finish line many minutes or—in the case of very long races like the marathon—even hours after the winner. These slower runners have pushed themselves just as hard as the winner and, like him, have overcome fatigue and the agony of too much pain too long endured. In the context of the race, they have become as excellent as they are capable of being. It is a rare and wonderful feeling.

Sport also does other things if we let it. For example, it teaches us

* This is why we care so little about an athlete's moral character or his or her "niceness." In the face of athletic excellence, such considerations are irrelevant.

lessons in human limits. Because sport offers no hiding places, it also teaches honesty and authenticity. In short, it teaches us something about personal wholeness and integrity. And if we give it the respect and attention it deserves, it teaches us something about joy.

These are not lessons in any formal, schoolroom sense. Rather, they are scraps of knowledge received piecemeal through Bannister's "extra sense." Because they are won by so much effort, they are that much more impressive and memorable. In *Leisure: The Basis of Culture,* Josef Pieper remarks that people mistrust rewards that come with too little effort: "[Man] can only enjoy, with a good conscience, what he has acquired with toil and trouble." There is enough "toil and trouble" in running to ease the conscience of the most puritanical of athletes, and this is one of running's clearest pleasures.

The simplest way to understand this apparent paradox is to consider the pain of running. It is possible to run without pain, but as soon as you start trying to improve, pain—or at least some mild distress—will be your companion. Let's assume you are accustomed to running a mile a day. You want to increase that distance, so one day you decide to try running two miles. No doubt you will be able to do it, but toward the end you will be tired and your legs will feel heavy. Then, as you push on, you will feel worse. Pain is the result of a struggle between your mind ("Keep running," it tells your body) and your legs ("For God's sake, let us stop!" they plead).

The severity of pain in running depends on the intensity of the mind-body struggle. If you just want to cover the two miles, you can slow down, ease the discomfort, and probably experience nothing more than a persistent ache. But if you try to run really hard despite the pain—the way you might, for example, if you were battling a rival in a race—it can be fairly intense. (One doctor has compared it with the pain of childbirth: not unbearable but not particularly pleasant, either.)

Yet pain of that intensity or greater is something runners regularly experience. Rick Wohlhuter once declared, "I'm willing to accept any kind of pain to win a race." Still, to assert that discomfort is a reasonable price to pay for the fruits of victory doesn't get to the heart of the pain question. In most races, even important ones, the prizes are inconsequential—an inexpensive trophy or medal, a round of applause. And in a training run the prize is only what you make it—a rest, a long, cold drink, the satisfaction of finally being home.

Why, then, do runners so willingly accept and even embrace pain? I suspect that it is because there is a close kinship between

pain and pleasure. Almost two thousand years ago, Seneca remarked that "there is a certain pleasure which is akin to pain." And Socrates said, "How singular is the thing called pleasure, and how curiously related to pain, which might be thought to be the opposite of it . . . yet he who pursues either is generally compelled to take the other; their bodies are two but they are joined by a single head." In his book: *Pain: Why It Hurts, Where It Hurts, When It Hurts,* Richard Stiller sheds light on the pain-pleasure phenomenon: "We think of [pain and pleasure] as opposites. Yet our language betrays the confusion that can exist between the two. We describe pleasure as being so intense as to be 'unendurable,' something we 'can't stand.' We talk of 'exquisite' pain. From the physiological point of view, agony and ecstasy seem remarkably similar."

The pleasure that conceals itself in pain is familiar to most runners. At the finish line of the 1975 Boston Marathon a spectator named Kitty Davis noticed a runner crying. His face was contorted like a child's, and tears were running down his weather-tanned cheeks.

"Why are you crying, sir?" Mrs. Davis asked. "Are you hurt?"

"No," the runner replied, "I'm crying because I'm so happy."

Perhaps, then, there is in us a need to experience pain, and through it, pleasure. Aside from this, however, a number of other needs are fulfilled when we run, among them:

The need for movement. Watch a child at play. It runs for a while, rests, runs again. Now it runs quickly, now slowly, now briefly, now for a longer time. After we enter school our running becomes more institutionalized. We run a few yards on a football field or ninety feet on a baseball diamond. Once out of school we hardly run at all—our style of living slowly squeezes the running out of us. Yet the need to run never leaves us, and we are the poorer if we do not somehow find a way to keep at it.

The need for self-assertion. In *Science and Sport* Vaughan Thomas observes that we spend much of our lives dominated by others—sergeants, bosses, mothers-in-law. As a result, our need for self-assertion is constantly being pushed out of sight. Running gives us a socially acceptable way of asserting ourselves, of being as competitive—either with ourselves or with others—as we want to be. If at work you try too noticeably to claw your way upward at the expense of your fellow employees, people frown on your behavior. But in a race, improving your position at the expense of others is considered admirable, so long as it is done with at least an outward show of humility.

The need for alternations of stress and relaxation. Dr. Hans Selye of the University of Montreal has been studying stress for four decades. Each of us, he believes, possesses at birth a given amount of what he calls adaptational energy. When that energy is used up, we experience a mental or physical breakdown. One way to avoid such a breakdown is by deliberately directing stress at varying body systems. "Often," Dr. Selye writes in *Stress Without Distress,* "a voluntary change of activity is as good as or even better than rest. . . . For example, when either fatigue or enforced interruption prevents us from finishing a mathematical problem, it is better to go for a swim than simply to sit around. Substituting demands on our musculature for those previously made on the intellect not only gives our brain a rest but helps us avoid worrying about the frustrating interruption. Stress on one system helps to relax another." Dr. Clinton Weiman, medical director of Citibank, one of the world's largest banks, found that employees had less disease—high blood pressure, overweight, and so forth—if they worked under an optimum amount of stress. Either too much or too little was associated with more disease.

Suppose you work in an office and you come home tired, washed out, your energy gone. You dread the thought of running; yet as soon as you start, you feel better, and by the end of a half-hour you are restored. You may have felt tired, but you'll find to your surprise that you weren't tired at all. It's a pleasant discovery.

The need for mastery over ourselves. Too many of us live underdisciplined lives. By giving us something to struggle for and against, running provides an antidote to slackness. "This urge to struggle lies latent in everyone," Roger Bannister has written, "and the more restricted our lives become in other ways, the more necessary it will be to find some outlet for this craving for freedom. No one can say, 'You must not run faster than this or jump higher than that.' The sportsman is consciously or unconsciously seeking the deep satisfaction, the sense of personal dignity, which comes when body and mind are fully coordinated and they have achieved mastery over themselves."

Mao Tse-tung agreed. "In general," he wrote in 1918, "any form of exercise, if pursued continuously, will help to train us in perseverance. Long-distance running is particularly good."

The need to indulge ourselves. When we run regularly we get into such good physical condition that we can afford occasional excesses. Five hundred calories of chocolate cake replace every last one of the calories we burn up during a five-mile run, but at least the balance is zero, not an excess of five hundred. And the effects of an extra drink are quickly burned off the next morning. A runner and actor named Jack Gianino likes to eat chocolate-covered candies while he watches television at night. "They're not good for me," he says, "but I don't care. I run enough to get rid of the calories." Gianino is right; despite his secret vice he is as thin as anyone could want to be.

The need to play. Although many of us virtually stop playing at some point in our lives, we never outgrow our need for it. Play not only keeps us young but also maintains our sense of perspective about the relative seriousness of things. Running is play, for even if we try hard to do well at it, it is a relief from everyday cares. As a result, these seem less pressing. Look at a group of runners at a race. Among them may be a heart surgeon, a judge, an airline vice president, a best-selling author. All of them have heavy responsibilities, yet they are as lighthearted as schoolchildren. When they return to their responsibilities later, some of the lightheartedness remains, for they know that tomorrow there will be another hour of play. Thorstein Veblen understood this phenomenon well, referring to "the peculiar boyishness of temperament in sporting men." He attributed it to "the large element of make-believe that is present in all sporting activity. . . . Make-believe does not enter in the same proportion into all sports, but it is present in a very appreciable degree in all."

Many people ask nothing more from running than this sense of play. For example, Dale L. Van Meter, of Sharon, Massachusetts, exults in the way the world looks when he runs. He described running early one spring morning while on a visit to Manhattan: "I had never seen the beauty of Fifth Avenue before. The streets,

empty of people, were filled with early-morning light. The New York Public Library appeared newly washed and clean. The spires of St. Patrick's Cathedral seemed to stand straighter in the early dawn of that March morning. It was a great experience and one of the high points of my trip." Van Meter's feeling for the sensual pleasure of running is echoed in the words of Janis Taketa, a twenty-six-year-old Fort Defiance, Arizona, runner. She said: "For me, running isn't drudgery but an effortless joy. Fort Defiance is on the Navajo Indian reservation, at an elevation of 7,000 feet. We are in a canyon surrounded by mountains, trees and sagebrush. Running while it's snowing is breathtaking. There are many places to run here, the air is clean, and there is no traffic. You can't get bored running in a place like this. I prefer running while the sun is coming up. By the time it's light, you're warmed up, you've got your second wind and your whole body feels right. It's great!" I asked a Massachusetts runner who took up the sport nine years ago how he thought his life would be different if he had not started running. His reply was an eloquent summary of the pleasures many people find in running: "My life has been much more exciting, much more *fun,* as a result of running. The first bird in the spring, cardinals singing in snow, the perfume of early morning—I would have missed those things and many others. Life is so much richer as a result of running. Running gives me more than I have ever given."

The need to lose ourselves in something greater than ourselves. The appeal of religion and of many mass movements lies, as Eric Hoffer demonstrates in *The True Believer,* in their capacity for allowing us to forget ourselves, to submerge our egos in what we regard as a cause greater than ourselves. Something like this happens in running. Running is such an intense experience, both physically and psychologically, that we shed self-consciousness and live solely in the moment of running. A psychologist named Mihaly Csikszentmihalyi has done research at the University of Chicago on activities that are intrinsically rewarding. Whenever we are involved in such activities, he has found, we experience a feeling he calls "flow." In this state, according to a recent report by William Barry Furlong in *Psychology Today,* "we are completely immersed in what we are doing. . . . the person loses a self-conscious sense of himself and of time. He gains a heightened awareness of his physical involvement with the activity. The person in flow finds, among other things, his concentration vastly increased and his feedback from the activity enormously enhanced." Dr. Csikszentmihalyi's "flow" is a common experience in running.

The need to meditate. Unless we make a particular effort to set aside periods of time, our lives seldom allow quiet intervals for thought. Even people hired specifically for their thinking ability usually become so mired in daily minutiae that they don't have a chance to do much thinking at all. Running changes that. While we run, we have time to follow our thoughts. Phones don't ring; visitors don't intrude. Even if it is only twenty minutes, we can count on that time as our own. We can, if we wish, address ourselves to specific problems. While writing two books on games, puzzles and human intelligence* I often solved problems as I ran. It was hard

* *Games for the Superintelligent* (1972) and *More Games for the Superintelligent* (1976).

work (I'm not much good at doing math without pencil and paper), but if I concentrated, I could usually accomplish something. The kind of thinking I most like to do while I run, though, is just to let my thoughts wander wherever they wish. What is important is not *what* we think about, but the fact that we are free to think at all. Even many people who for one reason or another are not eager to face all their thoughts find that thinking while running is a pleasant and restoring experience.

The need to live to our own rhythms. Large portions of our lives are plagued by schedules imposed upon us by other people. Running offers an escape from that. We can run where we want to. We can go fast or slow, hard or easy. We can run by ourselves or with friends. We can get out seven days a week or fewer. We can think or let our minds go blank. All these choices are entirely up to us; furthermore, we can change them according to the minute-by-minute requirements and fancies of our minds and bodies. "Rhythm is as much a part of our structure as our flesh and bones," says Bertram S. Brown, director of the National Institute of Mental Health. Running lets us adjust our lives to our rhythms. When our rhythms are at a low ebb, we can baby ourselves by running slowly and for a short time. When we feel strong and purposeful we can test ourselves by running up steep hills, by finding trails that require us to wade streams and vault fallen trees, by sprinting until we gasp for air. Whatever our need of the moment, running offers an answer.

If what I have been describing as needs are in fact true human needs, and if they are met through running, it should follow that runners are somehow different from other people. It has already been mentioned that runners *sense* they are different, but is there any way to demonstrate that the benefits runners think they gain are really there?

Two ways evidence might be mustered are by demonstrating that running has influenced specific people's behavior in specific ways, or by showing that where objective evidence is absent, so many people report having the same feelings that giving them credence is justifiable.

As I was working on this section, for example, I received a letter from Dr. Shew K. Lee, an optometrist in Washington, D.C. Lee, who is in his early fifties, started running seven years ago for his health; he had become worried when at a convention he felt his heart beating too rapidly. *My God,* he thought, *I'm not even fit enough to relax!* Here is how Dr. Lee feels now: "Some days I feel so energetic that I can fly up to my second-floor office, taking two steps at a time. My patients sense my new enthusiasm for life and work. They're glad to refer their families and friends to an optometrist with such eagerness and vitality."

Like Dr. Lee, most runners find they have considerably more energy than nonrunners, and this contributes to a feeling of greater control over their lives. Recently Les Anderson, the mayor of Eugene, Oregon, and a runner himself, said, "I feel a lot better generally. I know that I can do more things physically and that I recover from them quickly. I also think my mental processes are better." Jack N. Rosenberg, a New Jersey physician who gives frequent lectures, agrees. "Writing a lecture is easier after a run," he says.

Experiences like these were scientifically corroborated by a study conducted at Exxon's physical fitness laboratory in New York City. Dr. Albert M. Paolone, the lab's supervisor, said that after six months on an exercise program practically everyone reports an increased capacity for work, and a significant proportion say they feel less tired at the end of the day. This reflects my own experience. Before I became a runner I was often sleepy after lunch and had to force myself through a difficult hour or two before my brain came back to life. Now I have high energy all day long, and at night I invariably sleep well.

Most people who take up running find that their morale and general outlook improve. In his book *Running Scarred,* Tex Maule tells how running helped him find his way back to normal living after a heart attack. Of the psychological effect of running, he writes: "Although jogging is not an unalloyed pleasure, it *does* have a very pleasant side effect. I can't think of anything which relaxes you more mentally or eases tensions more completely than a leisurely run. While you are running, you do not worry about anything. It is an all-absorbing occupation. When you have finished, the pleasant fatigue combined with the sense of accomplishment keeps tension away for a long time."

Similarly beneficial results have been reported by the psychiatrist Thaddeus Kostrubala, who was mentioned earlier. In *The Joy of Running* he tells how, when he was in his early forties and weighed 230 pounds, he started running, lost 55 pounds, felt better, and eventually wondered what effect running would have on his patients. As it turned out, running accomplished what conventional treatment had not: "To my own surprise and pleasure, the running therapy opened up a new therapeutic aspect. For as I ran along with my patients, my own unconscious was stimulated. And as we explored the meanings and stimuli for both the patient and therapist, it became quite evident that I could no longer adhere to any stereotyped rules as a therapist. . . . I hold this first group very dear to my soul."

Kostrubala reports on the improvements not just in his patients but also in himself: "We all changed our life habits. . . . Smoking decreased, then stopped for one. Drinking followed the same pattern. My obesity fell away. Depressions lifted. Destructive relationships were ended by improvement or separation. Excessively bizarre thought processes were eliminated without destroying the verve and spontaneity of that person. New friends appeared. In short, the group was successful, and the combination of running and therapy seemed to be the key."

Diminished smoking and drinking are common by-products of running. A businessman named Frank Adams, who runs four to six miles a day in a Connecticut park, told me, "When I used to get tense at the office I'd stop off on the way home and have a couple of martinis. Now I take a run instead." And Dr. Ronald M. Lawrence, founder of the American Medical Joggers Association and a fellow of the American College of Sports Medicine, said not long ago: "You quit smoking in order to run long distances. Your consumption of alcohol drops for the same reason. You simply have more fun if drinking and smoking don't slow you down. Eating habits change because good nutrition is an integral part of aerobic exercises. Your total well-being improves. You sleep better but require less sleep. Your sex life is enhanced. Anxieties decrease and you're better prepared to cope with stress. Work productivity improves. You get away from the television and begin seeing a new world around you."

Another doctor, William Glasser, has written a book on what he calls "positive addiction"—the abandonment of bad habits like drug-taking and excessive drinking through the substitution of good habits. "A positive addiction," Dr. Glasser writes, "increases your mental strength and is the opposite of a negative addiction, which seems to sap the strength from every part of your life except in the area of the addiction. . . . Negative addicts are totally involved with their addiction, having long since given up on finding love and worth. The positive addict enjoys his addiction, but it does not dominate his life." Glasser thinks running is the surest route to positive addiction, an almost infallible way to shake yourself loose from habits that make life more difficult than you want it to be.

Glasser is not the only person to have noticed that running is a powerful enemy of bad habits. Some years ago Kurt Freeman, who is in charge of a rehabilitation center, noticed that alcoholics tend to lack any leisure activities other than drinking. What would happen, he wondered, if alcoholics could be induced to develop an interest in something else? By chance, one of his patients was a former high school sprinter who was interested in getting back into shape. Freeman encouraged him to enter some local track meets. The sprinter's condition improved so rapidly that Freeman started urging other alcoholics to take up running. Today Freeman puts on an annual Alcoholics Olympics in California. In 1976 some 1,500 athletes, both men and women, participated. One of Freeman's first alcoholic runners said recently of his running: "It has helped me more than anything to stay sober, to understand myself, to find out what the good points of myself were."*

Other people have reported still other benefits. Writer and researcher Robert Bahr takes issue with the argument that competitive sports like running encourage aggression. On the contrary, he says, what it teaches is how to *control* aggression. "The next time you're running," says Bahr, "when your lungs are burning, your feet are blistered, and you think you can't go another step, look at it this way: every mile you cover may be putting more distance between you and your destructive tendencies."

Most people who feel psychologically out of tune muddle along alone, doing the best they can by themselves. Yet they may be no less analytical about their problems than those in formal programs. In *Guide to Distance Running,* for example, a Santa Cruz, California, educator named Benjamin Sawyer wrote:

> I find that I do not fit into our culture, not very well at all. I have not been able to relate to the predominant values and modes of thought. Because of this, there has been an inevitable problem in viewing my own reality and valuing it for what it is. Running has helped me enormously in this. When I have slid down into melancholy blackness, my running has sometimes been the single bright thing I could turn to. The beauty and excitement of the artistic expression of running have helped me to cope with the defects of a mass, technological culture that I have been unable to enter on its own terms.

Another runner, Edward Epstein, told me that before he started running ten years ago he was shy and introverted. "What running did for me," he said, "was, first, to build my confidence and then to help me come to grips with the unnecessary limitations under which I existed. My self-confidence has risen to a level where I can set goals that were previously unthinkable."

There seems little doubt that running does enhance mental health, but does anyone know why? Not really, though there are some theories. One is that the brain, nourished by an unusually rich supply of oxygen because of running, responds by calling into play its self-correcting mechanisms. Another is that the body and the mind are so closely linked that when you help the body you

* In a puckish letter to *Runner's World,* Syl Ludington of Naples, Florida, agreed with a physician who had condemned running because he felt it could damage joints. "I have found," Ludington wrote, "that it *is* hard on the joints that I no longer frequent because it is more enjoyable to run six miles after work."

inescapably help the mind as well. You listen to your body and you hear from your mind.*

Listening to your body is not only a technique for monitoring your day-to-day condition, but also one of running's pleasures. Most members of our sedentary society feel remote from their bodies; knowing little about how their bodies work or what they are capable of, people fear and mistrust them. Runners, on the other hand, like their bodies. It is those bodies, after all, that carry them across all those miles and bring them all the pleasant experiences discussed in these pages. Because runners do like their bodies and think about how they function, they learn more about them than most people do. "Do you realize how privileged runners are?" Nina Kuscsik asked me as we were running one day. "We discover things about our bodies that most people, even doctors, never learn. We're so much more in touch with ourselves."

Consider, too, runners' attitudes concerning bodily functions, both those freely talked about and those that are ordinarily left undiscussed. For example, most of us don't think a great deal about how much water we drink or when we drink it. Runners, however, especially when a run is long or the weather hot, must think about this. They know that physical efficiency drops sharply if they drink substantially less than they lose. Instead of drinking merely because they feel thirsty (or not drinking because they don't feel thirsty), they drink consciously, deliberately, for the good of their bodies. They have learned how much their bodies need, and how often. What was once a mindless indulgence is elevated to an art.

Under the stress of hard exercise the functions we don't customarily talk about—belching, spitting, breaking wind—inevitably occur. If they happen when you are in the company of other runners, no one takes any notice. Runners come to accept the way the body works.

In the 1972 Boston Marathon, for example, Nina Kuscsik was on her way to winning the women's division when, at thirteen miles, she had a sudden attack of uncontrollable diarrhea. At the refreshment stations along the course she tried to wash her legs off with cups of water, but she wasn't very successful. As groups of spectators caught sight of her, she could hear their applause. Then as she passed and they saw her condition, the cheering would stop abruptly. "I got a little self-conscious," she told me at a party after

* Listening to your body is something you hear a lot about when you are a runner. Let's say your foot hurts. Should you run that day? If you pay attention to your body, it will give a virtually infallible answer. Simply *try* running on it gently, enough to warm up. If your foot continues to hurt or feels worse, your body is telling you not to run. But if the pain diminishes, it's probably safe to run.

the marathon. "I thought maybe I should stop. But I wasn't feeling nearly as bad as I looked, so I figured I'd just keep running if I could. After all, what was happening to me happens to everybody at one time or another; the only difference was that it was happening to me in public. I'd done a lot of training and I didn't want to stop if I didn't have to." So she kept running and beat her closest rival by a comfortable nine minutes.

A sign reading DEFEAT IS WORSE THAN DEATH. YOU HAVE TO LIVE WITH DEFEAT was once posted in a football team's locker room. Those words reflect our attitudes concerning winning and losing. Although there are indications today of a shift in these attitudes—we seem not to be quite so foolishly infatuated with victory as we once were—most of us still think it is good to win and bad to lose; what happens during the game or the race is of far less consequence. Of course it is not always possible to win. Occasionally, no matter how good we are, we fail—if our goal is always to win. When that happens, we don't feel good about it. We haven't learned how to handle not winning, and when it comes we don't know quite what to do about it.

Running changes our attitude concerning defeat. When we run, even in competition, we compete not so much against others as against ourselves. "You can succeed by finishing last," Joe Henderson said as we ruminated about running one day at the *Runner's World* office in California. "Maybe this is why so many people of small stature are runners. They've always done badly at athletics. Then they discover running. It's something small people can do well at. For the first time they succeed at a sport. So their attitude is 'Even if I'm not winning the race, I'm winning *something.*' "

To learn the meaning of not winning in running is to learn the meaning of not winning elsewhere in our lives. For what we learn through running radiates into the remotest corners of everything we do, making everyday failures seem less poisonous. Perhaps someday the lessons of running will radiate into other sports as well. The time will come, Mike Spino predicts, when athletics will change markedly. "They will remain serious but become joyful," he writes. "Old concepts of superiority and dominance will subside. Individuals who have prepared for an event will see it as their day to experience something special together. The training buildup will be seen as a preparation rite for a voyage into the physical/spiritual world. And we will have some sense that our bodies belong to us but may be a part of a vast oneness, and that each rite we enter takes us closer to our larger potentials."

Spino may underestimate the mud-spattered joy of a hard-fought, bone-wrenching football game. Still, his vision reflects an attitude that can already be seen in a great many runners. I know of no closer feeling between two athletes than to be running stride for stride in the twenty-fifth mile of a grueling marathon. Both know that one will cross the finish line first, and will thus, for the record book, win, but each also knows that his own fatigue and pain are indistinguishable from the other's. This shared experience draws them together far more strongly than their competitiveness drives them apart.

This is one reason runners become, to use Glasser's word, addicted to their sport. I recently talked with a friend who had been training for a marathon when an ankle injury forced him to stop. "I'm feeling suicidal," he told me with a bitter laugh. "I'm going to throw myself out of this twenty-fifth-floor window if this ankle doesn't clear up soon."

And Roger Bannister, though he was recently sidelined temporarily, feels the pull of running just as we lesser mortals do. Not long ago, in reply to an inquiry of mine about his running, he wrote with typical British understatement: "Though I was running five times a week until last year I was then involved in a car accident and the resulting ankle injury now prevents me from running at all. . . . I miss it very much."

Any account of running's psychological pleasures would be incomplete if it failed to mention the ways in which it enhances other activities. My wife, for example, is fond of traveling; to her way of thinking no year is complete without a trip abroad. Running makes travel more interesting, for there is no better way to explore a new place. I have had some of my pleasantest runs along the Danube in Vienna, in the hills above Florence, in the grassy fields near the Avon River in Stratford, along the mountain paths of Jamaica, and through the sheep pastures of Wales.*

The deeper pleasures of running are seldom experienced all at once, nor do they come to those who run only once in a while. To feel the profound changes that running can bring about, you need

* An account of the psychological element in running would also be incomplete without an acknowledgment of the problems running sometimes creates or brings to light. At least one doctor has expressed the view that the stress of too much running may make mental problems more acute. Runners' spouses, especially during periods of intensive training such as occur before a marathon, sometimes feel neglected. ("It isn't easy being the wife of an athlete," said the spouse of record-breaking Olympian George Young. "The season never seems to end.") Once addicted, runners sometimes put their running above all other activities, neglecting family, friends and jobs. A Lafayette College student named Daniel Glickenhaus told me: "I sometimes wonder whether running ten to thirteen miles a day has affected my ambition. My mother worries when I tell her that all I want out of life is to be a track bum out in California, with a job that allows plenty of time to run." Finally, a middle-aged runner told me, not without a certain pride, of an ultimatum his wife once laid down. Tired of changing plans and schedules to accommodate her husband's training, she finally said, "You're going to have to make a choice between your running and your marriage." "That," her husband replied, putting on his running shoes, "is a very easy choice."

to run for forty-five minutes or an hour at least four days a week. It takes that much running for its insistent, hypnotic rhythms to induce what some runners describe as a trancelike state, a mental plateau where they feel miraculously purified and at peace with themselves and the world.

As committed a partisan as I am, however, I am bound to admit that a few people seem simply not to be cut out for running. This has nothing to do with one's body structure; some large-boned people, though they have precisely the wrong build for running, thrive on it. What it does reflect, I believe, is a cast of mind that

---

ARE YOU CUT OUT TO BE A RUNNER?

Runners come in all sizes, ages, and aptitudes. Yet most of them—especially the ones who stick at it year after year, enjoying all its physical and psychological benefits—share certain characteristics. If you're a nonrunner, this rough-and-ready test will give you an idea of whether or not you're long-term running material.

	YES	NO
1. Are you ten or more pounds overweight?	____	____
2. Do you smoke?	____	____
3. Would you like to lose weight permanently, stop smoking permanently, or both?	____	____
4. Have you ever worried about someday having a heart attack?	____	____
5. Would you like to reduce your risk of heart attack?	____	____
6. Do you feel you're not in the shape you once were?	____	____
7. Would you like to get back into shape?	____	____
8. Would you like to feel better about the amount of exercise you're getting?	____	____
9. Would you like to sleep more soundly?	____	____
10. Would you like to be able to get along comfortably on less sleep?	____	____
11. Would you like to feel more relaxed?	____	____
12. Would you rather spend an evening by yourself, or perhaps with one close friend, than go to a big party?	____	____
13. At large gatherings do you ever feel like an outsider?	____	____
14. Are you usually happy when you're alone?	____	____
15. Are you self-assured enough not to mind seeming a little different from other people?	____	____

If you answered yes to twelve or more questions, running is right for you; eight to eleven, you'd probably enjoy it; five to eight, no guarantee but it's worth a try; four or fewer, the odds are against it.

makes it difficult to tolerate running's enforced contemplativeness, its meditative aspects. (To determine your own Running Quotient, see the test opposite.) Dr. Moe, whose thoughts on physicians I quoted in Chapter 1, often encourages patients to take up running, but even he, a dedicated runner, has had little success. "I have tried every approach I have been able to think of," he told me, "and my batting average is still poor."

An overweight neighbor in his mid-thirties once asked me to help him get started on a running program. One weekend afternoon we shuffled through a slow quarter-mile. Since he had not been more than mildly out of breath at any time, I hoped that his introduction had been pleasant enough to prompt him to stick at it. As it turned out, it had not. "Never again!" he told me the next day. "I'm so stiff I can hardly walk. Besides, running is so *boring*."

If you try running and find it worse than a trip to the dentist, perhaps you're one of the people whom nature never intended to run. But you should at least know that many runners don't begin to enjoy the sport until they have been at it for several weeks or even months. So give it a fair trial; if you don't, you could end up missing an extraordinary experience.

Precisely why running is so profound an experience is, to repeat, not fully known. Unlike running's physiology, which is fairly well understood, its psychological aspects have so far been only dimly glimpsed. In the years ahead, much that is new will no doubt come from individual runners as they pay attention to what happens in their minds. This is the main reason that running, old as it is, is still such an adventure. There are frontiers in it for us all.

3

Why Running?

It's Not the Only Sport, but It May Be the Best

Several years ago I was working in an office in midtown Manhattan. One day at lunchtime a friend invited me to accompany him to a health club where he was a member. The club had a ping-pong table, a chinning bar, a stationary bicycle, a steam room, a pool, and weights for lifting. It was frequented mostly by midtown businessmen, and during the hour or so I was there a number of them dropped by to work out. There was a prescribed program. The instructor, a muscled young man named Dan, would have a group of members lie on mats, then would put them through a ten-minute program of sit-ups, leg lifts, push-ups, and stretches. Once finished, they were free to do whatever else they wanted to—lift weights, ride the stationary bicycle, play ping-pong, swim, or sweat off a pound or two in the steam room.

Currently the United States has thousands of health clubs; there are locally owned clubs, nationwide chains, and vast numbers of so-called spas (which are really nothing more than health clubs with a European-sounding name). Men and women of all ages pour hundreds of thousands of dollars into them annually. (In early 1977, a year's membership in a Jack LaLanne health club I consulted cost $195.) It would be money well spent if health clubs really improved health, but they don't—not much anyway. They might make you look more muscular, give you a firmer midsection, and enable you to do more push-ups and lift heavier weights. But in general they cannot make you fundamentally healthier, because for the most part they attack symptoms, not problems. The average participant doesn't do enough swimming, bicycle riding or anything else to improve fitness significantly.

Commenting on a survey of health clubs in *The Physician and Sportsmedicine,* Allan J. Ryan, the magazine's editor-in-chief, wrote: "With few exceptions, the instructors and managers of these gymnasiums and studios were not persons trained in physical education or exercise physiology but salespersons whose principal functions were to recruit members and keep them coming back. Few, if any, precautions were taken in prescribing exercise for the physically unfit and those who had been inactive physically for some time."

Still, people do keep coming back, lured by the promise of someday looking like Atlas or a California beach bunny. In an illuminating lecture on the aesthetics of sport, Dr. Ernst Jokl of the University of Kentucky Medical School projected on a screen a photograph of Mr. Universe in full flex and said, "Look at those muscles. How wonderful they are. But don't ask what they're good for. They're not good for anything. They can't throw the javelin or put the shot. They're just beautiful."

Obviously we need to do something other than visit health clubs, but part of the problem is that everyone likes the idea of getting something for nothing. Fitness in thirty minutes a week, sweatless exercise and drinking man's diets have a mesmerizing appeal. A former Harvard high jumper I know has an apartment full of springs, weights and exercise devices of various kinds bought over the years whenever he was moved by a recurring impulse to get back into shape. But, he admits sheepishly, he has never stretched, lifted or otherwise used any of them more than once or twice. When we last talked, he had his eye on a $325 Abercrombie & Fitch treadmill.

The something-for-nothing phenomenon is so widespread that the American Medical Association's Committee on Exercise and Physical Fitness recently issued a formal statement condemning so-called effortless exercisers. "They do not," said the committee, "provide any hidden benefits or values. Their most serious shortcoming is that most of them do little to improve the fitness of the heart and lungs, which are most in need of exercise today. . . . Real physical fitness results only with regular overloads (in both the intensity and duration) of physical activity."

There is no lack of information on what various types of physical activity do for our health. Not long ago seven exercise experts were asked by the President's Council on Physical Fitness and Sports to rank popular forms of exercise on the basis of how much they help cardiorespiratory endurance, muscular endurance, muscular strength, flexibility, balance and general well-being. Each panelist was permitted to award a given activity anything from no votes (signifying no benefit) to three (maximum benefit). Thus twenty-one is a perfect score. Their findings for selected sports are summarized in the table below.

EIGHT SPORTS: HOW MUCH THEY HELP WHAT

	RUN-NING	BICY-CLING	SWIM-MING	HAND-BALL/SQUASH	TENNIS	WALK-ING	GOLF	BOWL-ING
Physical Fitness								
Cardio-respiratory endurance	21	19	21	19	16	13	8	5
Muscular endurance	20	18	20	18	16	14	8	5
Muscular strength	17	16	14	15	14	11	9	5
Flexibility	9	9	15	16	14	7	8	7
Balance	17	18	12	17	16	8	8	6
General Well-Being								
Weight control	21	20	15	19	16	13	6	5
Muscle definition	14	15	14	11	13	11	6	5
Digestion	13	12	13	13	12	11	7	7
Sleep	16	15	16	12	11	14	6	6
Total	148	142	140	140	128	102	66	51

Or consider, for the same activities, calorie costs per hour, a direct measure of intensity:

Running	*800–1,000*
Bicycling (13 mph)	*660*
Swimming	*300–650*
Handball/squash	*600*
Tennis	*400–500*
Walking briskly (4 mph)	*300*
Bowling	*270*
Golf	*250*
Walking slowly (2 mph)	*200*

Running, it is clear, is not the only sport that improves health. Bicycling, swimming, handball and squash all confer worthwhile benefits and may seem pleasanter to some people. In *Sports in America* James A. Michener writes: "As one who has jogged many weary miles I personally agree . . . that this is one of the world's dullest pastimes." And William F. Buckley, Jr., once confessed: "All I ever managed on those few occasions when I jogged was to concentrate on what a miserable form of self-punishment jogging is."

Nonetheless, for those who like running's subtle and solitary pleasures, there is no sport like it. But forget the fun of it for a moment and consider only its unique contributions to physical fitness.

Chapter 1 pointed out that running can serve as an antidote to many of the hazards of twentieth-century living. Moreover, running appears to confer long-term benefits that are now only beginning to be appreciated. Nathan Pritikin, director of the Longevity Research Institute in Santa Barbara, California, told me that in checking *Who's Who in American Sports* he discovered that the average life-span of former football players is fifty-seven years, of boxers and baseball players sixty-one years, and of track competitors seventy-one years. And Dr. Paul S. Fardy, a cardiac rehabilitation specialist at St. Catherine Hospital in East Chicago, Indiana, reports that in a study of more than 500 people, the hearts of former athletes—runners prominent among them—tended to function better than the hearts of those who had never participated in athletics.*

Fardy is one of a growing number of investigators who are discovering that running has distinct advantages over many other

* He adds, however, that sedentary people who take up a strenuous activity can improve cardiac function markedly, and in many cases perform as well as long-time athletes.

sports. In a recent article in the *American Physical Therapy Journal* he wrote: "Walking and/or jogging is the simplest and probably most popular aerobic activity." And Dr. Moe, the physician mentioned earlier, wrote in a letter to a medical magazine:

> It is hard for me to see how something with such great merit can be so largely ignored by the medical profession. We profess interest in preventive medicine, and we know that arteriosclerotic diseases, especially of the coronary arteries, account for over 50% of our annual death rate. It has been shown in animal and human studies that endurance-type training increases cardiac perfusion, enhances cardiopulmonary efficiency, lowers the resting pulse, and reduces blood lipids. Why, then, is it not obvious to more of us that we need to do endurance training ourselves and teach it to our patients?

Dr. Moe is plainly, and justifiably, a frustrated man—perhaps the price of being so far ahead of his time.

Even if we grant that there are other sports that are as good for one's health as running, there remain good reasons to choose running. One is the time devoted to it. When I played tennis, I was a member of a regular foursome who played from nine to eleven every Saturday and Sunday. What with time for dressing, showering and driving to and from the courts, I was spending six hours a weekend at tennis. Furthermore, I was burning up 2,000 calories at most. Nowadays, unless I am trying to put in high mileage to get ready for a marathon, I run ten miles a day—a total, on a weekend, of about two and a half hours, and even the world's longest showers could not possibly raise it to more than three hours. Thus in half the time it used to require, I get the same 2,000 calories' worth of exercise.

An incidental benefit is that running widows or widowers, if not unknown, are at least rare. Even a long run can be tucked away in some unnoticed corner of the day—either early in the morning or at a time when other members of the family are busy with cooking, homework or other activities. All it takes is some foresight and good manners.

The inner spirit of running is also different from that of most other sports. It can be as competitive or noncompetitive as you choose to make it. In touch football, there's no convenient way not to try hard. In tennis, you've got to try to put the ball out of your opponent's reach. Golfers become so immersed in the game that they tie themselves into tense, tangled knots even during a friendly round. Runners, on the other hand, can run as gently or as hard as they want to. With a stopwatch you can try to run a course faster than you've ever done it before. You can attempt to run your friends into the ground, or you can treat a run as if it were nothing more than a romp through the countryside, bouncing along only hard enough to set the juices to bubbling gently. Even in a race there's no need to run at full throttle if you don't want to. You'll get a good workout even if you run at less-than-maximum speed.

Many runners, some of them very good ones, never race at all. All they want is fitness and the good feelings that come from a daily run. Jack Gianino is one such runner. He puts in an hour and a half a day in Central Park and even when acting assignments take him out of town never misses a day. But Gianino does not race. "I tried it and I didn't like all that hard breathing," he says.

The noncompetitiveness of running makes it a perfect family sport. If a man wants to run ten miles, he can run the first two miles with his wife and children, then drop the kids off and run a second loop with his wife alone. When she's had her four-mile run, he can go bashing off through the countryside for a few more miles.*

Running is also probably the world's most democratic sport. Runners are almost totally lacking in discrimination based on race, sex, age, class or anything else. At a recent race in New York City I saw a cardiologist, an orthopedic surgeon, and a preventive medicine specialist for a major corporation, a foundry worker and a printer, a retired postman and a shoe salesman, a judge, an author, and a film-maker, a Rockefeller Foundation executive and a man who has long been on unemployment, along with an assortment of office workers, housewives, students and senior citizens. If they met at a cocktail party instead of a race I suspect they would not have much in common, but here there was little if any sense of social hierarchy. Running is an egalitarian and distinctly unsnobbish sport, one that meshes with much that is excellent in the American spirit.

I would be misleading you if I tried to force upon you the impression that there is nothing wrong with running. You can be forced into a ditch by a car. You can get Achilles tendinitis or a

* Will running always allow such noncompetitiveness? I have no idea. One reason it is possible now is that distance running, for all its recent publicity, is still a relatively obscure sport. It is also by all odds the most difficult spectator sport. If you doubt this, try watching the Boston Marathon some April. To see a given runner more than once requires not only split-second timing but some breakneck driving and more than a little luck. Running's obscurity gives it something of the quality women's sports have had until just recently. As Paul Weiss writes in *Sport: A Philosophic Inquiry*, "Women are fortunate in that few of their games come to the attention of the public; they are thereby enabled to avoid most of the misconstructions which beset male athletes." Perhaps there will always be a place in running for those of us who are more interested simply in doing it than in comparing ourselves with others. But perhaps not. If running ever becomes trendy, as tennis has during the past decade, might it not become just another activity for the display of machismo? I hope not. Whatever eventually happens, it remains for the moment wondrously free of the irrational, brain-numbing competitiveness that has soured so many people on Little League baseball. But as the mass media give increasing attention to running, who can predict what eventually may happen?

pulled muscle (see Chapter 16). You can find yourself, at five o'clock on a January morning, cursing the moment you first thought of running. (Don't worry; you'll feel fine once you get moving.)

But an even more general—and more serious—charge has been made against running: that it simply isn't good for you, that the harm it does outweighs the benefits. As I write this, the most visible proponent of this view is a physician named J. E. Schmidt, who practices in Charlestown, Indiana. The March 1976 issue of *Playboy* carried an article by Schmidt entitled "Jogging Can Kill You!" (exclamation point his—or *Playboy*'s). In a spirit of fair play Dr. Schmidt starts out by acknowledging that running can help your legs and heart and give you "that tanned, outdoorsy look." But his enthusiasm fades quickly. "The fact is," he writes, "that, for both men and women, running or jogging is one of the most wasteful and hazardous forms of exercise. Jogging takes more from the body than it gives back. It exacts a price that no one can afford or should be willing to pay for leg and thigh muscles or for that specious indicator of good health—the tan." Specifically, Dr. Schmidt says jogging can loosen the linkage between the sacrum and the hipbones, cause slipped discs, contribute to varicose veins, dislodge the uterus from its "perch," produce droopy breasts and, in men, bring on inguinal hernia. Jogging, he asserts, can even harm the heart by causing it to "tug" on its blood vessels and shake crusted material loose, inducing heart attack. Furthermore, he says, jogging can cause such architectural anomalies as "dropped" stomach, loose spleen, floating kidney and fallen arches.

When Dr. Schmidt's article came out, it created quite a stir.

Although no one I spoke to gave up running because of it, there was concern that beginners might be frightened away. As for me, I simply found the article puzzling. I had been a fairly close student of the medical literature on running, and I thought I had a clear sense of what the hazards were. Although the ones Dr. Schmidt cited were not among them, it was, of course, possible that I had missed something.

One day, therefore, I talked with Dr. George Sheehan about the article. Sheehan is one of the world's most widely consulted physicians concerning the effects of running on the human body, having for years combined running and medicine in such a way as to establish himself as the one man to be consulted when you've got a stubborn or baffling injury. Sheehan shrugged and told me he knew of no studies that support Schmidt's views. "He went by what I suppose we would call common sense," said Sheehan. "But when you start using common sense where the human body is concerned, you sometimes are brought up short. The body doesn't always operate the way you think it does. These indictments of jogging are done on the basis of *a priori* thinking, but that's not the way to do it. I'm suspicious when people say, 'It stands to reason.' I think the thing to do is go and find out for yourself whether something does occur."

(Sheehan, who exercises his sense of humor as assiduously as he does his body, told me he took modest revenge on Schmidt after a similar article by him appeared in a newspaper. The article, said Sheehan, was accompanied by a biographical sketch of Schmidt that mentioned his hobby was gardening. Sheehan wrote to warn Schmidt that working in a garden was a hazardous avocation. "I told him," said Sheehan with a grin, "that he might accidentally stick a pitchfork in his foot and get lockjaw.")

Schmidt's criticisms of running nevertheless stuck in my mind, troubling me. If there were any truth in them, no matter how slight, I didn't want to be guilty of ignoring them. So I finally wrote to him, saying in part:

> Your article in the March *Playboy* has, as you no doubt know, stirred up quite a bit of interest among runners. Right now I find myself in the thick of the flurry because I am writing a book on running . . . and in one way or another I'm going to have to deal with the questions you raise.
>
> Specifically, I am puzzled by the fact that none of the physicians most closely identified with running have acknowledged the truth of very much of what you said in the *Playboy* piece, and some have said publicly that there are no studies to support any of it. . . . I would be most grateful if you could tell me your sources. . . .

Schmidt replied:

> ... Let me say, first, that I would not be writing an article for *Playboy* in which I rehash well-known medical facts. To do that would be very boring. The understanding of the relationship between running and the traumata I described—plus a few others!—is now in its nascence, but I discovered it through fortuitous medical events more than twenty years ago.
>
> For centuries, scientists held that the earth is flat and that the sun revolves around the earth. You know of the obloquy that fell upon those who first proposed that this is not so! The physicians to whom you refer are unaware of the jogging hazards because they don't suspect jogging. The loving husband is the last to know about the faithlessness of his spouse. To suspect jogging is outré.
>
> Alas, I cannot go beyond these meager generalities, because I expect to do a book of my own on the subject, and there is where I will present the evidence.

A few months after Schmidt's piece appeared, I attended a conference, sponsored by the New York Academy of Sciences, on the physiological, medical, epidemiological and psychological effects of running. The conference brought together some seventy authorities who for four days, from early morning until far into the night, discussed the results of their studies. Most of the authorities documented the benefits of running, but four or five did mention occasional adverse effects. Schmidt's were not among them. Until convincing evidence appears, perhaps in the book he promises us, it seems not only perfectly safe to run but a smart thing to do.

4

The Longevity Factor

Running's Effect on How Long You'll Live

On June 11, 1958, one of the most extraordinary runners of all time died at the age of seventy. His name was Clarence DeMar, and he had run for almost a half-century, from 1909, when he placed fourth in a cross-country meet at the University of Vermont, until 1957, when he competed in a 15-kilometer race (9.3 miles) in Bath, Maine. He was twenty-one when he first ran competitively and sixty-nine when he retired. During his forty-nine years of competition he probably covered as many miles as any athlete in history. He ran in thirty-four Boston Marathons, winning seven times and finishing in the top ten no fewer than fifteen times, and competed in well over one thousand races in all, more than a hundred of them full-length marathons. In an article published after DeMar's death in the staid and stately *New England Journal of Medicine,* he was referred to as "Mr. Marathon."

Aside from his running, DeMar's history is unremarkable. He was born on a farm in Ohio. When he was eight his father died, and two years later the family—he was one of seven children—moved to Massachusetts. In 1915 DeMar received a degree in applied arts from Harvard, and a few years later a master's degree in education from Boston University. He taught part-time at the Concord Reformatory, worked as a night proofreader at a newspaper, managed a small farm in his later years, and ran practically every day. On the morning of the Boston Marathon he would come home from his proofreading job, look after the cows and chickens, nap for a while, and then get up and head for the starting line.

DeMar's years of running had some interesting effects on his body.* After his death (from cancer), an autopsy was performed. His heart was found to be large, but within normal range. He had some atherosclerosis, but for his age it was mild. His coronary arteries were two or three times the usual size. In its report on the autopsy (written by Paul Dudley White, a great champion of running and a physician to President Eisenhower) the *New England Journal of Medicine* said: "Strenuous physical effort, so far as is known, does not adversely affect the heart. Few athletes have had such a long period of physical effort during their lifetime as DeMar." A doctor with whom I discussed the autopsy findings said simply, "There was no way DeMar could have died of a heart attack. It had to be something else."

If we judge by the commonly accepted indicators of age, Clarence DeMar was younger than his years. His unusual vigor allowed him to compete in races even after cancer was diagnosed. His coronary arteries were large and allowed a free flow of blood. In his sixties he was capable of athletic feats beyond the ability of most people many decades his junior. In many significant respects DeMar was still a young man. Nor is he the only example among runners of a seemingly delayed aging process.

But do runners actually live longer than other people? This is not an easy question to answer. If exercised daily, rats live as much as 25 percent longer than their sedentary brethren. But people are not rats, and responsible researchers are cautious about extrapolating such findings to human populations. There are also statistical problems. Dr. Paul Milvy, a biophysicist and epidemiologist at the Mount Sinai School of Medicine, cautions that it is difficult to prove a cause-and-effect relationship between exercise and longevity. "The criteria for demonstrating causality," he says, "are quite severe and difficult to satisfy."

The history of the longevity question is instructive. Hippocrates thought sports contributed to an early death, and such was the

* In strict logic it is possible, of course, that running had had no effect at all on DeMar, that he was an excellent runner because he already had excellent physical equipment. Most doctors, however, do not believe this was the case.

force of his opinion that for centuries most people held to this idea. Then in 1873 an iconoclastic English physician, Dr. John E. Morgan, compared the longevity of the average Englishman with that of men who had rowed in the Oxford-Cambridge races between 1829 and 1869. He found that the rowers lived two years longer than insurance tables predicted they should have.

This seemed to settle the question, especially when several subsequent studies of college athletes turned up similar findings. In time, however, researchers realized that it might be fallacious to compare the general population with people who'd had the advantage of a college education. In 1926, to nullify this possible source of error, J. C. Greenway and I. V. Hiscock compared the life-spans of Yale graduates who had been college athletes and the life-spans of those who had not. Curiously, it now turned out that the nonathletes lived slightly longer.

The results were puzzling but not conclusive, because the Greenway-Hiscock sample had been a small one and thus might very likely have been skewed. Six years later, therefore, L. I. Dublin used records from the classes of 1870–1905 at eight Eastern colleges to compare the life-spans of 4,976 letter-winners and 38,269 other graduates. There proved to be a three-month difference in life expectancy—in favor, once again, of the nonathletes.

What are we to conclude from this? It is possible, of course, that athletics are simply bad for you, though most investigators do not think so. A more likely possibility is that athletes are more inclined to enter hazardous occupations.* Most studies also suggest that to have been an athlete at one time does not confer long-term protection. One must stick at one's sport if it is to continue doing any good.

But the central question still remains unanswered: does running lengthen lives?

Several recent studies shed light on the matter. Drs. Arthur S. Leon and Henry W. Blackburn of the University of Minnesota reported recently that thirty to sixty minutes of endurance exercise three or four times a week "without question can improve health and quality of life for most people . . . and perhaps increase longevity." A cautious appraisal, certainly, but in the context of current research a significant one.

Dr. Thomas Bassler, whose comments on loafer's heart and kindred ailments were mentioned in Chapter 1, is less cautious. A California pathologist, Bassler has made something of a name for himself by his insistence that finishing a marathon in less than four

* A number of studies have shown that athletes have a higher incidence of violent deaths. Despite considerable speculation about the reason, none has conclusively shown why this occurs.

hours gives years of immunity to heart attack. Although not all of Bassler's medical colleagues agree with him, he does have a wide following. Bassler states clearly that simply running the marathon itself does *not* confer the immunity, but that it develops from 1) the daily training required and 2) the marathoner's customary life style, which includes, among other factors, no smoking and a diet low in harmful fats such as cholesterol. Studies done in Ecuador, Pakistan and the U.S.S.R. of people who live well past the age of one hundred have shown that a high level of physical activity and low-fat diets are significant common denominators.

An unusual opportunity for studying the relationship between continued exercise and aging occurred in 1975 when the World Masters' Championships, an international track meet that attracts participants from thirty years old to over ninety, was held in Toronto. Dr. Terence Kavanagh of the Toronto Rehabilitation Center and Dr. Roy J. Shephard of the University of Toronto's Department of Preventive Medicine and Biostatistics examined 128 men and 7 women participants. They found, among other things, that the aging athletes' oxygen-processing ability declined more slowly than it does in the general population, and that heart abnormalities were rarer. Purists will point out, of course, that this conclusion doesn't take into account the self-selection factor. True enough. The findings are impressive nonetheless.

Another relevant study was conducted by Dr. Fred Kasch at San Diego State University's Exercise Physiology Laboratory. Kasch began with the premise that a key indicator of aging is a person's capacity for work, since work capacity is known to decline 35 to 40 percent between the ages of thirty and seventy. If, therefore, work capacity could somehow be sustained longer than usual, aging would in effect have been delayed. Kasch signed up 43 middle-aged men, forty-five to forty-eight years old, for a ten-year program of running and swimming. As the years passed, the results were astonishing. During the course of the study the men's maximum heart rates declined far less than predicted from data on "normal" men. Their resting heart rates declined because their hearts had become more efficient, and their oxygen-carrying capacity either increased (in the case of the subjects who had been sedentary before the program began) or remained constant at 36 percent above average for age and sex (in the case of subjects who had previously been active.)* In effect, the program had acted as a kind of time machine in which the subjects aged less quickly than their nonexercising contemporaries.

* Both heart rate and oxygen-carrying capacity are closely related to age. The relationship of heart rate to running is discussed in the next chapter.

One of the most ambitious recent efforts to explore the relationship between exercise and longevity was undertaken in Boston in 1965 by Dr. Charles L. Rose and others. They interviewed the next of kin of five hundred men who died in Boston that year, asking hundreds of questions about diet, drinking habits, recreation, occupation and exercise, both on the job and off. In all, he took into account some two hundred factors. Then, using complex statistical techniques, he sought to discover which were most closely correlated with a long life. One of his findings was odd and significant: physical exertion during leisure hours benefited people more than exertion on the job. Furthermore, exertion off the job, particularly during the decade from forty to forty-nine, was among the best of all longevity predictors. An even more recent study, made public in early 1977 by Drs. Ralph S. Paffenbarger, Jr., Wayne E. Hale, Richard J. Brand, and Robert T. Hyde, shows, however, that San Francisco longshoremen who work hard have fewer heart attacks than those who do only light work. The conclusion is clear: If you're active, whether on or off the job, chances are you'll live longer.

Though hopeful, the scientific community remains cautious about making claims that cannot yet be fully substantiated. Until someone does a study specifically relating running not to mere *indicators* of aging but to how long runners actually *live,* it is not possible to say with certainty that those who run stay alive longer. Nonetheless, many scientifically sophisticated students of the subject think that this is true.

There is as yet no single, tidily assembled body of evidence to support such a view. Rather, there are hundreds of tantalizing bits of evidence. As one example, let's look at one of the fragments, a project currently being conducted by the Longevity Research Institute in Santa Barbara.

Some people, many doctors among them, think the Longevity Research Institute is up to very little good. In a long letter to the local newspaper, the *Santa Barbara News-Press,* one physician insisted that the LRI's approach doesn't attack the real problem, that the results are merely short term, and that—in his own words—"the center takes a Band-Aid approach."

All the same, its claims are worth examining. Typically, patients come to LRI for an alternative to coronary bypass surgery, a complex and costly* treatment for coronary artery disease. A coronary bypass involves replacement of arteries that have become blocked by cholesterol and other materials, much as a water pipe is narrowed by mineral deposits. Although coronary bypasses may bring

* One patient reports having paid $25,000; $10,000 to $15,000 is common.

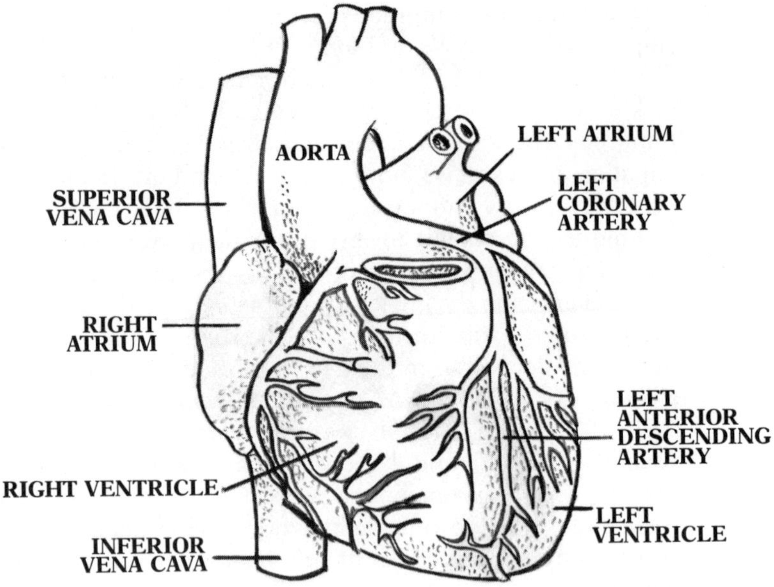

The human heart, with coronary arteries

impressive results in some cases, they are not a foolproof cure; some 20 percent of them close up within a year. The LRI alternative is to put patients on a program of exercise—walking and running—and a rigorous low-fat diet that LRI officials say will clear clogged arteries without the need for bypass operations.

After six years of intermittent chest pains, one fifty-five-year-old patient was told he needed a bypass. An angiogram (an X ray of the heart, made after the blood vessels have been injected with a radiopaque fluid) showed that all three coronary arteries were severely blocked. He started on the LRI's program; in thirty days he was walking four miles a day and no longer needed the medicine he had been taking for chest pains. Most significantly, his cardiologist reported that the disease had reversed itself and that he was now "capable of high-intensity exercise."

The relevance of such cases to the longevity question is that degenerative diseases, among them coronary artery disease, go hand in hand with the body's aging. If, therefore, they can be arrested or reversed, the aging process itself has in effect been reversed.

The LRI also reports the case of an eighty-three-year-old man who had become increasingly senile (the result of degenerative changes in the brain's blood vessels) and couldn't walk without help. Under a diet-and-exercise program he regained his mental faculties and was able to walk again.

Finally—and this is the case LRI officials most enjoy citing—an eighty-one-year-old Santa Monica grandmother named Eula Weaver started on the program after suffering from, among other things, the symptoms of high blood pressure and degenerative changes of the heart and joints. She could walk no more than a hundred feet and had such bad circulation that she had to wear gloves even in summer. Four years later, at the age of eighty-five, she entered the half-mile and mile races in the Senior Olympics at Irvine, California, and won gold medals in both. (The literature is vague about just how good her competition was, or indeed whether she had any, but does it really matter?) The following year, 1976, she won two more gold medals and was running a mile each morning, putting in ten of fifteen more miles on a stationary bicycle, and working out in a gym twice a week. At last report she was eighty-eight years old and still going strong.

Although the evidence on longevity, including LRI's, is inconclusive, most of it clearly suggests that running is more likely to increase than decrease longevity. Fewer and fewer people these days argue that running shortens lives, while a lot of people say that it may lengthen them. If that's all we've got for the time being, it seems a good enough argument for running. Not airtight, but good enough.

Eula Weaver, at 88, trains for the Senior Olympics

I was convinced each day that I had strained the limits of human endurance. Then, gradually, a strange thing happened . . .
—David T. Burhans, Jr., Pasadena, California

Part II
THE ART of RUNNING

5

Getting Started

What You Need to Know as You Take Your First Steps

Running may well turn out to be one of the most significant experiences of your life. Yet it does not always seem fun when you first try it. For one thing, chances are you're out of shape. Not irreparably, but if you're beyond your teens you're probably not in the best condition. Your muscles are soft. Your joints are stiff. Your heart and lungs aren't used to working hard. As a result, you'll feel slow and awkward when you run and will ache a bit afterward. But even if you're severely out of condition it only means it will take a bit longer to get back in shape.

I ask you to trust me. The goal, I promise, is worth the struggle. Within a few weeks you'll be covering a mile or two at a time. After a run you'll feel refreshed. You'll have more energy, more zest. You'll take more pleasure in both work and play. You'll sleep more soundly, lose weight if you need to, and feel better than you have in years.

You won't get those results from your very first day, but there's no hurry. Running isn't something you do only in the spring in order to look good in a bathing suit. It's best when it's worked into the fabric of your life, as an indispensable part of each day. So start slowly. If you read a lot about running you'll often come across the phrase "Train, don't strain." It could be the most important advice in this book. You'll improve just as quickly if you take it fairly easy rather than continually flogging yourself to go farther and faster. Furthermore, you won't get injured as often. That's important, for the fewer running days you lose, the easier it is to stay in shape.

BEFORE YOU RUN

First, spend a few minutes taking stock of what kind of condition you're in. Beginning runners who are badly out of shape or who try to do too much too fast almost always have trouble. Don't let your good judgment be warped by wishful thinking. Dr. Leroy H. Getchell of Ball State University directs a popular adult physical fitness class in Muncie, Indiana. This is his advice for getting started: "If you're overweight, or have a tendency toward high blood pressure, or have a family history of heart disease, ask a doctor to check you over thoroughly. But if you can walk for a mile or two and not feel discomfort or dizziness, and then alternately jog for thirty seconds and walk for a minute and still not have any problem, you're probably okay. If you have the slightest doubt about your health, though, I recommend an exercise stress test of the heart. I don't work with people in my classes or start them out without a stress test. However, if everyone who wanted to begin a program had to have a stress test, many wouldn't start. People under thirty-five generally need only a checkup or the approval of their family physician.

"Most people can start out with just a little activity and gradually build themselves up. If there's a problem, they'll have some indication—chest pains or dizziness or something else.* But they shouldn't feel fatigued an hour after a workout. If they are, that's a sign that it was probably too vigorous for their condition and that they should modify the next day's workout by easing up."

Some doctors are more cautious than Getchell is, insisting that anyone over forty should have a stress test before undertaking a running program. Most people are familiar with the electrocardiogram, or ECG (as it is commonly called). Because it is a record of the electrical changes that take place in the heart with each beat, it provides information about how the heart is functioning. If an

* A few conditions may rule out exercise altogether, if only temporarily. Among them: infectious diseases, recent surgery, kidney diseases, fractures, certain electrocardiogram abnormalities and extremely high blood pressure.

A stress test

ECG is taken while a patient is resting, it does not reveal changes in heart function that exercise can cause. A stress test, therefore, is performed by taking an ECG while the patient exercises. The physician watches the ECG for changes in the electrical patterns that may indicate potential trouble.

Stress tests cost about a hundred dollars. If you're inclined to be cautious, you'll want to set your mind at ease by having one. (They are included in some medical insurance plans.) Some, though by no means all, doctors administer stress tests right in their offices. Or you can go to a professional testing organization like Cardio-Metrics at 295 Madison Avenue in New York City. Not long ago a middle-aged runner I know was evaluated by Cardio-Metrics. Although he had been running for three years and had completed several marathons, he had never undergone a stress test. At Cardio-Metrics he ran on an inclined treadmill under the direction of a cardiologist and was examined by other doctors. After an hour of intensive scrutiny he was told that he was in excellent shape and was in virtually no danger of experiencing difficulties with his heart. As a result, he is enjoying his running more than ever.

If you have no adverse medical history, and no symptoms that concern you, it's probably safe to start right in with some easy running, bearing in mind Getchell's warnings.

Stress test or not, some beginners are more comfortable if they have at least some idea about what kind of shape they're in before they start. One of the quickest ways to find out how fit you are is with the Harvard Step Test, which is described in Appendix C.

How hard you should run, particularly when you're starting, depends on your condition. If you score low on the Harvard Step Test, limit your workouts for a while. Alternately walk and run slowly, and do it for only a few minutes. Two or three weeks later, when you take the test again, your score will almost certainly have improved. That's the time to start working out a little harder.

Incidentally, if you're overweight you'll probably score lower than you'd like to. A recent report by Dr. Merle Foss and three of his associates shows that extremely overweight people may need as much as eight weeks of training simply to be able to walk a mile. You probably won't have that much trouble getting started, but keep in mind that extra weight will slow your progress.

WARMING UP

You're wearing the clothes you're planning to run in* and you're ready to start. Don't—not yet, anyway. Your mind may be ready to go, but your body isn't. It has probably been doing nothing all day, and the last thing it wants to do is spring suddenly into action. Before you start running, you've got to prepare it. This is where warming up comes in.

Some people think a warm-up isn't important. (As you get more deeply into running you'll find that there are diametrically opposed views about almost every aspect of it.) Vaughan Thomas writes in *Science and Sport* that warming up contains a "witchcraft element"—it does some good, he implies, but not as much as is popularly believed. "Physiologically speaking," he writes, "there have been more races lost due to energy expenditure during warm-up than have been won due to the raising of levels of organic function." He may be right. Still, warming up does serve some important purposes, so it should never be neglected.

Dr. Paul Fardy, the cardiac rehabilitation specialist who was introduced in Chapter 3, reports that a warm-up stimulates the circulation and raises body temperature, thus enhancing the efficiency of muscle contraction. "Increasing coronary circulation," he writes in the *American Physical Therapy Journal,* "is especially important in middle-aged and older adults, since myocardial ischemia [an insufficient blood supply to the heart] has been observed at the onset of strenuous exercise without preceding warm-up." Studies by Dr. R. James Barnard of UCLA's School of Medicine support Fardy's argument. When forty-four healthy men ranging in age from twenty-one to fifty-two were asked to run on fast-moving treadmills without warming up, more than two-thirds of them had abnormal ECG's. When, on the other hand, two minutes of warm-up preceded the treadmill runs, in almost all cases the ECG abnormalities were eliminated or lessened.

The flexibility warm-up. Running, as discussed in Chapter 3, rates low in promoting flexibility—much lower, for example, than swimming, handball and tennis, and only slightly higher than walking,

* For sartorial notes and a word or two about shoes, see Chapter 12.

golf and bowling. Practically all runners develop tight muscles, particularly in the backs of their legs. The reason is that the muscles used in running go through a relatively small range of movement and repeatedly perform the same actions. You can increase their range slightly by doing different kinds of running—fast and slow, uphill and downhill—but you need flexibility exercises, too.

If you have enough time it would be desirable to do a half-hour or so of flexibility exercises every time you ran. But which of us has such time to spare? (I'll confess that when I'm in a hurry I often neglect to stretch because I'd rather spend the time running. I hope you'll be more sensible than I am.) Luckily, you can get in an abbreviated stretching session in about ten minutes—certainly time well spent.

First, for your stomach muscles, do some sit-ups with your knees slightly bent to minimize help from the hip muscles. You needn't do them fast, and fifteen is enough, but do more if you want to. (When you start out, you may find it easier to do sit-ups with your arms stretched out over your head. Later, as your stomach muscles get stronger, do them the hard way—with your hands clasped behind your head.)

Next, to stretch your hamstring and calf muscles, lie on your back with your right knee flexed, foot on the floor, and your left leg straight. Slowly raise your left leg until it's perpendicular to the floor and your toes are pointing straight up. Lower your left leg slowly and repeat the whole sequence with your right leg. Stretch both legs this way three or four times.

Now face a wall or tree, put your palms against it, and slowly shuffle backward, keeping your feet flat on the ground, until you feel strain in the backs of your legs. Hold that position for twenty or thirty seconds, letting the muscles relax. Repeat the exercise two or three times.

Finally, lie on your back. Keeping your legs together, slowly bring them over your head and, with your knees straight, hold your legs parallel to the floor for twenty or thirty seconds. You should feel strain on your hamstring muscles.

"A flexible and free-flowing body," the physical fitness specialist Bob Glover explains, "is more efficient and tension-free. Proper stretching before and after vigorous exercise will eliminate undue stiffness and fatigue and prevent injuries. It will also increase your athletic efficiency. Runners will increase their stride and fluidity. Less muscle tightness and leg cramping will result."

If you're over thirty, stretching is especially important. At about that age, muscles start tightening noticeably, unless they are stretched frequently, and as a result, injuries are likely to be more frequent. Jim Nolan, a marathon runner in his mid-fifties, told me: "My daughter came home from college for vacation and I went out running with her without stretching first. I got sore. Younger people may be able to do without it, but we old fellows really need it." Nolan, who is a writer and has a schedule as flexible as he himself is, sometimes puts in as many as ten brief stretching sessions a day.

Incidentally, don't stretch jerkily. When a muscle is pulled suddenly, it fights back and shortens. Only when it is stretched slowly does it lengthen and stay that way.

In Chapter 15 you will find some other useful exercises. For the time being, however, those four will be enough.

The running warm-up. At the West Side YMCA in New York City, where I occasionally run when the winter weather is particularly severe, inexperienced runners sometimes stand beside the track, anxiously watching for an opening. When one appears, they spring into it, sprint two or three laps at top speed, then stop. That's the wrong way to run. First, it isn't nearly enough to do any good. Second, as mentioned, in the warm-up you need to raise your body temperature and increase circulation. Those changes don't occur in only a minute or two. They take time—six or eight minutes at the very least. That's why it's a good idea to shuffle along slowly for a while when you first start out. I remember watching John Vitale, one of the country's top distance runners, warming up before a 10,000-meter race in Darien, Connecticut. He was moving so slowly that a toddler would have had little trouble keeping up with him, but later he covered the hilly, winding 6.2-mile course at well under five minutes a mile.

After a few minutes of easy running you'll start to sweat. That's a sign that your warm-up is taking effect and that you're ready to move a little faster.

WHERE TO RUN

At last you're ready to run in earnest. The important thing is to go outside and *do* it. Many people feel they have to have a special place, but actually any place that's relatively smooth and safe from traffic will do. For what they're worth, a few thoughts on where to run:

I'd be inclined to stay away from tracks, because I find a quarter-mile track one of the world's dreariest places. The chief problem is the treadmill effect. To run a mile you've got to pass the same point four times, and this makes even a short run seem endless.

It's more fun to run in parks or on country roads. Not far from my house is a pretty little park with broad grassy areas, a stream and a pond, two gazebos, and a year-round flock of Canada geese. If I'm just coasting, it takes me about eight minutes to run around the circumference; I call it a mile. I never run for long in the park—the treadmill effect again—but occasionally I'll do a couple of turns there for variety's sake.

Or I go out on the roads, heading either north into hills and undeveloped country or south toward Long Island Sound with its shoreline of woods and beaches. It depends on what I feel like looking at. If you're not fully familiar with the roads and trails in your area, a U.S. Geological Survey map will help.

You'll find that every course has its own peculiar character. Not far from my house is a mile-long stretch of pavement—it's called Laddins Rock Road—that does to me what the poppy field did to the Cowardly Lion. Every time I run there I feel sluggish, but as soon as I'm through it I feel fine again. There's another stretch of road that always makes me feel good. Even though part of it is uphill, I can count on feeling fine there. I can't explain either case.

What about simply staying at home and running in place? If for some reason that's what you want to do, fine. So long as you make your heart beat fast enough (see below) you'll be getting a measurable training effect whether or not you go anywhere while you're doing it. But you'll be missing most of the fun of running—the variations of scenery and seasons, the sun and wind, the pleasure of running with friends. You may find running in place an ideal form of exercise, but you couldn't pay me to do it.

ON NOT FEELING LIKE A FOOL

Some people feel conspicuous and foolish when they first go out in public wearing running clothes. I know I did. I used to wait until I thought nobody was around; then I'd dart out my back door and head for places where I was sure no one would see me.

I've discovered that running in secret is unnecessary. First, most people admire what you're doing. Second, people are generally wrapped up in their own thoughts, and the sight of a runner scarcely penetrates their minds. You're just part of the scenery. Furthermore, the longer you run, the more permanent a part of the environment you'll become. Where I live I'm just one of the neighborhood characters. Children call out cheerfully; adults wave, or if I stray from my accustomed time, remark, "Hey, you're early today." I smile and wave back and we all get along fine. You will, too.

THE FINE, EASY ART OF RUNNING

Do you remember the first time you tried to play tennis or golf? Wasn't it awkward to hold the racket or club the way your instructor told you to? Running isn't like that. Everybody knows how to run. Furthermore, the more you run the more efficient your style becomes.

The secret of style is to run naturally. Your body is a unique biomechanical system. It's different from everyone else's. It has its own centers of gravity and articulations. That's why it's a mistake to imitate anyone else's running style. Just keep your body straight and your head up, and lean slightly forward. Don't exaggerate arm motion. Run with your elbows bent but not held tightly against your chest. Your hands should be relaxed. not made into fists. (Tension in one part of the body causes tension in other parts.) As you run, don't worry about the length of your stride; just do what feels natural. Keep your hips, knees and ankles relaxed. Each foot should strike the ground at the heel and roll forward, finally pushing off with the toes. If this feels unnatural, try landing flatfooted. Don't run on your toes; you'll only get sore calf muscles and possibly strain your Achilles tendons.

Breathe naturally. If you're running slowly you won't need to open your mouth wide, but as you move faster don't be afraid to gulp in all the air you can get. (For some reason many beginning runners have the mistaken notion that they're not supposed to open their mouths.)

As you run, keep these guidelines in mind but don't let them dominate or sour your running. Remember that you're running not just for fitness but for fun. Running is a vacation from everyday chores, a special treat for your mind and body. If you concentrate on the fun, the fitness and style will take care of themselves.

HOW FAST?

If you're just beginning, don't think about speed. Move along easily, letting your body get used to the unaccustomed actions of running. Stop if you get tired, then run some more. Don't strain. A crash exercise program can be just as harmful as a crash diet. You should be able to carry on a conversation while you run, so don't run so fast that you can't talk comfortably with a friend.

As you get stronger, you'll be able to run faster and sustain a given pace longer with the same effort. Only then should you think about how fast you're running.

David T. Burhans, Jr., of Pasadena, who took up running in 1970, told me how pleased he was, after an initial period of difficulty, to see how quickly he improved: "I'd like to be able to say that the process was an easy one. It wasn't. At the end of my daily jaunt I was totally exhausted. I was convinced each day that I had strained the limits of human endurance and that no amount of pleading or promises of future health could possibly move my body any faster. Then, gradually, a strange thing happened. I began to realize that it was taking me less and less energy to run a mile. I was beginning to get in shape!"

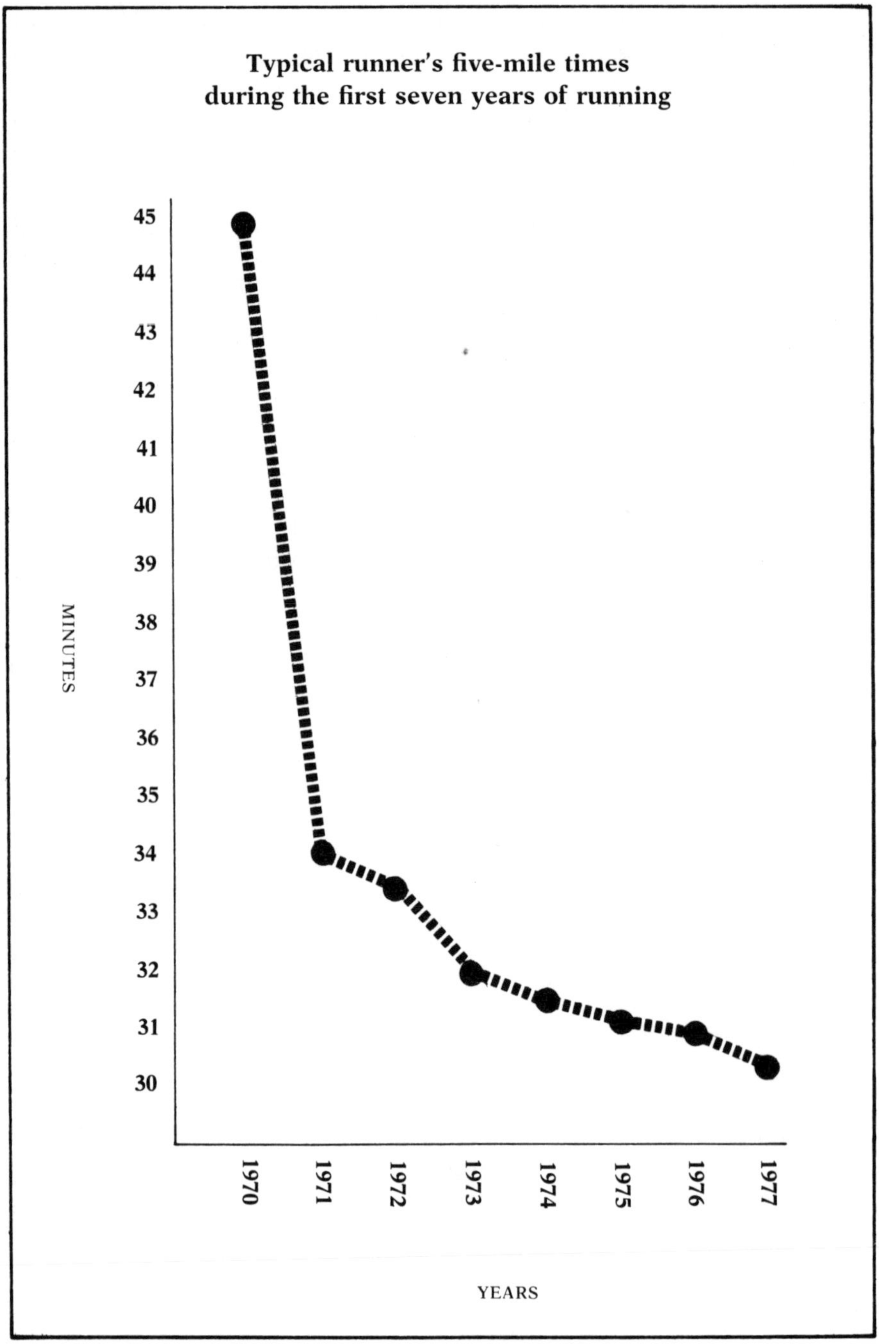

Adaptation to training depends on the overload principle. If you ask your body to do more than it can easily perform, it responds by becoming not just strong enough for that task but even stronger. To become fitter, therefore, simply make use of the overload principle. Figuring out how much of an overload you need isn't hard. Each of us has a maximum heart rate; our hearts are able to beat that fast and no faster. Although it varies from person to person, your maximum heart rate is roughly 220 per minute minus your age. If you're forty years old it's about 180; if you're thirty it's about 190, and so forth. For most people, training should be at resting heart rate plus 75 percent of the difference between resting and maximum heart rates. (In the medical literature you'll usually find it called "maximal heart rate." *Maximal* is doctors' jargon for maximum; it means exactly the same thing.)

To find out how hard you should train, figure your maximum heart rate. Then find your resting heart rate by taking your pulse after you've been sitting still for a few minutes. Subtract your resting heart rate from your maximum, multiply by .75, add that figure to your resting heart rate, and do most of your running at a speed that will make your heart beat about that fast.* To save yourself the trouble of computing, you can simply refer to the chart on page 68. It does the same thing as the formula, although of course it does not take into account individual variations in resting heart rate. The figures labeled "Optimum" are recommended, but it's all right to stay anywhere between "Minimum" and "Maximum."

To take your pulse, use a watch with a second hand. Stop running and check your heartbeat either at your wrist or at your neck just below the angle of your jaw. Count the beats carefully for six seconds and add a zero. Some authorities recommend taking it for longer to increase accuracy, but heart rate declines so fast when exercise stops that six seconds is best.

By far the easiest way to take your pulse, however, has recently been introduced by the Pulsar watch people. It is a wristwatch that, in addition to giving the time, provides a digital readout of your heart by monitoring capillary blood pressure. Its only drawback is that you must momentarily stop running to obtain an accurate reading.

Don't bother taking your pulse every time you run. With a little practice you'll learn how fast you have to go to hit that 75 percent heart rate. But you should check it every few weeks, since you'll have to run faster to achieve the same rate as your condition improves.

* Use .65 if you smoke or are more than twenty pounds overweight, or if you've recently had surgery or a serious illness.

THE HEARTBEAT TEST

Using Your Pulse as a Training Guide

WOMEN			
Age	*Minimum*	*Optimum*	*Maximum*
25	130	157	185
30	126	153	180
35	123	149	175
40	119	145	170
45	116	140	165
50	112	136	160
55	109	132	155
60	105	128	150
65	102	123	145
MEN			
25	137	166	195
30	133	162	190
35	130	157	185
40	126	153	180
45	123	149	175
50	119	145	170
55	116	140	165
60	112	136	160
65	109	132	155

Source: The Jogger

Don't consider the 75 percent figure sacrosanct. The maximum heart rate you'll arrive at by subtracting your age from 220 is merely an estimate. If yours is lower, you may find yourself tiring as you try to keep your pulse at 75 percent of the hypothetical maximum. In that case, slow down a bit and don't worry about it. Each of us is different. All we can do is make the best of what we've got.

The reason for the 75 percent level is that cardiovascular fitness—the kind that really counts and, happily, the kind that running gives us—depends on how efficiently the body uses oxygen. The rate at which the heart beats is directly related to how much oxygen is being used. When we make the heart beat faster, therefore, we are calling the oxygen-processing mechanism into play and thus strengthening it.

More is not better, incidentally. You won't get faster results by trying for 85 or 90 percent.

HOW FAR?

The first time you run, don't plan to go far. Try running a couple of hundred yards. If you become tired or winded, walk for a while. When you feel rested do another couple of hundred yards. When you've run a total of half a mile, quit if you don't feel like doing more. The important thing is to work out at least four times a week. It's the repeated running that brings improvement.

It may take you several months to get to the point where you're running two, three or four miles at a time. Don't be in a hurry. Gradual improvement is safest. If you try to do too much too quickly, you're likely to hurt yourself. When I first started I had all sorts of injuries. I was trying to do too much too fast. Now, even though I run a lot, I almost never push really hard. It's been two or three years since I had an injury that kept me from running.

If you find that your training increments are causing soreness or fatigue, slow your progress down. Incidentally, it's a good idea not to plan your regimen too many days in advance; if you're as compulsive as I am, you'll be reluctant to change it. But try not to be. It's important to monitor your body closely to see how it's responding. After a while you'll get so that you can fine-tune your workouts.

ON NOT OWNING A STOPWATCH

By this time you've no doubt gathered that I'm fairly relaxed about how fast and far I run. It's more fun that way, and I suspect I improve almost as much as I would under a more spartan regimen. So even though you may be curious about how fast you can run, don't buy a stopwatch—not yet, anyway. Stopwatch runners tend to be haunted, driven souls. What counts most is what one researcher has called "perceived exertion." That means nothing more than how strenuous a run seems to you. If you feel that your workout is a good one—not ridiculously easy but not bone-battering, either—that's about right. The beauty of the perceived-exertion formula is that it takes into account such factors as heat, humidity, terrain and wind. Sometimes you may fly along; at other times you'll plod. It doesn't matter. What counts is how you feel.

WATCHING FOR YOUR SECOND WIND

After you've been running for a few minutes, especially as you begin to get in shape, a nice thing happens: you get what is known as second wind. Second wind follows an initial period of breathlessness. When it comes, the breathlessness abates, and you suddenly feel light, strong and fast.

Over the years there has been a lot of argument about whether there really is such a thing as second wind. There is. Dr. Roy Shephard reports that when researchers questioned twenty students at one-minute intervals during a hard twenty-minute treadmill workout, eighteen said their breathing improved after a while and fourteen said their legs felt better. You'll experience a second wind, too. Watch for it.

WEATHER

In Chapter 13 you'll learn how to run when it's hot, cold, snowy or rainy. When you're just starting out, there are really only two factors you have to be cautious about: heat and humidity. Both will slow you down, so on a mid-August day don't try to run as if it were April. Heat and humidity can upset your body badly. If it's likely to be above eighty degrees F. at midday, try to run early in the morning, or else wait until after sunset.

After you've been running for a while heat will be less of a problem because your body eventually gets used to it. It takes about a week of running in the heat to become fully acclimated.

As for rain, it need never stop you if you follow the suggestions in Chapter 13.

AFTER A RUN

When your run is over, don't stop suddenly. Take time for a cooldown (sometimes, somewhat illogically, called a warm-down). This should consist of a brief relaxed walk and some stretching of the same kind you did before you ran. Stretching after a run is particularly beneficial. Your muscles are warm and supple; they stretch most easily then. Try to devote eight or ten minutes to cooling down in order to help work the metabolic wastes out of your muscles. By the time you stop, your pulse should be within twenty beats of what it is when you aren't exercising.

WHAT TO DO ABOUT SORENESS

When you first start running, you'll probably get sore legs. They're pretty much unavoidable. If you have severe pain, you're running too hard or too far. The soreness should be nothing more than a pleasant tingling. It's your body's way of telling you that long-dormant fibers are back on the job. A hot bath, followed by a massage with some liniment, will make you feel better. If the soreness isn't bad, you needn't curtail your running. A slow run the next day, preferably on a cushion of soft grass, will make your muscles feel better.

As you get further into your running program, you may experience occasional pains that seem to be in the bones and joints. Shin splints—pains in the front of the leg that are common in beginning runners—are a good example. They're perfectly natural. You're asking your body to do things that it's never been called upon to do—at least not for a long time—and it responds by obligingly restructuring itself to make its various parts more efficient. Small and large pains are therefore bound to crop up from time to time as your body makes adjustments. Most will disappear without any treatment, and very few will make you stop running altogether. A good rule of thumb is: if it feels better when you run, keep running; if it feels worse, take a rest.

MAKING IT A HABIT

Running, as we have seen, brings not just physical benefits but a number of psychological benefits. It does not bring either, however, unless it is done regularly. From the beginning, therefore, make running a habit. Set aside a time solely for running, and make it long enough to give yourself plenty of time for dressing, warming up, running, cooling down, taking a leisurely shower and dressing again. Running is more fun if you don't have to rush through it.

GETTING OVER SETBACKS

If for one reason or another you don't run for a while, don't say, "Well, there goes all my training down the drain." Unless the layoff has been a long one, you will still be enjoying some of the effects of your earlier training. It takes about as long to get completely out of shape as it took to get trained. Just get back to your running as quickly as you can. After checking with some light experimental running to see how much of your training has slipped away, start right in again. It won't take you long to get back where you were.

The more you run, the fewer excuses you'll make for not running. In the beginning you may miss quite a few days. Later on, you'll hardly ever let a day go by without running. In a recent two-year period I missed only five running days, and they were all spent on rocky trails high in the White Mountains. Any run there might easily have been my last.

So don't worry about setbacks. Just get back on your good behavior as soon as possible. (Incidentally, you can preserve many of your training benefits during a layoff by avoiding overindulgences and weight gain.)

KEEPING A DIARY

Most runners keep a journal in which to record their running experiences. Joe Henderson, the editor of *Runner's World,* has kept one for years. It is very detailed, a record not just of miles but of his thoughts along the way. Mine is simpler: "Wed., Nov. 11—10. Hills." The "10" means I ran ten miles that day. "Hills" is a code meaning that I ran my hilly northern course and ran hard on the upward portions of the hills. Some runners keep records of their diet, weight, how they felt, and so forth. Keep whatever kind of journal you like, but do attempt one, and from time to time record your resting heart rate. That way you'll be able to check your progress from the beginning. You'll find it fun a year from now to look back and say, "Why, I only ran half a mile at this time last year. Today I did five! And my heart rate is twenty beats slower!"

6

Getting Thin

The Mathematics of Looking Like a Runner

First, the good news: If you run, you'll almost certainly lose weight, whether you change your eating habits or not. Furthermore, you'll start losing even if your weight is on an upward trend right now. Because runners burn significantly more calories than nonrunners, women typically lose ten to twelve pounds in the first year of running; men lose twenty or more. One woman runner, Kathryn Lance, said: "Soon after I took up running my body changed completely. All my friends had always been the kind of people who looked good whether they were athletic or not. Not me; I'd been flabby my whole life, even as a teenager. Then I started running and suddenly I wasn't flabby any more. It was a weird experience. I would touch my body and it felt different. My posture improved, too. I lost maybe ten pounds during the first year of running, but I lost inches even more quickly than that. Almost immediately I looked thinner. And my dress size went from fourteen to ten."

Now, the bad news: Unless you're already fairly lean, the weight you lose won't be enough to make you a really good runner. Good runners are startlingly thin. At a recent gathering of marathon runners one observer looked around the room and said in disbelief, "Some of you people look like chickens that are only fit to make soup out of." He was right. A runner in good condition weighs not more than two pounds per inch of height. A man is not more than 5 or 10 percent fat; a women, not more than 15 or 20 percent. (The average nonathletic man is about 15 percent fat, the average nonathletic woman 22 to 35 percent.) Ted Corbitt, the former Olympic marathoner mentioned in Chapter 2, says, "When people tell you how good you look, you can be sure you're not fit. If you don't look gaunt, you're out of shape." Dr. Alan Clark, the same physician cited in Chapter 2 as an advocate of aerobic exercise instead of tranquilizers, told me that after six months on a running program "friends would approach my wife in private and speak with a concerned air about my gaunt appearance and ask how long I had been ill. Her explanation—that I was a long-distance runner—would leave them scratching their heads."

Let's say that according to the life insurance charts you're ten pounds overweight. In clothes you look quite trim. It's only when you're undressed or in a bathing suit that you look slightly puffy around the waist. Are those ten pounds anything to worry about? Unfortunately, yes. After the age of forty-five, people ten pounds overweight experience an 8 percent increase in their death rate. If they are twenty pounds overweight, they are subject to an 18 percent increase; thirty pounds, 28 percent; and fifty pounds, 56 percent. A study conducted a decade ago in Alameda County, California, demonstrated the close relationship between weight and health. Researchers asked 6,928 adults a battery of questions designed to determine their state of health, past and present, and their eating, sleeping, smoking, drinking and exercise habits. Answers to the two sets of questions were compared. The researchers reported that "the relationship between overweight, especially the higher degrees of overweight, and poor health is evident. . . . Men with the best physical health were those less than 5 percent underweight up to 19.99 percent overweight; among women, those who were underweight or less than 10 percent overweight were slightly more healthy than the average."

Complicated as the body is, in one respect it is remorselessly simple: it is an unfailingly accurate calorie counter. It keeps track of calories in exactly the same way a bank keeps track of your money. If you put in more calories than you take out, your weight goes up. If you take out more than you put in, your weight decreases. If you want to lose weight you must therefore eat less, exercise more, or do a bit of both.

Curiously, the first possibility is the least effective. In a recent study Dr. Grant Gwinup of the University of California at Irvine refers to the futility of treating overweight by diet alone. As an experiment he therefore decided to try exercise alone. He selected eleven overweight women whose weights ranged from 134 to 218; in some cases they had been overweight all their lives. All eleven had tried dieting with at best only temporary success. Gwinup instructed the women not to make any changes in their diets, but in addition to whatever else they normally did, to walk rapidly for thirty or more minutes each day. Weight loss in the first year averaged twenty-two pounds.

Another study, this one by Drs. W. B. Zuti and L. A. Golding, had as its subjects twenty-five women ranging in age from their mid-twenties to their mid-forties who were as much as forty pounds overweight. The women were assigned to three groups. Under the study's ground rules, all three undertook a 500-calorie daily deficit, but they did so in different ways. The first group did it by diet alone, the second by exercise alone, and the third by a combination of diet and exercise. After sixteen weeks the weight loss was 11.7, 10.6 and 12 pounds, respectively. Although the combination group lost more weight, the difference was not statistically significant. What was significant was that the combination group lost more fat and gained proportionately more lean tissue than either of the other two. "On the basis of these data," concluded Zuti and Golding, "we recommend that those interested in losing weight combine a lowered caloric intake with a physical fitness program."

Some aspects of losing weight by exercising seem curious and even illogical. For example, running does not increase one's appetite. On the contrary, it usually diminishes it. Says one researcher: "Exercise may be a suppressant rather than a stimulant to appetite." This phenomenon is borne out by studies in which animals exercised for an hour a day ate less than animals that weren't exercised at all.

It is also curious that how fast you run has little effect on how many calories you burn. A 150-pound person running at an eight-minute pace uses 102 calories during a one-mile run, while the same person running at a twelve-minute pace uses 98 calories.*

* What counts considerably more than your pace is your weight. A 220-pound person running a mile at an eight-minute pace uses 150 calories, while a 120-pound person running the same distance at the same pace uses only 82 calories. The following are the calorie figures for other weights: 130 pounds, 90 calories; 140 pounds, 98 calories; 160 pounds, 110 calories; 170 pounds, 116 calories; 180 pounds, 124 calories; 190 pounds, 130 calories; 200 pounds, 136 calories; 210 pounds, 144 calories.

Studies have also shown that calorie costs are not affected much by the length of your legs or how long a stride you take. It doesn't even matter whether you're a world-class runner or a beginner: the mechanical efficiency of top runners is only slightly greater than that of novices.

It's easy to figure out how much you'll lose through running and how quickly you'll do it. Suppose you now weigh 180 pounds and, after an initial training period, you regularly run five miles a day. At 180 pounds you burn 124 calories during every eight-minute mile, so each time you run your five miles you burn 620 calories. Your body—anyone's, in fact—requires an intake of 3,500 calories to add a pound and a deficit of 3,500 to lose a pound. At your rate of running, therefore, if you don't vary your intake you'll lose a pound every 5⅔ days, or about five pounds a month. (You'll have to adjust the mathematics slightly from time to time, since as your weight goes down, you'll burn fewer calories per mile.)

Eventually, of course, your weight will stabilize. Exactly where it stabilizes depends on how much you eat and how far you run. When I started running, I lost weight rapidly. Soon I had to take all my clothes to a tailor for alterations. That was wonderful! I was eating and drinking all I wanted to, and still losing weight. In my ignorance I supposed this would continue until I was a mere wraith. Soon, however, the rate of loss slowed, and ultimately my weight steadied at 170—less than I had weighed originally but still twenty-odd pounds above my ideal weight—142.

Something like this will no doubt happen to you, too. You'll lose effortlessly for a while, but eventually, sad to say, your weight will stop declining. Then you need to become really clever—and determined. You can, of course, run—and even race—even though you're well above your ideal weight, but you'll never perform up to your potential. Not long ago *Runner's World* published an article showing what extra weight does to running times. One example given was a 161-pound runner who had finished a marathon in 3:13:01. The runner reduced his weight to 147. With no other changes in his training, he finished his next marathon in 3:04:26. In other words, every extra pound costs some two-thirds of a minute. It may not sound like a lot, but it adds up to a big difference.

Extra weight slows you down for several reasons. A given amount of energy carries you a little less far. Suppose your steps are shortened by only an eighth of an inch. If your feet strike the ground 800 times per mile, this adds up to a difference of a hundred inches—more than eight feet. In a ten-mile race, you'll end up eighty feet or so behind a similarly trained runner who isn't carrying extra weight.

Extra weight also means that, since your body obeys Newton's laws, it takes longer every time it shifts from downward to upward motion. Watch a fat person run. One reason he or she runs so clumsily is that at each stride the excess weight is still in mid-descent when the rest of the body is already moving upward. Fat tends to keep moving in its original direction, and only valuable energy can change its direction. Fat thus acts like an anchor, slowing every step.

Finally, extra weight isn't confined to the outside of your body. Some is on the inside, too, lodged in the muscles, where it keeps the fibers from operating efficiently. This is true, incidentally, even if your extra weight is only a temporary increase in water. For this reason medical specialists recommend avoiding certain foods for three days or so before competition. The *Journal of the American Medical Association* lists them as:

Salt
Monosodium glutamate
All heavily salted foods
Sauerkraut
Bread and rolls with salt toppings
Potato chips, corn chips, other salted snacks
Pretzels
Salty and smoked fish and meats
Bacon and bacon fat
Bologna
Chipped and corned beef
Frankfurters
Ham
Koshered meat
Luncheon meat
Salt pork
Meat tenderizer
Prepared mustard
Relish
Pickles
Crackers
Worcestershire sauce
Sausage
Anchovies
Herring
Sardines
All cheese
Peanut butter
Salted nuts
Popcorn
Olives
Bouillon cubes
Catsup
Celery salt
Onion salt
Garlic salt
Chili sauce
Horseradish
Canned soup
Salted cottage cheese
Dry cereals
Instant cocoa mixes
Soy sauce

How, exactly, do you continue to lose once your weight is stabilized? Remember, to lose weight, you must use up more calories than you put in. As mentioned earlier, you can eat less, run more, or do a little of both. The chart opposite shows how this works.

Let's say that you'd like to weigh 150. Since fifteen calories are

THE RUNNER'S DIET

A Mathematico-Physiological Excursus

1. Calories Required Per Day

Desired weight ____________ × 15 = ____________
(in lbs.)
+ Miles run ____________ × 100 = ____________
Total$_1$ = ____________

2. Calories to Be Eaten Per Day

Calories from Normal Diet = ____________
+ Calories from Runner's Bonus = ____________
(must be less than line 2 under "Calories Required Per Day")
Total$_2$ = ____________

3. Calorie Deficit Per Day

Total$_1$ = ____________
− Total$_2$ = ____________
Total$_3$ = ____________

4. Rate of Weight Loss

$$\frac{3{,}500}{(\text{Total}_3)} = \text{Days to lose 1 lb.}$$

5. Time required to Reach Weight Goal

Days to lose 1 lb. ____________ × total lbs. to lose ____________ = ____________
(from above) (total days)

---

required to maintain every pound of weight, your proper intake per day, if you were not a runner, would be 2,250 calories. Let's assume you run six miles a day. Since the energy cost of running a mile is approximately 100 calories, multiply the number of miles you run by 100. (If your weight is appreciably lower or higher than average, make appropriate adjustments from the calorie-per-mile information given on page 76.) Call this number the Runner's Bonus—that is, the number of extra calories you're burning every day because you're a runner and not a sedentary person—and add it to your basic calorie requirement.

Now we arrive at the dieting part of the equation. On "Calories from Normal Diet" enter the figure from "Desired weight × 15" (in this case 2,250). On the next line enter a figure that is less than the

Runner's Bonus. Let's make it 100. Add the two together and you get the total number of calories you're going to permit yourself per day. Notice that even though it's less than the number of calories you're burning, it's still enough to provide for an entirely adequate and even filling diet (and, if you balance the budget properly, for such extras as cake, beer or an occasional highball).

We could stop here, for you can be sure that so long as you eat and drink fewer calories than you burn, you'll lose weight. But let's see how *fast* you'll lose. In the example given, Equation 3 shows that you're incurring a deficit of 500 calories a day. Enter that figure in Equation 4 to see how many days it will take you to lose a pound. In this case it's seven days. How long, therefore, will it take you to reach your desired weight of 150? It depends, of course, on what you weigh now. Let's say you've been running for a while and now weigh not 180, but 170. You still want to lose twenty pounds. Thus it will require 7 × 20, or 140 days—about four and a half months.

Notice that the rate of loss I have cited is not extremely high. It's exactly what many doctors recommend for patients who need to lose weight. A 500-calorie daily deficit is the equivalent of only one container of fruit-flavored yogurt and two pieces of toast lightly spread with jam. If you want to lose faster, you would probably be able to do so without much trouble.

Furthermore, I have mentioned only one way to unbalance the equation—by eating less. You can also unbalance it by running more. If, for example, you add two and a half miles a day—only an additional twenty minutes or so—you'll burn an extra 7,500 calories a month, or better than two pounds' worth. Even if you don't eat a calorie less than you do now, you'll lose the twenty pounds just as surely as you would by the first method. (If you use both methods simultaneously—eating less and exercising more—your weight will go down that much faster.)

If you want to run well, try not to be satisfied with staying at "normal" weight. Frank Shorter, who won an Olympic gold medal in the 1972 marathon, is 5 feet 10½ inches and weighs a scrawny 134. Bill Rodgers is 5 feet 8½ inches and weighs 125. Jeff Galloway, another top runner, says, "I'm convinced you run much better the skinnier you are."

7

Getting Good at It

The Techniques of Training for Speed and Endurance

If you've been following the counsel in Chapter 5 for a few weeks, by this time you can probably run a couple of miles without tiring. After a run you feel exhilarated, buoyant. Work is easier and play more fun. Perhaps you're content to leave matters exactly as they stand, running no farther or faster. If so, fine. So long as you cover a mile and a half four or five days a week at a moderate pace, you'll stay in decent shape. The only thing you won't do is improve much. When you first take it up, your fitness increases rapidly. Then, as your heart, lungs and muscles, responding to the unaccustomed work, become stronger and more efficient, improvement tapers off. Finally you reach a state of equilibrium; your body is able to perform its appointed tasks fairly easily, but it no longer becomes detectably fitter.

I have already mentioned the first race I ever entered—a five-mile run in which I came in last, despite the fact I had been running more or less regularly. It wasn't until I started reading about the sport that I discovered that my slow training shuffle wasn't enough. In order to evoke the desired responses from my body I needed to run harder some of the time. When you always run slowly, I learned, you aren't teaching yourself to run fast. When you run fast but not far, you aren't building endurance. When you run on flat terrain, you aren't learning to run on hills. "We learn what we practice and at the velocity at which we practice it," writes J. Kenneth Doherty in *Modern Track and Field.*

When we train, a number of adaptations take place in our bodies. Among them are these:

1. We increase our capacity for using oxygen.
2. Our hearts are able to pump more blood at a lower pulse rate and blood pressure.
3. Our lung capacity increases.
4. Our heat-dissipating ability increases.
5. After exercise, our pulse rate and blood pressure return to normal more quickly.
6. We develop greater muscular strength.
7. We produce less lactic acid—a work-limiting substance—for a given amount of work.
8. Our bodies become more efficient mechanically, using less oxygen per unit of work.
9. We develop greater endurance.

To a limited degree these changes occur even if we do very little running. To produce continuing adaptations, however, we need to train more consistently and purposefully. Probably the most effective way to train is under the eye of a knowledgeable coach. He can tell when we're not working as hard as we could or when we're getting too tired. He knows how to prescribe a workout that will leave us refreshed, or at least appropriately fatigued, rather than exhausted. However, most of us—including me—have no coach. Even the typical running club has no formal coaching system. An experienced runner may occasionally offer some pointers to a friend, but most of the time we coach ourselves, picking up a fragment here, a scrap there. "Training is my creativity," Edward Epstein told me. "I wouldn't want a coach even if I could have one. The fun is in trying to figure things out for myself." I agree. Right now I'm doing a lot of hard uphill running, trying to strengthen my quadriceps, the muscles at the front of the thighs. My theory is that if those muscles get stronger, I'll be able to take longer and faster strides. If this approach doesn't work I'll try something else.

This chapter is written on the assumption that you've been running for a while and would now like to become more serious about improving. How much improvement you want is entirely up to

you. You can try to improve just a little, or you can set out to improve a lot. How you train depends on your goal, but whatever that goal is, four principles are applicable:

Principle 1. Make running a lifetime activity. It's wasteful to train for just one race and then let all your hard-won conditioning evaporate. Plan, therefore, to make running a daily habit, or at most skip only two or three days a week. Both your body and mind will benefit.

Principle 2. Don't expect quick results. If you try to do too much too fast you'll pull muscles or be so tired you'll feel terrible. Gradual improvement is best.

Principle 3. Alternate hard and easy periods. Beginners often buy a stopwatch and try to run faster than they did the last time every time they run. "I made many mistakes in that first year," Tex Maule writes in *Running Scarred,* "the most painful being a tendency to run the first mile too fast. I began doing that when I got the stopwatch, trying to break my personal record each time I ran, a manifest impossibility." The hard-easy principle applies to individual workouts, to successions of workouts, and even to entire years. After a tough quarter-mile the body needs a rest; after a hard day, an easy day; after a few weeks of hard training, a period of slower

---

HOW GOOD DO YOU WANT TO BE?

The Road Runners Clubs of America and England have established standards of excellence (in hours, minutes and seconds) for races of ten miles and more.

MEN

	World Class	Champion Class	First Class	Second Class	Forty and Over	Fifty and Over
10 Miles	0:49:10	0:50:30	0:53:00	1:01:00	1:03:00	1:10:00
15 Miles	1:14:25	1:17:30	1:23:00	1:37:00	1:40:00	1:50:00
20 Miles	1:41:40	1:47:00	1:54:00	2:16:00	2:20:00	2:30:00
Marathon	2:15:00	2:23:00	2:35:00	3:04:00	3:10:00	3:25:00

WOMEN

	World Class	Champion Class	Class A	Class B	Class C
10 Miles	0:56:16	1:00:25	1:05:14	1:10:54	1:17:37
13.1 Miles	1:14:51	1:20:25	1:26:52	1:34:26	1:43:05
20 Miles	1:57:38	2:06:27	2:16:41	2:28:44	2:43:06
Marathon	2:37:57	2:49:53	3:03:45	3:20:04	3:39:35

running. Soon after New Year's Day each year I start taking longer and harder runs in preparation for the Boston Marathon in April. Over a three-month period, I increase my mileage. While I am doing so I sometimes feel tired, and by the time the marathon is over I'm ready for a rest. For the next few months, particularly during the heat of summer, I run as I feel, seldom pushing myself and treating many of my runs as if they were just walks through the countryside. Under this relaxed regimen, my zest soon returns, and almost without realizing it I'm taking an occasional run of fifteen or eighteen miles. When this occurs, I know my tanks are full again.

Principle 4. Increase your weekly running mileage very gradually in order to give your body plenty of time to adapt. Too quick a change produces fatigue and injuries.

Training can be made into a forbiddingly complex matter. Listening to runners' jargon, to their talk of "intervals" and "fartlek," is enough to make you want to forget the whole sport and take up golf. But training need not be complicated if you understand that there are really only four principal ways to do it.

Intervals

Interval training is the most scientific training method. Commonly attributed to Woldemar Gerschler and Hans Reindell, two German physiologists who are said to have developed it in the 1930's,* interval training consists of repeated hard runs over a measured distance, with recovery periods—the intervals—of relaxed jogging in between. Interval training is particularly versatile because depending on the effect sought, five factors can be varied: the total distance run fast, the duration of each fast run, the number of fast runs, the time between fast runs, and the type of activity between fast runs (walking or slow running). A champion like Olympic marathoner Bill Rodgers may run a half-mile, three-quarters of a mile, a mile, and then two miles at a 4:40 pace, with only a four-minute interval of slow running between each hard run. Then he may—and in fact often does—repeat the entire set. Less accomplished runners necessarily do lighter workouts. A little experimenting will show what works best for you. Remember, though, that since in interval training you run all the fast portions at the same pace, your first couple of fast runs should not be all out. If you're planning to do, say, six fast runs, only the last two or three

* Its parentage is disputed by some writers. It has been attributed to, among others, Lauri Pihkala, a pre–World War I Finnish runner, and George W. Orton, at one time Penn State's track coach.

should be really difficult. If your pulse doesn't return to 120 within ninety seconds, you're running too hard.

Interval training produces results, but you pay a price. Since it is usually done on a track, the scenery is monotonous and the runs are repetitious. "Interval training," writes J. Kenneth Doherty, "lends no ears to the singing of the birds . . . no eyes to the beauties of sand, sea, and sky." Especially if you're doing it alone, it's tempting to slack off and easy to lose interest.

Don't, by the way, attempt interval training until you've laid down a solid foundation of long, slow distance. It's hard work and can easily cause injuries unless you're in top shape. Be sure you're fully warmed up before you start an interval workout. A mile of slow running is the minimum, and two miles is better. Don't do intervals more than twice a week, and don't let interval workouts add up to more than 5 percent of your total mileage.

Since interval workouts are infinitely variable, I have deliberately not prescribed any specific programs. One runner I know, a middle-aged marathoner, runs twenty 220s twice a week, doing each in thirty-five seconds. Rodgers, as we just saw, runs considerably longer distances. You may decide that something in between is right for you. Whatever you choose, be patient; it will take at least three months to get results.

Fartlek

This is a Swedish word meaning "speed play," and this is exactly what the fartlek method is. Codified by Gösta Holmer, chief coach of the 1948 Swedish Olympic team, it consists of fast untimed runs over varied distances and terrains. Although the alternation of fast and slow runs varies from runner to runner, the goal is always the same: a good workout that is also fun. In *How They Train,* Raoul Mollett offers this description:

> Fartlek was perhaps the most alluring discovery since the beginning of the century in the realm of training. . . . A window was opened on the forest, and at the same time an idea of training emerged which one would classify as "happy." Fartlek, with its walks, its runs at slow pace through the woods, its short sprints, was able to revolutionize the training of the track world. . . . There is without doubt not a single irreconcilable sedentary person who would not feel a twinge of nostalgia when faced with the thought of a man running barefoot on springy moss, in a setting of forests and lakes reflecting the sky. Faced with this picture, the track world felt an irresistible rise in spirits.

Fartlek is not intended as a way to avoid working hard, but only as a way to avoid repetition and monotony. It is an effective way to train only if you have the self-discipline to perform a tough workout. One day I ran with the members of the Oberlin College cross-country team on a ten-mile fartlek workout. At the start of the run they carried a couple of tennis balls. One runner would sprint ahead, like a football player going out for a pass, and another would toss the ball to him. There was conversation and laughter. We came to a rutted road deep in mud. Splashing our way through it, we ran through a field of wildflowers, forded a waist-deep stream, vaulted a few fences and finally finished with a fast mile on a country road. It was a hard workout, but it was fun all the way and neatly illustrated one of the special joys of fartlek: you take conditions as you find them. A stream, a muddy road or a foot-deep snowfall is not an occasion for lamentation but a welcome challenge.

LSD

LSD isn't a drug but a way of training; the initials stand for "long, slow distance." Its invention is often attributed to Ernst van Aaken, a highly regarded German physician and coach, but in this country its chief popularizer has been Joe Henderson, the editor of *Runner's World.* "LSD isn't just a training method," Henderson has written. "It's a whole way of looking at the sport. Those who employ it are saying running is fun—all running, not just the competitive part. Training isn't an exhausting, anxiety-filled means to an end that's barely tolerated. The simple, unhurried, unworried, nearly painless daily tours of the countryside come to be as much fun in their own way as racing." Running this way offers all the pleasures of walking, but you go seven or eight miles in an hour instead of three or four.

Although it seems paradoxical, a number of impressively fast runners do all their training by the LSD method. A young New York lawyer, Frank Handelman, can race six miles in thirty minutes and a few odd seconds, yet he rarely exceeds an eight-minute pace in training. The key, I suspect, is that he competes so often that he gets in enough hard running that way. Most runners and coaches feel that you need to run fast only about 5 percent of the time—a mere one mile out of every twenty.

Long, fast distance

I mention this method only because some people, under a misapprehension about how our bodies function, try to train this way. There are two reasons why it won't work:

1. The body will eventually rebel and break down. If you're lucky the breakdown will be in the form of a cold or persistent tiredness,

but it could be something worse—painful knee trouble or a stress fracture.

2. Long, fast distance conflicts with the physiology of athletic improvement. In training we wear ourselves down in order to let the body repair itself during an ensuing period of rest and become stronger than ever. Without rest, scientific studies show, repair is severely limited.*

Which training scheme is best for you? The only sure way to find out is by experimenting. If you're a highly disciplined person and always accomplish what you set out to do, interval training may work for you. If you like to hang loose, fartlek or LSD may suit you best. Some people do one kind of training during part of the year, another kind during the rest. After a while, as you learn to read your body, and as you come to trust your readings, you'll come to know what's best for it.

Not everyone should train the same way. The kind and amount of training you do ought to be based on what you're training for. If you're getting ready for a five-mile race, your training will be different from that of a marathon runner. The reason, as discussed earlier, is that how you train determines how you'll race. Take two extremes, the quarter-mile and the marathon. The chemical reactions that produce energy require oxygen. When you run a fast quarter-mile you go so fast that during the run itself you get only about 25 percent of the necessary oxygen. The other 75 percent—your so-called oxygen debt—has to be made up after you've crossed the finish line. That's why a quarter-miler has to do a lot of anaerobic training—running in the absence of sufficient oxygen. A marathoner, on the other hand, gets 98 or 99 percent of his oxygen during the race itself. His is mostly aerobic running, and that's the way he does most of his training.†

If the weather is likely to be hot during a race, try to do some training in the heat. If it's cool outdoors, create your own hothouse by wearing a sweatsuit (or even two sweatsuits), gloves and a wool hat. Because it takes only a week or so to become acclimated to heat, you won't have to put up with the burden of so many clothes for long. Anyway, the slight discomfort will be worth it. At the start of the 1976 Boston Marathon it was 116 degrees in the sun. Few runners had supposed it could possibly be so hot on a mid-April

* Science has recently been working its way into the running world with increasing insistence. Today there are even computerized training systems. A runner named Jim Gardner, for example, has written (with J. Gerry Purdy) a book called *Computerized Running Training Programs* that prescribes day-by-day workouts based on a runner's current ability.

† In-between distances require different ratios of aerobic and anaerobic running—70–30 for the mile, 80–15 for two miles, 90–10 for three miles and so forth.

day in Massachusetts, so practically nobody had trained properly. As a result, most people's times were terrible.

The same specificity principle applies to terrain. If you want to do well on a hilly course, you need to get in some hill running beforehand. Running up and down is different from running on flat terrain. Going uphill requires strong quadriceps; coming downhill gives the feet and knees a hard pounding. The only way to do well at hill running is to train for it.

How far should you run when you train? One answer is to run as far as you feel like. Not many years ago I thought six miles was a pleasant distance—enough for a good workout, but not enough to bring on exhaustion. Now it takes ten miles to satisfy me. (Where it will end I have no idea; I try not to think about it.) If you're preparing for a race, though, you should put in the proper number of training miles to get you safely past the collapse point—the mileage beyond which you simply can't do anything more than what has been called a survival shuffle. Your collapse point is easy to compute, at least theoretically. If you never miss a day of running, it's your daily mileage multiplied by three. If you occasionally miss days, figure your collapse point by adding up your most recent monthly total and dividing by ten.

The collapse point, needless to say, is only a rough rule of thumb. Some runners can run farther than theory indicates; a few can run less. Top runners, of course, think about attaining their potential, not about collapsing; that's why some of them train twenty miles a day or more. Nor do collapse-point computations take speed into account. All they tell you is that if you train enough, you'll probably be able to make it to the finish line. They don't say what you'll look like when you get there. You'll have to experiment to find *that* out.

There are at least three ways to find out how far you're running. You can drive over your course in a car, checking it with the odometer. Most odometers aren't all that accurate, so your measurement won't be accurate, either, but it will be reasonably close.

Or you can run at your usual pace around a quarter-mile track four times to see how long it takes. Let's say it takes nine minutes. Thereafter, figure that you cover a mile every nine minutes. From time to time, as you improve, recheck yourself.

Or, most accurate of all, buy a little mechanical device that counts a bicycle wheel's revolutions. First, to calibrate it, measure off a half-mile with a steel tape, put the revolution counter on the front wheel of a bicycle, and ride over the measured half-mile on that bicycle, noting how many revolutions are in a half-mile. Then, without adding any air to the tire on the wheel with the revolution counter (to do so would change the circumference), ride over your intended course and mark each mile with a spot of paint. (Put the marks someplace where cars and pedestrians won't obliterate them. I marked a course seven years ago. The mile markers I sprayed on horizontal surfaces—curbs and the like—have long since disappeared. The ones I put on vertical surfaces—stone walls, for example—are as good as new.) If you'd like to buy a revolution counter, see Appendix A.

Once you've run a few races you'll start to notice that you do better at some distances than at others. There are a number of reasons, among them your age, your physique and the type of muscle fiber that predominates in your body.* You may want to confine your racing to the distances you're best at—if you do, it will simplify your training—but most people enjoy racing a variety of distances, treating victory and defeat like the impostors Kipling said they are. If you've trained well, there isn't much point in fretting about bad performances, since research suggests that your

* For more on this scientific frontier, see Chapter 23.

basic speed is largely an inborn quality, one that can't be greatly influenced by training. You're either fast or you're not. What you can improve through training is endurance—the ability to run at a given pace for a long time.

Endurance comes with running a great deal. Top runners work out two and sometimes even three times a day. There's no need for you to do so, though, unless you simply like the idea and have lots of extra time. It may not even do you much good. In a study conducted by Edward W. Watt, B. A. Plotnicki and Elsworth R. Buskirk, college distance runners were divided into two groups. For nine weeks both had a training session every afternoon. In addition, one of the groups ran six fairly hard miles every morning. At the end of the experiment the one-mile times of the two groups were indistinguishable. (Differences might, of course, have showed up over a greater distance.)

What appears to be more important than the number of workouts per day is their regularity over a long period—months, years and even decades. Doherty investigated the time it took twenty champion runners to reach their top performances. The average, from the time they first raced until they had their best run, was 10.4 years. (They had trained an average of 5.8 days a week for 10.2 months of the year.)

Some runners and coaches think weightlifting is essential to good performances. Emil Zatopek, the champion Czech runner of the 1950's, used to do squats while holding his wife, Dana, on his shoulders. Weight training may make a difference if you're getting ready for the Olympics, but most runners don't bother with it. They'd rather spend their time running.

Whatever training method you choose, stick with it long enough to evaluate its effects. Some runners impatiently switch from one regimen to another so often that they never really have a chance to find out whether anything works. The body adapts slowly; some changes occur within days or weeks, but others take years. If you give your body enough time, you may be pleasantly surprised. There's no shortcut to experience.

When we train we also are exercising our minds. The indefatigable Ted Corbitt told me of running twelve hours at a time when he was preparing for fifty-mile races; it was as much for his mind, he said, as for his body. Even if you're not planning to run fifty miles, the same principle applies. You need to demonstrate to your brain that certain things are going to be required of it—among other things a toughness that doesn't fold under pressure or fatigue. This is why Zatopek used to hold his breath repeatedly until it hurt. He wanted to teach his mind not to panic if his body didn't get enough oxygen.

When we race, strange things happen to our minds. The stress of fatigue sometimes makes us forget why we wanted to race in the first place. In one of my early marathons I found myself unable to think of a single reason for continuing. Physically and mentally exhausted, I dropped out of the race. Now I won't enter a marathon unless I truly want to finish it. If during the race I can't remember why I wanted to run in it, I tell myself, "Maybe I can't remember now, but I know I had a good reason when I started." I've finally learned how to fight back when my brain starts using tricky arguments.

As a race continues, it's also easy to find reasons to slow down: the pain is unbearable, you tell yourself; an old injury is acting up; blisters are coming on; it isn't an important race anyway. Such arguments can sound beguilingly persuasive in the heat of a race. Only later, after you've yielded to their spurious plausibility, are you disappointed in yourself. If you're going to race at all, it's only sensible to make a maximum effort.

This is where mental training comes in. There are several ways to strengthen your mind for running. One is always to run the distance you set out to do. If you plan to cover two miles, do it even if you have to walk part of the way. Thus you'll learn to endure the bad runs and thereby toughen yourself for the occasional discomforts of running. If you quit when training goes badly, you only learn how easy it is to avoid discomfort. When I have a bad run I write "Ugh" in my training diary. Strangely, a day or two after an "Ugh" run I almost always have an unexpectedly good one. The reason, I think, is that an "Ugh" is always slower than usual. It rests me, making a faster and easier run possible next time.

Another good way to train your mind is to do exactly the type of workout you plan, no matter how hard it seems or how badly you're running. You're bound to have days when everything seems sluggish and ungainly and you'd just as soon not be training at all. That's a good time to persist. As mentioned earlier, studies show that the effort an athlete feels he is putting into a workout is very close to the actual effort as measured by such criteria as heartbeat and oxygen consumption. So even if you're moving a lot more slowly than you'd like, chances are you're getting a decent workout.

A third way to train your mind is occasionally to run an unusually long distance. Instead of running three miles a day on two successive days, run a mile on the first day and five on the next in order to accustom yourself to running for long periods. When you train in this way, after a while even marathons don't seem intolerably long.

Still another way to train your brain is by rehearsing in your imagination what you hope to do. Richard M. Suinn, a psychology professor at Colorado State University, recently described his work with Olympic skiers. Suinn found that if they first imagined themselves skiing down a course, their performance improved. In addition, he found that not just their minds but also their muscles were helped—that true learning apparently took place:

> I recorded the electromyograph responses of an Alpine ski racer as he summoned up the moment-by-moment imagery of a downhill race. Almost instantly, the recording needles stirred into action. Two muscle bursts appeared as the skier hit jumps. Further muscle bursts duplicated the effort of a rough section of the course, and the needles settled during the easy sections. By the time he finished this psychological rehearsal of the downhill race, his EMG recordings almost mirrored the course itself. There was even a final burst of muscle activity after he had passed the finish line, a mystery to me until I remembered how hard it is to come to a skidding stop after racing downhill at more than 40 miles an hour.

Other athletic researchers confirm Suinn's belief that mental training is as important as physical. At the University of Rochester, a psychology professor named Robert M. Nideffer found that mental rehearsal significantly improves performance in nearly all sports. Similarly, in *Sports Psyching* Thomas Tutko and Umberto Tosi write: "The psychological factors are the most important yet the most neglected in our approach to sports. . . . Most great athletes acknowledge state of mind as the key to success."

Mental rehearsal is particularly helpful when applied to relaxation, a crucial aspect of running. You can't run well unless you're relaxed. The reason is that every muscle used in running has an opposing muscle; if both are tensed at the same time, movement is necessarily slowed. For example, the quadriceps is used to swing the leg forward. If its antagonist, at the back of the upper leg, is relaxed, the leg can move quickly and easily. If, however, it is tensed, the action of the quadriceps is inhibited. Mentally rehearsing a proper running style makes relaxation easier when you get tired and your legs want to tighten up.*

To talk about such things as fatigue, tightness, blisters and pain might seem to suggest that training must be nothing but drudgery. It doesn't need to be this at all. Sometimes it's hard work, but

* A runner and transcendental meditation student named John Hale uses a related technique. In the late stages of a race, when relaxation is difficult, he ticks off a mental check list of the various parts of his body, urging each one to relax. "Relax, ears," he will say. "Relax, mouth . . . head . . . neck . . ." and so forth. I've tried it while running with Hale. It works.

because you have a worthwhile goal in mind it's not only tolerable but fun. If you find that it's becoming more work than fun, ease up. After all, we run chiefly for pleasure, not for pain.

One thing that will add to the pleasure of training is occasionally to run with a friend. Having a companion makes the time pass easily and takes your mind off incidental discomforts. Another is to run different courses for the sake of variety, or run by the time rather than the distance. Sometimes, wearing a watch, I simply go out and run, wandering wherever I want to go and exploring new places. If I feel I'm running at about an eight-minute pace, I'll call an hour's run seven and a half miles. I may be wrong by a few hundred yards, but it doesn't make much difference.

Some people seem to become more bored with running than I do. They're the ones who carry transistor radios or wear those funny earphone receivers that make them look like Mickey Mouse.

If you need Bach or the Beach Boys to get you through a workout, by all means take your radio along. I've even seen runners carrying them while competing in marathons. Most people soon discover, though, that the running is entertainment enough.

After a few months of conscientious training you'll find that you run more easily, cover the same distances in less time, and, if you race, beat people who used to beat you. When these things happen, you may be so encouraged that you'll be tempted to step up your training. That's the time to be wary. For just as you can do too little training, you can also do too much. Your body, as noted, needs time for repairs after a hard workout. Rest periods are an essential part of training.

8

The Mythology of the Woman Runner

Why She Usually Gets More Out of Running Than She Expects

It was an early September day, cool and bright and just right for running, and I was in the first few miles of a 10½-mile race over a course sadistically boobytrapped with steep, exhausting hills. Still, I felt rested and springy; despite the hills it was going to be a fine run.

Just ahead of me was Peggy Mimno, a teacher from Mount Kisco, New York. She too was running easily, moving along efficiently at my speed. The pace felt comfortable, so I decided to stay where I was; why bother concentrating on pace when she was setting such a nice one? I'd overtake her later on when she tired.

So I tucked in behind her. The course headed north for five miles, wandered west for a hilly mile, then turned south again along a winding road. The race was getting tougher. We had four miles left and already it was beginning to be real work. I was breathing hard, and my legs were turning to mush.

Peggy overtook a young male runner. Apparently she knew him, for they exchanged a few cheerful words as she passed him. Their exchange worried me. You don't chat during a race unless you are feeling good, and Peggy plainly was. There was still a discernible bounce in her stride, but whatever resilience I'd once possessed had long since left me.

Still, I was close enough to overtake her if she tired, so I didn't give up hope completely. We were approaching a long, punishing hill now and it would be the test. We were a mile from the finish line, so whatever happened on the hill would almost certainly determine who crossed it first.

As I moved up the hill, working hard, my attention wandered for a few minutes. When I looked up, Peggy was moving away—first five yards, then ten, then more. Finally it was clear that there was no hope of catching her. She beat me decisively.

There is an important lesson in that race. Much of what you read about running makes a sharp distinction between the sexes. Women are assumed to be weaker, slower and not nearly as adept athletically. (For example, women are always being told how to

place their feet and hold their arms; the assumption is that any man simply knows such things, perhaps through some kind of male osmosis.) Yet as Peggy Mimno so clearly demonstrated, the similarities between male and female runners are more important than the differences. I have run with a number of women, both in training and in competition, and I can testify that it is often hard work. As I was gathering information for this book I took a seven-mile run in Central Park with Nina Kuscsik, the 1972 Boston Marathon women's division winner, thinking I would interview her as we ran. I finally got so winded I had to abandon my questions until we finished.

Men in general are faster than women in general, but that's only part of the story. As I write this I have before me the results of the annual Labor Day race held in Westport, Connecticut. Because it is well organized and the course is picturesque, it attracts contestants from hundreds of miles around. There were 127 finishers in the race in question. The first 51 were men. Then Frances Goulart, a runner from Wilton, Connecticut, finished, and other women promptly began to stream across the finish line. For 51 runners, in other words, the race was mainly a man's race, but for the other 76 it was entirely mixed.

Far from being inferior to men as runners, there are certain distinct ways in which women excel. Their running style is likely to be tidier and more economical than men's. "Women seem to run with greater ease than men," writes Thaddeus Kostrubala in *The Joy of Running.* "Their style is easy. The natural style of most twelve-to-fourteen-year-old girls is almost perfect. . . . They roll their feet, their pelvises move. They look at ease and ready to play; in fact, they are playing. Is all this because they have not been the victim of male cultural expectation—that of competition?"

Kostrubala's impressions about women's running style are borne out by a study conducted at Penn State by Dr. Richard C. Nelson and Christine M. Brooks. Comparing forty-two top runners, both male and female, they found that women had longer strides compared to their height, took more strides per minute, and were in contact with the ground less. The clear conclusion is that women shouldn't try to mimic the running style of men; their own is every bit as good.

One important exception manifests itself when previously unathletic women let their style be influenced by mistaken notions about running. A knowledgeable woman runner told me: "I maintain that women do *not* run as well as most men without some training tips. Maybe if all men and women had the same sort of athletic background, women would have some kind of advantage because of pelvic build or whatever, but I notice a lot of common mistakes in almost all beginning (and some experienced) women runners. Most of these mistakes I myself made and had to correct. Most common: running daintily, on the toes. I think this is because women have observed sprinters running this way and also because women have greatly shortened Achilles tendons as a result of wearing high heels. Another mistake seen more in women than in men: shuffling. Another: carrying the arms too high, almost at the shoulder. Another: too much swiveling from the pelvis, or throwing the feet out too much to the side. I think these faults are common because few women have had a chance to engage in sports where a lot of running is involved, and so have had no opportunity to observe correct running form or to be corrected as men are."

Women tire less noticeably than men and, especially in long races, become less stiff. By the eighteenth or twentieth mile of a marathon many male runners are out of gas. The fuel in their muscles has given out, and they must finish—if they do so at all—on sheer guts. Any television watcher who saw Frank Shorter's ragged and halting stride as he tried to hold his pace toward the end of the 1976 Olympic marathon witnessed precisely this phenomenon.

Women, on the other hand, have a larger natural supply of fat—about 10 percent more, as noted earlier, than an equally well-trained man. Because fat is an extremely efficient fuel in endurance work (birds use little else when they are migrating), women can run great distances without "hitting the wall"—that painful moment when the fuel tank is suddenly empty and the legs are capable only of a slow, anguished shuffle. "In thirty-five marathons," Nina Kuscsik told me, "I've never hit the wall. I get tired, but I can always keep going."*

Nor, contrary to the old wives' tales, are women any more prone to injuries than men are. After gathering data from 361 schools, more than 125 athletic trainers and all manner of published reports, Dr. Christine E. Haycock of New Jersey Medical School and Joan V. Gillette of the University of Nevada concluded that well-trained women are no more likely to be hurt in athletics than are well-trained men. The one exception is that because women's joints are looser, their knees are slightly more subject to injury.

Furthermore, women derive just as much benefit from training as men do. In a comparison of males and females during a carefully controlled program, Leroy Getchell and J. C. Moore report in the *Archives of Physical Medicine and Rehabilitation,* women's physical condition improved just as much as men's did. It is simply

* A greater proportion of fat means, admittedly, a smaller proportion of muscle. Yet pound for pound of muscle, studies show, women are just as strong as men.

a myth that men need and can benefit from exercise while women don't and can't. (This idea is particularly dangerous after menopause, when women's partial immunity to heart attack disappears and they become just as susceptible to heart trouble as men.)

Why, then, are women so commonly treated like second-class athletic citizens?

The chief reason appears to be cultural. Kathryn Lance has not only thought deeply about the subject, but has put many of her conclusions into a practical and wise book entitled *Running for Health and Beauty.* When I talked with her, she spoke feelingly about the way society conspires to keep women from discovering the pleasures of athletics.

"Women know they're too sedentary," she said. "But no one tells them to go out and learn a sport, the way men are supposed to do. Women are told to get their exercise by bending over daintily while they're doing housework. If you're a woman, people are always giving you silly exercises to do at home or at the office or on the way to the market. It's the result of a whole cultural bias."

Joan Ullyot, a San Francisco physician and marathon runner, has written of sitting in Golden Gate Park some years ago with a friend and watching her husband run on the grass. Suddenly she was startled by a thought: "Maybe I can do that." She recalled later: "It was a revolutionary idea. I'd never seen a woman running. The whole concept was foreign to me."

Understandably, this stereotype makes some women angry. Nina Kuscsik told me of feeling "cheated" by not having been offered a chance to enjoy the benefits of running when she was growing up. And in *Against Our Will* Susan Brownmiller writes with passion of the same phenomenon: "There are important lessons to be learned from sports competition, among them that winning is the result of hard, sustained, serious training, cool, clever strategy that includes the use of tricks and bluffs, and a positive mind-set that puts all reflex systems on 'go.' This knowledge, and the chance to put it into practice, is precisely what women have been conditioned to abjure."

Sport and Society, an evenhanded treatment written and edited by two males, John T. Talamini and Charles H. Page, puts it succinctly: "To note [sport's] emergence as a two-sex activity . . . should not obscure the persistence in sport of male domination, male prejudice, and discrimination against girls and women."

But a bad situation is not necessarily a hopeless one. Although at this point only some 5 percent of race participants are women, their numbers are growing rapidly. Bruce Ogilvie, a clinical psychologist at San Jose State University, recently offered some relevant advice at a sports seminar in Seattle. Women, he said, have no

lack of natural ability; they are merely subject to cultural prejudices. "Culture pressures are created by what people think a woman should be," he said. "Remember the old bromide—horses sweat, men perspire, women glow." The woman who wants to turn to athletics must therefore "make a leap—a psychological leap. She has to have the courage to redefine herself as a human being." If she wants to get to the top, Ogilvie went on, she must go even further: "She must be fiercely independent, even to the extent of telling her coach to 'go stick it in your ear.' "

Women agree with Ogilvie about the need for determination. "When I first began to run I found it tremendously exciting to feel so good," said one. "Girls practically never have that experience in our society the way boys do. But it did take courage." Another said, "Sister joggers should each get a medal just for breaking out of the cast-iron stereotype."

More and more women *are* breaking out. In my own family, my sister runs regularly. My wife, Alice, has run as much as seven miles. At Binney Park, just down the hill from my house, a number of women run every day, and in Central Park, where I run when my work takes me to Manhattan, there are always women runners on the path around the reservoir.

Most female runners find their way into the sport as part of a search for physical fitness. Dr. Ullyot recalled what she had felt like at the age of twenty-nine: "My body, like all of ours after about age twelve, started going downhill because I wasn't keeping fit. I lost my endurance, if I'd ever had any. If you looked at my list of physical complaints—not just absence of good health, but actual complaints—I had insomnia, constipation, migraine headaches twice a month like clockwork that would last a couple of days. I was rather ill-tempered and tense. Looking back, I think I never was really alive."

Kathryn Lance started running for another reason: "I had this job where I was under enormous pressure. I was smoking a lot and I was overweight. Then I got high blood pressure. I got really scared. I had this idiot doctor who said, 'Stop worrying. Don't eat any salt, and if your blood pressure's still elevated in a few months we'll put you on pills.' I had read about those blood-pressure pills, how they make you depressed and have weird side effects, and once you're on them you may have to stay on them for the rest of your life. I didn't want to start taking them. I had heard that jogging can lower your blood pressure, so I went out and bought Dr. Cooper's book [*Aerobics*] and read it and started jogging." Today Ms. Lance's blood pressure is normal—*low* normal, in fact—and like most women runners she reports a number of other beneficial side effects. (More about these later.)

How should a woman get started in running? As suggested at the beginning of this chapter, it isn't much different from running for men, so the principles outlined elsewhere in this book are applicable for the most part to both sexes. However, there are a few differences dictated by women's anatomy and physiology, as well as by certain hazards more common to the female than to the male.

Women have more trouble than men when they buy running clothes. Men's running shorts often don't fit them properly, but so far there are practically none made especially for women. Shorts cut like men's running shorts can be found in tennis shops, but they cost more. Many women solve the problem by wearing bathing-suit bottoms in the summer. In colder weather, sweat pants, leotards or warm-up suits—finally available in women's sizes—are fine. Not all manufacturers make running shoes for women, as for example, Saucony does. If your foot is fairly wide this presents no problem; if you can find a pair that fit, men's shoes are fine. But if your foot is narrow you may have a hard time. One woman told me that she has to wear two pairs of socks to get her running shoes to fit. One solution is to try Adidas and Pro-Keds shoes first; some models tend to be fairly narrow. And the new Converse line of running shoes comes in three widths.

The Great Bra Controversy is probably a good subject for a man to stay out of. Yet I would be remiss if I didn't mention that some women insist you need a bra when you run, others say you needn't bother, while still others specify certain kinds or even brands. Nina Kuscsik takes a no-nonsense approach: "Women need a firm bra, not one of the flimsy all-elastic ones. That's especially true if you have large breasts. Otherwise they'll bounce and you'll always be waiting for them to come down before you take the next step. Also, you can get abrasions from skin rubbing repeatedly against either skin or clothing." However, most women feel that you're not going to injure yourself if you wear a loose bra, or even if you don't wear one, so it's safe to experiment to see what works best for you.

Many women are reluctant to take up running because of a fear of 1) ridicule, 2) muggers and rapists, or 3) male hasslers. To take the three in order:

Ridicule is something you quickly learn to live with, especially once you realize that it usually signifies disguised envy. Just accept the fact that some people are going to make such derisive remarks as "Hey, honey, if I catch you can I keep you?" Some women prefer to ignore such needling, some reply with oaths that would shock a stevedore (on the reasonable theory that if they reply in kind no male will want to have anything to do with them), while others find it effective to give what one called "half a peace sign." It's all a matter of style.

Fear of muggers is largely unfounded. Anyone worthy of that name can easily figure out that a runner, male or female, isn't going to be carrying anything of value. Why bother to mug such an unpromising victim when there are plenty of others carrying purses and wearing expensive jewelry? And why pick a moving target—one that may even be able to outrun you—when you can find lots of people sitting on benches or simply strolling? Still, it's a good idea not to tempt fate by running alone in remote places or when it's dark.*

Some people are simply up to no good. It's not necessary to find out what their precise variety of evil is; all you want to do is encourage them to stay away from you. Such encouragement can take numerous forms. I once saw a woman in Central Park carrying a four-inch blanket pin—menacingly opened for action. Male runners on the same path were giving her a wide berth. (I know *I* was.) Another woman carries a large stick when she runs; others carry dog repellent or whistles. Running with someone else, either

* Even this isn't an invariable rule. One woman has run at night in New York City's Riverside Park for several years and has never been bothered.

a man or a woman, is also an effective deterrent. So is running with a good-sized dog.

Another hazard women worry about is damage to their bodies. A while back, as noted in Chapter 3, a physician wrote in *Playboy* that jogging is one of the most hazardous forms of exercise. In the case of women, he said, it can displace the uterus and "snap" ligaments in the breast, causing it to droop "like a partly deflated balloon." Every last one of the numerous doctors I have talked with about these hazards has expressed puzzlement. There simply seem to be no citations in medical literature to justify such conclusions. On the contrary, women report that on taking up running their breasts characteristically become firmer, probably because the action of the arms strengthens the pectoral muscles. Nor has any female runner I have spoken with reported any problem with her uterus.

Many women are afraid of becoming musclebound and looking like something out of *Pumping Iron.* The fact is that women runners simply don't become any more musclebound than men runners do. The next time you see a woman running, look carefully at her legs; you'll see long, supple, nicely shaped muscles, not lumpy ones. Futhermore, they'll stay exactly that way no matter how hard or long or fast her exercise program is.

Some women even do weightlifting to improve their running. But Jack H. Wilmore of the National Athletic Health Institute points out that it's not true that strong muscles have to be big ones. "Contrary to the misconceptions created by the comic books," he says, "the skinny kid on the beach might be as strong or stronger than the full-necked ruffian who kicks sand in his face." Wilmore, who is well known for his work with women athletes, says some women have increased their strength by as much as 44 percent with almost no increase in muscle size.

In fact, the odds are that if you're a woman who runs you'll lose both weight and girth even if you don't change your eating habits. As noted in Chapter 6, most women report that in the first year of running they lose ten pounds or more. Furthermore, they do it painlessly and with no recourse to will power because running doesn't make you any hungrier than usual. After a few months or running, Kathryn Lance writes in *Running for Health and Beauty,* "I had the spooky feeling that I was dressed up in somebody else's body."

Far from experiencing difficulties as a result of having taken up running, most women report that their lives become pleasanter and easier. Dr. Ullyot's testimony reflects what many women say: "All of my physical problems have disappeared now that I run. I've gone from a size fourteen to a size ten dress. My pulse is down to 45–50 from 70–75. I haven't had one migraine in five years. . . . I have no problems with constipation; the reverse, if anything. And no insomnia; I sleep like a log the minute my head hits the pillow."

Dr. Kenneth Cooper, one of the founding gurus of the running movement, may underestimate the benefits of running for women. "Women suffering from cramps find exercise extremely uncomfortable," he writes in *The New Aerobics.* "Common sense alone tells them to skip exercise during those days." Not every woman agrees. In *The Jogger* Natalie Browne wrote: "I have found jogging during my period beneficial for two reasons: first, it cuts down on the severity of the cramps (perhaps because I am in better physical shape). Secondly, if I jog at the time my cramps are particularly intense, the pain dissipates."

Marge Albohm, head women's trainer at Indiana University, maintains that most women feel better during their periods if they run. She also reports that "physical performances are not dramatically altered by the menstrual cycle. Some phases of the cycle may put the female in a condition more conducive to efficient performance,* but the differences have been found to be so slight in average daily performance that they are unnoticeable.... Full participation in athletics should be allowed at all phases of the menstrual cycle."

Other investigators report that cramps are by no means the only menstrual condition that is helped by exercise. In one study, Dr. G. J. Erdelyi of Cleveland points out that "athletes had the fewest symptoms of premenstrual tension, especially headaches and dysmenorrhea" (the medical term for painful or difficult menstruation).

Dr. Evalyn S. Gendel goes even further, reporting that women who are in top physical condition not only experience less menstrual discomfort but also have fewer backaches, digestive disorders, colds and allergies and less fatigue. Once they have taken up running, most women are pleasantly surprised by their increase in stamina. A runner named June Cheek tells of having to wake up three times a night to nurse her newborn baby: "I would begin to drag in the midafternoon. By six I was ready to take a nap instead of preparing dinner. Jogging changed all that. I couldn't believe how much better I felt."

The moral would seem to be: during your period, keep running even if you don't much feel like it. You may be pleased with the results. If you aren't, you can always stop.

What about running during pregnancy? Most doctors say that this isn't a good time to start. If you're already running, however, there's no reason not to keep on—unless, that is, your doctor says

* Principally the phase following menstruation, when water retention (and therefore weight) is lowest.

you shouldn't. You'll not only feel better, but after delivery you'll return to your normal shape more quickly. Carol Dilfer tells of running following the birth of her second child, Erin: "I kept it up until Erin was born, sensing that there was some intrinsic value in this whole business of jogging during pregnancy. After I delivered Erin, I *knew* that exercise during my pregnancy had been a tremendous help. I went into a long labor which began at one A.M. after a week-long bout with the flu. I expected to be totally exhausted. Instead, I felt great, took a shower an hour after delivery, chatted with my friends, and never did experience that terrible fatigue that frequently follows childbirth. My recovery was very rapid, my stamina inexhaustible, my sense of well-being tremendous. To top things off, I was able, the very day I brought Erin home, to wear clothing that I hadn't been able to squeeze into for six months after my first child was born."

Sandra Davis finished one marathon when she was four weeks pregnant and another when she was eight weeks pregnant. Trina Hosmer went out for a four-mile run two hours before her first son was born. (She had miscalculated the due date and didn't realize that her feeling of malaise came from being in labor.)

Running performance, incidentally, need not suffer after childbirth. "There are many examples that women do as well after pregnancy and delivery as before," Dr. Erdelyi said recently. "Some of these top-ranking athletes have been Olympic champions after having children. The only thing that could happen is that the children might keep an athlete away from the proper training, and then her performance might drop for lack of preparation."

Women well beyond childbearing age have also been helped by running. Recall the case of the octogenarian Eula Weaver, mentioned in Chapter 4. And even the condition known as idiopathic osteoporosis, in which older people's bones become brittle because of calcium loss, can be reversed through exercise, according to a study at the University of Wisconsin.

By far the most spectacular alterations, however, in women as in men, are those described in Chapter 2—the psychological changes. "It was the first time," Nina Kuscsik reports, "that I had experienced any confidence in myself. I knew I had disciplined myself, that running was my own doing, that no one had pushed me to do it. I knew that I was able to accomplish what I had because I had worked on it. It was very clear-cut."

One woman told me how running helped her during her divorce. "Even with all the emotional trauma, I began to run better and better. I wondered; How can this be? My insides were in such a turmoil that I thought that sooner or later this would take its toll. I ran a marathon four days before my divorce. I was on tranquilizers, and I don't know how I did it. But I knew the running would be good for me physically, and that the end result would be good emotionally. Running helped me through that whole time, and I came out of it healthy."

Where running is concerned, women, unlike men, are only at the beginning. Little more than a decade ago it was thought that no female could possibly run a marathon. Women who applied were refused entries on grounds that they "couldn't run that far." In 1966, however, the Boston Marathon was finally cracked by Roberta Gibb of Winchester, Massachusetts, who hid in the bushes until the gun sounded, then slipped into the pack unnoticed and covered the entire distance. A year later Kathy Switzer became the first woman to run while wearing an official number. (See Chapter 18.) It was 1972 before women were finally allowed to compete officially.

The women's marathon record, improving year by year, reflects the change in attitude. In 1967, it was three hours and seven minutes. By 1975 it was two hours and thirty-eight minutes, far faster than most men will ever run the distance, and it was recently estimated on the basis of scientific analysis that one day a woman will cover the course in two hours and twenty-three minutes. Records at other distances are also falling fast. There is no doubt that as more women take up running, thereby increasing the odds that some really gifted ones will enter the lists, spectacular performances will occur. For women, it's an interesting time to be running—perhaps the best of times.

SENIORS

9

When You're Over Forty

You'll Actually Start Looking Forward to Your Birthdays

After the Boston Marathon a year or two ago I went to a party given by some participants in their hotel suite. No one is more at ease than a runner in the company of other runners after a hard race, so it was a cheerful and convivial gathering, with people busily reviewing—and no doubt embellishing—their performances for the benefit of anyone who would listen. Eventually I fell into conversation with a white-haired man named Norman Bright. Bright was nearly sixty-five years old, yet had run the race that day in an astonishing 2:59:59 and had finished in 615th place, thereby defeating two-thirds of the field. Many of the younger runners at the party, exhausted by the race and feeling creaky, were sitting down or lay sprawled on the rug, but Bright stood and talked animatedly. He was planning to go abroad soon for some races in Europe, he told me, and was looking forward to the change of scenery. Opening an orange knapsack he had stowed in a corner of the room, he began showing me the maps, brochures and entry blanks he had gathered in preparation for his trip. He was as enthusiastic as a teenager.

Norman Bright is unusual chiefly because he is an American. In this country we have some odd ideas about how older people, even those barely into their forties, ought to behave. They should like Lawrence Welk, not Bob Dylan; it is more seemly if they eat porridge, not pizza; and they ought to be dozing in a Barca-Lounger rather than working up a sweat on the road from Hopkinton to Boston. Europeans have few such preconceptions. In West Germany the Deutscher Sportbund has formed more than 40,000 athletic clubs, many of them with programs for elderly people. In Italy some 4,000 senior citizens were among the 33,000 participants in a recent Stramilano, the fifteen-mile race held each spring in Milan, and 150 Italians over sixty entered a forty-three-mile ski race. Though exercising isn't likely to displace wine-drinking as the French national pastime, several thousand Frenchmen over sixty meet weekly for physical training. And in the Soviet Union the state-run *Gotov k truduy oboronye* ("Ready for labor and defense") sponsors cross-country runs and ski meets. In the winter it adds ice swims that are said to be good for the nerves, metabolism and will power.

All this is in contrast to what is expected of older people in the United States. "Our attitude is one of overprotection," says Dr. Theodore G. Klumpp, a New York cardiologist who hopes to help establish a nationwide exercise program for the elderly. "Our middle-aged and older people are encouraged and virtually compelled to reduce their physical activities to the point where atrophy of disuse sets in, with damaging if not disastrous results." As recently as a generation ago there was serious debate about exercise for middle-aged people. In 1950, in a book called *How to Stop Killing Yourself,* P. J. Steincrohn wrote: "Exercise is a state of mind. Like sheep we follow the leader. We have been told that 'exercise is good for you'; we have accepted this dictum without reason, and have subjected creaking joints and protesting muscles to unnecessary strain simply because we think exercise is a necessary adjunct to proper living. Remember: *you don't have to exercise.*"

Yet at long last there are some harbingers of change. One is the growing number of men and women over forty who have taken up running. A recent report from the National Running Data Center showed that of 18,466 runners who entered official races in 1975, some 2,250 were forty or over. Furthermore, many of these men and women train just as hard and race as well as runners who are decades younger. In meets where contestants are divided into five-year groupings, it is not unusual for the winner of, say, the fifty-to-fifty-four-year-old category to cover the course faster than the winner of the next younger group. Not long ago, at a race in Succasunna, New Jersey, I met Percy L. Perry, a seventy-two-year-old runner who started in his sixties after his doctor told him he ought to get more exercise. Today, as a member of the Old Guard Club at his local YMCA, Perry runs six miles a day and can outrun many people half his age. "The doctor says I'm good for another fifty years," he told me.

As mentioned in Chapter 4, Dr. Fred Kasch has demonstrated that several of the chief physical changes associated with aging can be arrested and even reversed by exercise. Furthermore, at the University of Southern California, in a study of women fifty-two to seventy-nine years old, Dr. Herbert deVries and Gene Adams, whose work was noted briefly in Chapter 2, showed that as little as three months on an exercise program can significantly improve the cardiovascular system and lower the resting heart rate. At Penn State's Noll Laboratory for Human Performance Research, scientists have demonstrated that previously sedentary middle-aged women benefit from a conditioning program exactly as men do, and are no more susceptible to injury. Finally, USC researchers have also shown that through a program of running and other exercises faithfully carried out for a year, men in their eighties can lower their blood pressure, body fat and nervous tension levels while significantly increasing their strength. In short, you can improve no matter how late you start.

Probably the biggest benefit to older people, however, is not health per se but the fact that they simply feel better and have more fun when they're in good condition. This, more than dry statistical measures of improved health, accounts for the large numbers of people over forty who are entering the ranks of runners these days. Whatever you do, whether it's work, a hobby, or something as pedestrian as carrying out the garbage, it's pleasanter to do it without having to breathe hard. Conversely, few things are more discouraging than being unable to do what practically everyone else your age can. "Disuse is the mortal enemy of the human body," says the U.S. Administration on Aging. "We know today that how a person lives, not how long he lives, is responsible for many of the physical problems normally associated with advanced age." A doctor put it another way: "Most of us don't wear out. We rust out."

Fifteen years ago, at a publishing house where I worked, I met a trim young editor in his mid-twenties whose name was Ted. He was a person of formidable intelligence, and we enjoyed each other. Eventually we both left the publishing house and lost track of each other. A year or two ago, Ted called and we made a lunch date. I hardly recognized him. He was forty pounds heavier and had developed a double chin that bounced as he talked. He asked me how I managed to stay thin, and I told him about running. A worried look came over his face. "But is it really a good thing for a person your age to do something like that?" he asked me with concern. "I'm forty years old, you know, and I try to take it as easy as I can."

So does most of the population, but by no means all of it. More than four decades ago, in 1935, a twenty-seven-year-old runner named John A. Kelley won the Boston Marathon. Ten years later he won it again, covering the course even faster than in his first victory. Today, though nearly seventy, Kelley still competes in the marathon, to the appreciative cheers of a crowd that regards him as a permanent fixture at the event. And in San Francisco, Larry Lewis was still running six miles a day—and working full time as a waiter at the St. Francis Hotel—when he was over a hundred.

The remarkable and wonderful thing about the world of running is that people like Lewis, Kelley, Bright and Perry are in no sense looked upon as intruders—or even as curiosities. They run in the same races as twenty-year-olds and receive equal respect for their accomplishments. They have their own magazines (including an excellent one called *Veteris,* published in England), their own organization, the Master Sports Association, and even their own annual International Senior Olympics. It is no wonder that far from dreading their birthdays, many runners actually look forward to them, figuring they'll be that much tougher to beat in the next age group.

There is usually little difference in the training of serious young runners and serious old ones. Many of the latter cover as many miles as their juniors, and in some cases even more. "Just because you're getting older doesn't mean you should do less," Ted Corbitt says. "If you step up from five-mile races to marathons you require more mileage." John Kelley runs an hour every day, much of it hard. Jim McDonagh, a top runner in his fifties, once did a 65-mile workout in preparation for the famed 52½-mile London-to-Brighton race, and Corbitt himself has been known to go out early in the morning and simply run all day long. A few years ago, when *Runner's World* put out a booklet called *Running After Forty,* the editors found that there wasn't really much to say about the training of older runners that hadn't already been said for younger ones, so they had to fill out the pamphlet with a lot of biographical information about top runners in their forties, fifties, sixties and seventies.

If you're an older runner, your training will necessarily be governed by two factors: the distance you're training for, and how much work you can tolerate. As Corbitt indicates, a middle-aged marathoner needs to run as many miles as a younger one—probably nine or ten a day at a minimum, and more if he hopes to do really well. However, if he's going to run only an occasional casual race of five or six miles, then a couple of miles a day is plenty. Many runners, as noted earlier, have no interest in racing, and for them, a total of eight or ten miles a week will confer the fitness and sense of well-being they're looking for.

Still, though older runners may run just as far as young ones, they do not, except in rare instances, run as fast. The reason, of course, is that the aging body gradually slows down. Countless scientific studies have shown that as we get older our muscle strength, coordination, maximum heart rate and ability to use oxygen all decrease. So does our ability to adapt to heat. One study showed that men from thirty-nine to forty-five work up a sweat only half as fast as men from nineteen to thirty-one, and that when they're through exercising it takes them longer to stop sweating. Furthermore, to add injury to insult, older people get hurt more easily and recover more slowly.

There are compensations, though. For one, athletic ability declines slowly up to the age of sixty. Strength, for example, rises from early childhood to the age of twenty, then starts an extremely shallow decline (see the graph on page 114). It is not until age sixty or so that the decline shows any appreciable steepening. Moreover, even though older people are more susceptible to injury, they compensate by being more careful. Young people—especially those who do hard interval workouts—are constantly pulling muscles, wrenching knees and bruising heels.

If you're over forty and just starting to run, the most important thing—and probably the most difficult—is to be content with slow improvement. The admonition "Train, don't strain" is especially pertinent. If you put on a pair of track shoes and start sprinting after a twenty-year layoff, you may improve for a while, but sooner or later you're sure to hurt yourself. Muscles and tendons accustomed to years of disuse need lots of time before they can readjust to a more vigorous regimen. During my first two or three years of running I suffered from lots of injuries. Then, mysteriously, the pains went away. Today, nearly a decade later, it is only infrequently that I feel even the faintest twinge of discomfort—and then a good run usually cures it. "A beginning runner has to remodel his whole body," a California doctor who runs marathons says. "He can't do it overnight."

Therefore run slowly at first, slowly enough to hold a conversation. In the beginning it's important to build endurance; speed can wait until later, when you've laid down what runners call a "base." You'll be doing exactly what world-class runners such as Bill

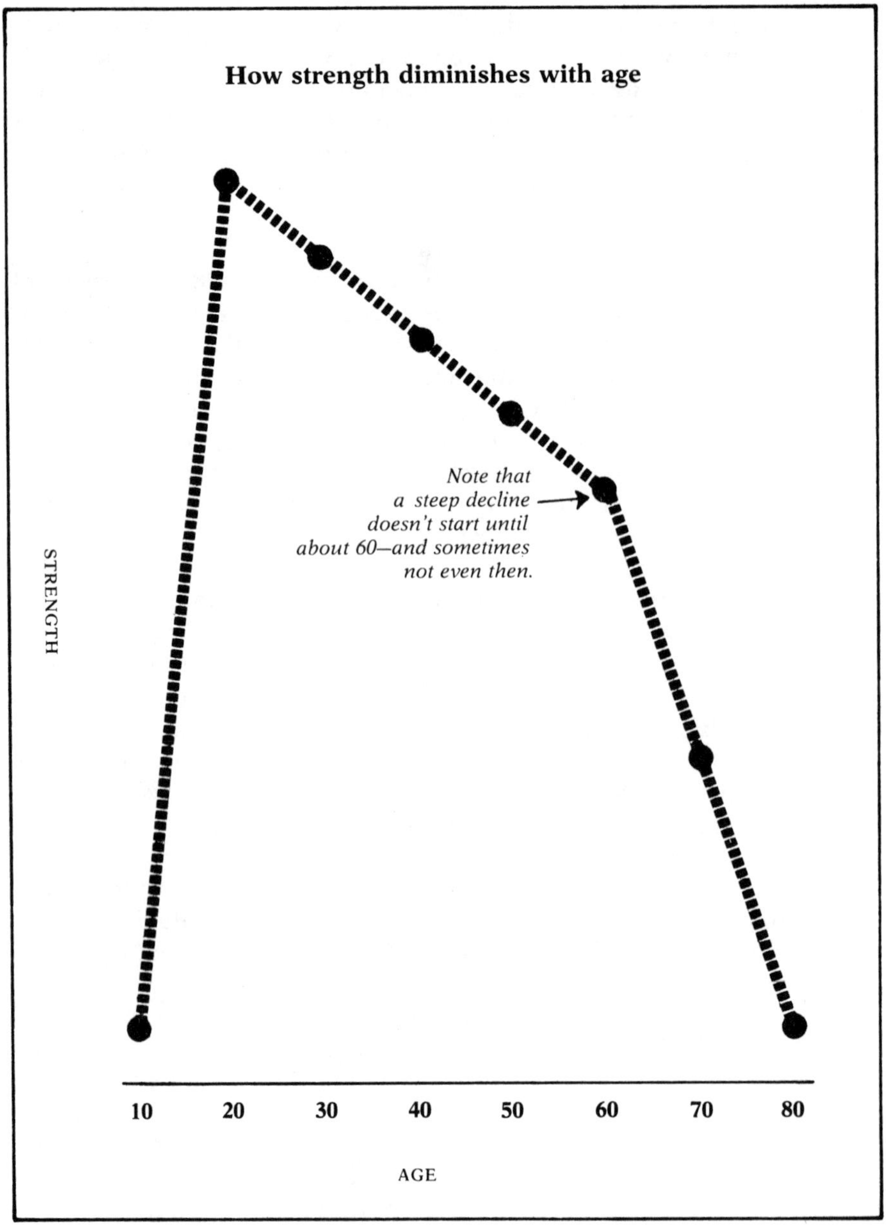
How strength diminishes with age
Note that a steep decline doesn't start until about 60—and sometimes not even then.
STRENGTH
10
20
30
40
50
60
70
80
AGE

Rodgers do when they train. First Rodgers makes sure he has the strength and endurance to run twenty-six miles without undue fatigue; only then does he start adding the grueling speed workouts that allow him to cover the course at an improbable five minutes a mile. To establish and maintain this base, Rodgers runs twenty miles a day, year in and year out. When asked if so much mileage left him tired, he replied, "No, I've been doing it for three years now and can handle it pretty easily." You may decide to run only a mile or two a day, but like Rodgers, make sure you can tolerate this distance at a moderate pace before you try to speed up.

Dr. Leroy Getchell, who, as mentioned, directs a physical fitness program for adults at Indiana's Ball State University, knows precisely how older people respond to exercise. He has written articles and books, among them the recent *Physical Fitness: A Way to Life,* and as a staff member of his university's highly regarded Human Performance Laboratory (see Chapter 23), has access to the latest research. Moreover, as a six-mile-a-day runner himself, he has firsthand experience. Getchell recommends that middle-aged beginners first have a physical, then ease into running by walking until they can continue briskly for an hour without shortness of breath, dizziness, chest pains or extreme fatigue.

The Ball State program, which meets from 6:15 to 6:45 four mornings a week, is a good model for an adult who wants to start running. Men and women work out together. (There's no point in depriving yourself of companionship just because you've decided to take up running.) After some warm-up exercises, participants run fast enough to raise their heart rates to 75 percent of the difference between their resting and maximum rates, added to the resting figure—the same method described on page 67.

Even in older people, exercise—in particular, running—can do a lot to reverse the long-term effects of smoking, drinking and overeating, the salient conditions of twentieth-century living. Studies have shown that sedentary old people who start training become as fit as long-time athletes. Dr. deVries has shown that through exercise, even octogenarians can increase their physical capacities enormously.* In the Connecticut town where I live, a group of runners gathers at a quarter-mile track on Thursday evenings during the summer for short races. There are no entry fees, no formalities, and the participants range from college competitors to mile-a-day housewives and children. During the past couple of summers a muscular white-haired man in his seventies has been coming to the track. Wearing shorts and tennis sneakers, he runs slowly in an outside lane while we race. One night I talked to him. He told me that his wife had recently died, that he lives alone now, and that he started running to see if it would make him feel better. When I asked him whether it had, he grinned like a kid and said, "You couldn't *pay* me to miss a day."

* His research has also demonstrated that people over sixty derive benefits from exercise so mild that it would have little effect on younger people. Even walking produces measurable results.

273

10 Kids

They're Faster— and Tougher— Than You Think

Oneupmanship starts early in my family. One Sunday when my son John was ten or eleven years old we drove to Hamden, Connecticut, to run in a five-mile race. I ran well, so I received the second-place trophy for contestants my age. (Following long-standing tradition, it was a sculptured pedestal of chromelike plastic surmounted by a rampant male runner. Runners' trophies are, I must report, among the world's ugliest.) A few minutes later, John's name was called; his trophy was for being the youngest finisher, and to his delight and my chagrin, it was twice as tall as mine.

A few days later, hearing about John's award, a friend asked, "But is it *good* for someone that young to run so far?" I realized that I didn't really know. I was aware that plenty of children, some of them much younger than John, run, and that many even compete in marathons. I also had heard of one boy, the son of a marathon runner, who'd had open-heart surgery and whose parents encouraged him to run long distances, presumably on medical advice. Still, I didn't know exactly what effect running had on kids and whether it was in fact beneficial to them, so I started reading and asking questions. After all, if running was going to hurt John, I didn't want him to continue, no matter how big his trophies. For all I knew, running might have quite different effects from those of baseball, football or basketball. In those sports, while there are bursts of all-out, heart thumping effort, there are also occasions for rest. But in running, especially competitive running, it's all-out continually. The heart pounds, the legs ache, breathing is labored. What might happen to a child?

As I pursued the question, pieces of evidence started to fall into place. Studies show, for example, that early signs of atherosclerosis–blockage of the arteries–are detectable in an alarming number of young children. Since aerobic exercise, especially if accompanied by a diet low in saturated fats, can arrest and even reverse atherosclerosis in adults, it seemed possible that running might also help children. I raised the question with a distinguished researcher mentioned earlier, Dr. Elsworth Buskirk, director of Penn State's Noll Laboratory for Human Performance Research. His answer confirmed my hunch. "Evidence in the literature," he said, "suggests that primary prevention programs should start with the very young."

A second piece of evidence came from the Department of Exercise Science at the University of Massachusetts. Three researchers there–William B. McCafferty, Arthur C. Cosmas, and Dr. Dee W. Edington–reported not long ago on a study they did which was designed to clarify aspects of the relationship between exercise and longevity. Specifically, they wanted to find out whether exercise begun late in life would help people live longer. Because they used rats and not people, the results of their experiment cannot be extrapolated in their entirety to humans. Still, the implication is clear, for if you get particular results with one organism, you're likely to get similar ones with another. McCafferty, Cosmas and Edington started with four groups of rats ranging in age from four to twenty months and exercised them on a treadmill for twenty minutes a day until they were three years old. The earlier the rats started working out, the better their survival rate. "It appears," said the researchers, "that there may be a threshold age above which an exercise program may not be beneficial. . . . It is reasonable to assume that exercise programs begun early in life (before a hypothetical threshold age) and continued into old age promote longevity more than an exercise program begun late in life."

Another good reason for a child to start exercising early is that he or she is less likely to become fat. Obesity, reported Dr. Nathan

J. Smith at a meeting of the American College of Sports Medicine, is not a dieting problem at all, but one of activity; usually it is too little exercise rather than too much eating that causes fatness. A professor of pediatrics and sportsmedicine at the University of Washington, Smith said, "Nutritional fitness and avoidance of obesity demand an increasingly active life style for the American child."

What about injuries? Might not running's continual stresses cause more damage than start-and-stop sports do? At least one study, conducted by Gregory W. Zoller in Seattle's public schools, suggests that compared with other sports, running isn't hazardous at all. On the contrary, running can even make other sports less dangerous. In *The Physician and Sportsmedicine,* Jack Wilmore, mentioned earlier, has written about the importance of matching the training to the sport. Cardiorespiratory endurance, for example, can help a football player even though what he needs most is strength. "The football player relies on short bursts of activity from play to play," says Wilmore. "Thus football is predominately a speed-and-power type of activity requiring considerable anaerobic metabolism. However, when it comes time to play the fourth quarter, the endurance component becomes crucial. A player with poor endurance will be fatigued . . . and will be more prone to serious injury." In fact, there are very few sports that cardiorespiratory endurance—the type developed by running—won't help.

Furthermore, young people benefit just as much as adults from the psychological changes running produces. Knowing at an early age that you can cover ground faster than all but a few people is a powerful stimulus to self-confidence. To run in a race as a teenager and, with a hundred yards to go, sprint past a fit-looking twenty-five-year-old is to enjoy a rare sense of equality. Roger Bannister has written: "Adolescence can often be a time of conflict and bewilderment, and these years can be weathered more successfully if a boy develops some demanding activity that tests to the limit his body as well as his mind."*

Even the period before adolescence is a vintage time for running. One fall day I traveled to Van Cortlandt Park, at the northern tip of New York City, to watch the National Age Group Cross-Country Championships. There 3,429 boys and girls, some of them only six years old, competed on a 1½-mile course around the perimeter of a broad, grassy field. Divided into two-year age groups, they ran in wave after stampeding wave—first six- and seven-year-old girls, then eight- and nine-year-old girls, and so on through

* Bannister made the observation more than a decade ago. Were he writing now, he would no doubt include girls as well as boys.

boys sixteen and seventeen years old. The results were astonishing. A girl in the youngest category ran the course at a pace well under seven and a half minutes a mile. A boy in the same category ran a 10:48—just over seven minutes a mile, and far faster than many adults will ever do it. But what was even more remarkable than their times was the spirit of the occasion. As the children fought for position in the last few yards, their faces wore the same agonized expressions you see on the faces of international runners, but once they crossed the finish line they were again grinning kids on a day's outing.

Despite the evidence mentioned above, some parents do worry that children so young will hurt themselves by running hard. They would probably also be concerned about events like the "Run-to-Mom 20-Yard-Dash" held at Duke University not long ago for infants six to thirteen months old. Since I have children of my own, I've asked doctors and physiologists what they think about such events. Most counsel a prudent degree of caution—don't urge your four-year-old to run a marathon, for example—but not one has mentioned any way in which a child, however young, can hurt himself permanently by running. What it comes down to is simply being sensible. You don't want your child to return from a workout so exhausted he or she can hardly crawl, any more than you yourself would want to. But if you don't push him to perform beyond his capacities, this isn't likely to happen. No matter what their age, most people have sense enough to slow down when they start hurting too much.

Most, but not all. Young people are less inclined than adults to ease up when the going gets too tough—as, for example, on a sweltering August day. On such a day I've seen high school kids in races, too proud to drop out, staggering dazedly or running on painful blisters. That's silly. There's always another race. Like the rest of us, young people should think of running as a long-term sport, not as something to be conquered in a single season.

It doesn't matter if young people don't race; that's just a bonus if they want it. What counts most is the continuity. There's a special pleasure in running every day in all sorts of weather, and young people are as receptive to it as the rest of us. Running is also something children and adults can do together, an occasion not simply for working out together but communicating with each other both verbally and through their bodies. There's nothing quite like two or even three generations running together, forgetting the differences that ordinarily divide them. The same David Burhans introduced in Chapter 5 spoke of the joys of running with his children: "The pleasure of running was greatly enhanced for me by the fact that right from the beginning four of my six children ran along with me. I bought them all inexpensive track shoes and University of Southern California track shirts just like Daddy's, and we soon had the makings of a family track team. Fortunately, one of the rules of our daily run was that 'nobody is permitted to run faster than Daddy,' so they patiently trotted along beside me as I gradually got into condition to run the kinds of distances and times that they could have managed much sooner. We have since run nine miles—on my daughter's ninth birthday!"

Young people will find most of the principles scattered through this book just as applicable to them as to older people. However, there are a few points that deserve emphasis.

Children's bodies adapt more quickly to training than older people's do, and because improvement comes so fast, it's tempting to push hard and do more than you're capable of. Under such a grinding regimen, everything will probably go fine for a while, but eventually the young runner will acquire a pulled muscle, a sore tendon, or if he's lucky, just a nasty stale feeling. Staleness goes away after a few days' rest, but a muscle or tendon injury takes longer than that. It's important, therefore, to start training slowly, building a foundation of endurance before making any effort to

increase speed. Bill Bowerman, who not only is the author of *Jogging* and the former coach at the University of Oregon, but also is the source of some of the wisest counsel on running ever uttered, suggests that a runner of any age shouldn't start hard running until he or she can run for an hour without becoming overtired. In early training, the emphasis should be on learning to cover distance, no matter how slowly.

Unfortunately, in many track and cross-country programs such leisure isn't possible. At the start of the season runners turn up untrained; since within a few weeks they're expected to compete in a meet, the hard training starts right away. The smart runner has an antidote: several weeks of slow pre-season training on his own. Then when his coach starts cracking the whip, he's strong, fit and ready for anything.

This is especially true if the runner has been eating a proper athlete's diet. Most of the nutritional principles in Chapter 14 are applicable to young runners, yet many young people find it hard to apply them consistently. They're tempted to snack on potato chips, soft drinks and junk foods and to skip breakfast in the morning rush. If you're a young athlete, try to avoid developing such habits. Junk foods provide you with calories but practically no nutritional benefits, and skipping breakfast leaves you without energy when you need it. Nutritionists say that a third of one's calories should be eaten in the morning.

If you're a girl, foods rich in iron are important to make up for the iron lost in menstruation. Liver and dark-green leafy vegetables are convenient ways to get this nutrient. It's also important for girls to stick undeviatingly to sound eating habits. In *Nutrition and the Athlete* Joseph J. Morella and Richard J. Turchetti write: "Males reach their maximum natural fitness during their late teens and early twenties; females, on the other hand, reach their peaks during puberty and the middle teens. There is a steady fitness decline from these ages on, unless it is maintained through proper exercise and diet."

It is generally agreed that an adult runner's diet during the hours immediately preceding competition makes no difference. In the case of young athletes, there is some doubt about this. Some authorities say that children fifteen and younger shouldn't eat for four hours or so before competition. Others dispute this. Among the dissenters is Dr. Robert L. Craig of Fernandina Beach, Florida, who has worked as volunteer physician for high school, Pop Warner and Little League teams. Recently he wrote: "As any parent knows, these youngsters seem to be eating constantly. Many of them are undergoing their growth spurt. If they are deprived of food for periods of four hours prior to a game, it is my impression that the second half of the game provides the setting for extreme fatigue or discoordination. Six hours is too long for this age group to be without food."

Much depends, I suspect, on the individual child. If a young athlete feels weak and tired after four hours without food, it's probably a reliable sign that he or she needs to eat oftener. As with much else in running, a little personal experimenting often yields answers that can't be found even in the most authoritative medical books.

If you're a young athlete who eats properly, trains wisely and toughens your mind for the rigors of competition, are you assured of going to the top? Unfortunately, no. An Israeli physician, Dr. Oded Bar-Or, has made a study of the early indications of athletic excellence and reports that such unchangeable factors as height, reaction time and inborn oxygen-processing ability are crucially important. As the Swedish researcher Per-Olaf Åstrand has said, "I am convinced that anyone interested in winning Olympic medals must select his or her parents very carefully."

On the other hand, there are a good many elements that science can't foresee—at least not so far. It can't take into account motivation, learning ability or willingness to endure discomfort, which is why a person with all the right genetic equipment may be beaten by someone who looks too clumsy to cover a hundred yards without tripping over his own feet. This is also why young runners are so full of fascinating surprises, and why you're in for some fun if you're one of them.

11

Fitting It into Your Life

Thoughts on the Problem of Finding Time

Jerry Noah (which is not, for reasons that will become clear, his real name) is an important Manhattan advertising executive with a big apartment in the city, a summer place on Long Island, two cars, a dog and children in good colleges. Manhattan advertising executives, especially important ones, work hard. To outsiders it may sometimes appear as if they aren't working at all, but that's because outsiders don't understand what they're doing. The main thing outsiders notice are the three-hour lunches. What they don't realize is that this is where much of the work gets done. The three-hour lunches are not, therefore, a luxury or indulgence; without them, there could be no advertising business as the civilized world knows it.

Thus Jerry Noah attracts only perfunctory attention as he leaves his big corner office each weekday at noon, not to return until three. He has been doing it for years and will be doing it for many more to come—if, that is, his luck holds. For Jerry Noah does not in

truth eat lunch at all, not with clients or anybody else. Instead he takes a cab to Sixty-third Street and Central Park West, enters the West Side YMCA and changes into running clothes. In a few minutes he is joined by a maker of documentary films, a securities analyst, a magazine editor and a man who works for a big accounting firm. Their stories are much like Jerry Noah's. Their employers imagine them to be having lunch with people useful to their businesses.

These are the closet runners, and their number is legion. Once you know what to look for, the closet runner is easily identifiable. He (or she, for many are women) has a windburned look all year long. He becomes restless, even dowright twitchy, if a late-morning meeting threatens to last beyond its allotted time. He invariably carries a commodious briefcase of sweatproof construction. Above all, he exhibits a vagueness akin to amnesia when anyone asks about his lunchtime activities. (In most American business offices it is perfectly all right to come back from lunch with your brains so shriveled by martinis that you can hardly find your own desk, but it is considered frivolous to spend an hour in a sweatsuit.)

To the closet runner, running comes first. Superficially he or she may look like anyone else, but there is an important difference. In a society that has not yet discovered what running is all about, the closet runner lives to run. He is a man ahead of his time. This creates problems, some of them with ugly moral overtones. For example, the closet runner will sometimes dissemble about his whereabouts or, to suggest that he has been honorably engaged at lunchtime, even surreptitiously adjust his expense account. This is why he is likely to be a troubled soul. But it is his deliberate choice; he would rather be troubled than miss a run.

Even world-class runners have problems with those who do not understand their love for the sport. Bill Rodgers, who set a course record in winning the 1975 Boston Marathon, is a schoolteacher. He is devoted to his students and often gives them souvenirs such as shoes and T-shirts that he has worn in important races. But he is also devoted to his training, and customarily runs during his lunch hour. "One day," Rodgers told me, "my principal took me aside and said, 'Isn't it about time you started giving as much attention to your vocation as you do to your avocation?' " The comment hurt, Rodgers said, but he knows that if he eliminated the noon run he'd soon be far back in the pack.

Cindy Bremser, a top-ranked runner at 1,500 and 3,000 meters and a nurse at Madison General Hospital in Wisconsin, has had similar difficulties. A ward supervisor once remarked, "She's going to have to make up her mind about what is more important to her—nursing or sports."

These cases are only extreme examples of a problem common to us all: how to find time for running. I have a friend named Wolfgang, a tall, handsome publishing executive in his late thirties. He knows that he is out of shape. He used to ski on weekends and, when he had time, run in Central Park, but in recent years the pressures of a volatile business have kept him from exercising. Lamenting the condition he has fallen into, he once asked me what I thought he could do about it. When I suggested that he set aside half an hour a day for running, a pained expression came over his face. "I just don't have the time," he said.

Whatever Wolfgang thinks, time isn't hard to find if you know where to look for it. Many busy and successful people run regularly. One thinks of the thousands of physicians, executives, financiers, lawyers, judges and others in posts of responsibility who would no more omit their daily run than neglect to brush their teeth. The trick lies in knowing where to find the time. Each of us has a different schedule. It may be impossible to run at one time of day, much easier at another. The first step, therefore, is to make an honest appraisal of your day.

What if no part of your day is perfect for running? In this case, sacrifices are necessary—giving up part of the cocktail hour, perhaps, or getting up earlier than you really want to. You'll find that any inconveniences are thoroughly compensated for by the pleasure of running.

Most people, however, can easily avoid being seriously inconvenienced. Simply settle on the right time of day and then summon the will power to get out the door. Or, alternatively, pick different times from day to day, depending on your schedule. You're luckiest if you're a student—just pick any time after school. For most of us, though, more planning is necessary.

The easiest time of day for running, the time least likely to be disrupted by unexpected intrusions, is early morning. All that's needed is to rise a bit earlier than usual. Even in winter there's a special joy in being oudoors at dawn, a peaceful sense of privacy found at no other time. In summer there's the advantage of getting your run in before the heat of the day.

Some people, it goes without saying, don't like to get up early, not even for running. If you're in that category, try to fit it in at lunchtime. Unless you're overfastidious, you don't even need a place to shower—just a place to change clothes. Jim Nolan, who was introduced earlier, used to work for a big Manhattan corporation and kept his gear in his office. When lunchtime came he closed his door, changed clothes, headed for the elevator and went running in Central Park. Afterward, he sponged off in the men's room with paper towels. (His fellow employees thought him eccentric at first but quickly got used to it; even the most bizarre behavior is taken for granted when it's repeated often enough.)

If you're appalled at the thought of going without a shower, it's worth recalling the comment of a top English runner who worked out three times a day. When an American commented that he must spend half his time in the shower, the Briton replied, "Who takes showers? You Americans have an obsession with smelling sweet." And so we do—a needless obsession, too, for the sweat of honest exercise is practically odorless.

For lunchtime running, it's convenient to join a Y or a gym. That way you can keep your running gear in a locker and avoid having to carry it back and forth. Even if the place has an indoor track, however, run outdoors unless the weather is really foul. You'll avoid joint problems that can result from continually turning the same way. Furthermore, it's less monotonous, and you'll find the fresh air and changing scenery exhilarating.

Running after work has advantages. It's the best time to sweep the day's tensions away. Furthermore, as mentioned in Chapter 6, exercise diminishes your appetite and keeps you from eating too much dinner. There's no reason, by the way, not to run in the dark as long as the footing is good and you wear clothing that can easily be seen by motorists.

Or if your office is a convenient distance from your house, why not run to and from work? Many people get in their running this way. Given the slowness of rush-hour traffic, it takes practically no extra time. Jerry Mahrer, a Bronx schoolteacher, runs the five miles from his home to his job and back again. Ted Corbitt, the former Olympic marathoner, runs to and from his office. "I've adjusted my route to make it as traffic-free as possible," he says. "I used to run around the periphery of Manhattan, but now I run right through the heart of town. To cut down on pollution I pick streets that have the least traffic."

Another way to fit running into your life is by being alert to every opportunity for it. When you take your car in for servicing, for example, run home from the garage. Run to and from the post office as well, or when you pay a casual visit on a friend. Bill Rodgers wears running shoes much of the time so that he can break into a run whenever he wants to.

If you're responsible for the daily care of young children, finding time for running is likely to be especially difficult, but it's seldom impossible. "It is common," writes Kathryn Lance, "for women runners to stop running altogether, or to cut back considerably on their time or mileage, as soon as they become mothers." Try not to. Perhaps you can run when it's convenient for your husband to look after the children. Or hire a babysitter; it's worth the cost. Or search out another woman runner and take turns looking after the children. There's no question that it's tough but you'll feel much better for it.

Certain circumstances put a special strain on even the most dedicated runners. Business trips are one. When you're out of town it sometimes seems as if there's no time for even a short run. If, as sometimes happens, you find yourself being entertained far into the night, facing an alarm clock early the next morning isn't appealing. I've found, though, that there's usually one period of the day when I can slip a run invisibly into my schedule: the hour or so before dinner. Meetings tend to break up about five o'clock, and dinner is commonly scheduled for seven. Some people go to their rooms for a bath and a rest; others gather for a drink or two. That's the time to go running. The chances are that you won't even be missed, but if your disappearance will be noticed and commented upon, don't hesitate to announce, "Well, time for a little jog."* People will admire you for it.

On vacations, running is both a pleasure and a problem. First of all, it is a way of doing some sightseeing. But fitting in a run when you're on vacation can be difficult, especially if you wait until the

end of the day. You're likely to be tired then, and eager to settle down in a warm tub or pub. Furthermore, unknown footing may make it hazardous to run in the dark. The best solution is to run early in the day. Still, it's always possible to be surprised. In England one of the pleasantest runs I had was after dark in Weston-super-Mare. My wife and I had been driving all day and I felt tired. Our hotel, a vast Victorian place of towers and turrets, was on the waterfront. Outside our window, to my delight, was a two-mile-

* Although for convenience we have agreed in this book to call all running, no matter at what speed, running rather than jogging, it's more tactful to refer to it as jogging when you're with nonrunners. "Jogging" sounds less arrogant. Even if you've just returned from a two-hour bout of interval training that has turned your legs to tapioca, refer to it as "a little jog." Why rile people up for no reason?

long lighted boardwalk. I got into my running clothes and went out. It was a mild evening and salt-water scents hung in the air. Suddenly I felt better, and I ran lightly and easily. A dentist from Scotland, who had recently established an office in Weston-super-Mare, was also working out, and we ran together for a while. In an hour I was my old self.

Don't always wait until nightfall, though, because you can't count on being as lucky as I was that time. If you have any doubt about what the day is going to be like, run early.

12 Gear

What to Wear, No Matter What the Weather

One of the nicest bonuses in running is that you need so little equipment. A pair of shoes and the right clothes to keep you warm when it's cold and cool when it's hot are practically all it takes. Yet dressing properly is more involved than it may seem at first because there's a lot to learn about the body's behavior under varying conditions. I had been running for five or six years before I finally learned how to dress in winter, and I made the discovery by accident after someone gave me a paper-thin nylon jacket that repels wind better than all the sweaters, coats, warm-up jackets and sweatshirts I had ever tried.

This illustrates probably the most important aspect of dressing for running: common sense doesn't necessarily help. For example, in winter you'll feel comfortable if you dress more lightly than common sense would suggest. (The heat your body generates is the equivalent of a lot of heavy clothing.) Hence, even though you've been choosing your clothes for most of your life and doing just fine at it, the notes in this chapter may spare you years of trial and error.

The main principles are simple. To start with, it doesn't matter what you look like. Dress as expensively or as cheaply as you like. Cut-off jeans and an old sweatshirt are fine. The only important point is to surround your body with as hospitable an environment as possible. Think of one of those wonderful spring days when the temperature is 55 or so, a light breeze is playing with the leaves, the sun is out to warm you, and the new grass is as springy as Astroturf. On such a day the best way to run would be naked. There's nothing that clothes could provide that nature hasn't already given you. On a cooler day, however, you need to give nature some help, and on a warmer day you want to stay out of nature's way by wearing as little as possible. And always, cold or hot, you need to have the right shoes on your feet.

Because running is such an individual matter, what works for 99 percent of the people may not work for you. So treat the observations that follow as guidelines, not gospel. If something seems sensible, try it. If it doesn't work, or doesn't work as well as you'd like, try something else. When I started running, I saw a lot of runners wearing sweatbands, so after sweat had dripped into my eyes a few times I went out and bought one. I didn't like it. I couldn't get over the feeling that my head was in an iron maiden, so I stopped wearing it, reasoning that I'd rather get sweat in my eyes than have my brains squeezed. Sweat bothers me only part of the time; the sweatband bothered me all the time.

Here, then, from the ground up, is a little primer on running gear. All but a few of its principles are applicable to women as well as to men.

SHOES

Think what you are asking your feet to do when you run. In fact, the remarkable thing is that you can run at all. Each shoe lands on the ground some 800 times a mile. In a ten-mile run, that's 8,000 times. Multiply that by the weight of a 150-pound person and you have a total impact of 600 tons for each foot during every ten-mile workout. That's quite a pounding, and it doesn't stop at your feet, either. The impact of those 8,000 jolts is carried through your feet to your ankles, knees and hips. If you're not wearing the right shoes, your chances of having trouble, either in your feet or somewhere else, are greatly increased.

Tennis sneakers or basketball shoes aren't sturdy enough and don't give your feet enough support. If I didn't have any bona fide running shoes and wanted to go out right now, I wouldn't hesitate to run a mile or two in sneakers—or even, for that matter, in street shoes—but I wouldn't do it as a steady diet. It's worth the expense—anywhere from less than $20 to more than $40—to own real running shoes. First, they treat your feet properly. Second, lacing on your running shoes brings a welcome psychological lift. Even if you feel sluggish, putting on a familiar pair of shoes makes you feel like running. It may sound strange, but it works.

For training—that is, for everyday running rather than racing—most runners like shoes with well-padded soles. The cushioning shouldn't be too soft, though. If you can compress it easily with gentle pressure, it's not firm enough. If, on the other hand, a shoe is stiff and feels unyielding when you stamp on the floor, the padding is too hard. Look for padding that's firm but gives a little. The shoes I've found best have a fairly hard sole with a layer of soft cushioning between it and the foot.

A running shoe should be flexible, especially at the ball of the foot where it bends as you push off with each stride. If it doesn't flex easily enough you'll be using unnecessary effort and putting needless stress on your legs. Before you buy a shoe, bend it. If it takes a lot of pressure, choose another pair.*

A stable heel is important. Look for one that's wide enough to provide a good foundation when your foot lands. Compare shoes, and don't buy any that have noticeably narrow heels. Also, most runners feel that the heel should be built up somewhat higher than the ball of the foot since that's the way street shoes are made; their theory being that they don't want to strain their feet—in particular, their Achilles tendons—by putting them into something radically different. I'm not so sure; I wear running shoes that have practically no heels. But I usually wear fairly flat street shoes, so maybe my feet are used to them.

Don't worry about the weight of a training shoe. A couple of ounces one way or the other aren't going to make much difference. What is important is that your feet be protected from road shock. Some people wear heavy shoes when they train and lighter ones when they race, in order to cut down on weight when they're looking for speed, but many runners wear the same shoe for both training and racing.

A few years ago most running shoes were made of leather. Now almost all of them consist mainly of nylon, which dries quickly and doesn't need breaking in. If you choose a nylon shoe, be sure to buy one that's firm where it grips your heel; that's where support and rigidity are particularly necessary.

* If you already own shoes that are too stiff, you can limber them up by cutting three or four slits across the soles where you want them to bend.

Good shoes are made by all the major manufacturers: Adidas, Puma, Tiger, Nike, Converse, Patrick, New Balance, Karhu and so forth. But don't just take a salesperson's word about what you need; carefully check any shoe you're thinking of buying. Pay particular attention to how it fits. Running shoes should be a bit snugger than street shoes, but they shouldn't pinch or cramp your toes and shouldn't let your foot slide forward so your toes can jam against the front. And it goes without saying that if you're going to be wearing socks when you run (see below), you should wear them when you try shoes on. The same Dr. Moe mentioned earlier has passed along a clever trick for making shoes fit well. "I take a short pair of laces," he says, "and lace up the toe of the shoe for maybe four sets of eyelets, and tie that. Then I take another short pair and go up the rest of the way. I can then adjust the fit of the toes as loosely as I want to, while using the upper set of laces to clamp the foot firmly. I've been lacing my shoes this way for over a year with good success." (Of course this won't work with shoes like New Balance, which have only a few sets of eyelets.)

No matter how well running shoes fit, break them in before you race or take a long run in them. I always start wearing a new pair before the old ones are completley worn out. In this way I can shift over gradually from one to the other. The first time I wear a pair of new shoes I run only three or four miles; then I switch back to my old ones for a day or two. Soon I start taking longer runs in the new pair and wearing the old ones less. By the time the old shoes are close to tatters, the new ones are well broken in and my feet are used to them. Such a cautious introduction may not be necessary if you don't run more than a mile or so a day, but if you're going to be running farther, and especially in anything like a marathon, it's essential.

The care of shoes isn't complicated. If they get wet, let them dry slowly (not over heat) with shoe trees in them. If the heels wear unevenly, repair them with an electric glue gun. Glue guns are simple to operate, and practically everyone nowadays uses one. All you do is drip pellets of glue onto the heels; they harden as they cool. If, after a few hundred miles of running, your nylon shoes begin to smell a bit gamy, just toss them into the washing machine. If the uppers are all leather, you're stuck with the smell; but washing doesn't seem to hurt the little incidental patches of leather on nylon shoes. They get a bit stiff when they dry, but they limber right up as soon as you run in them.

A note on spikes: Not long after I started running I bought a pair of shoes with spikes, thinking they'd make me faster when I ran on cinder tracks. They didn't. Unless you specialize in the 100-yard dash, the only thing spikes will do is make it more probable that your foot will catch on something and cause an injury. If you want extra traction, buy shoes with a deeply imprinted design on the sole—Nike's waffle pattern, for example, or Converse's stars.

SOCKS

Some runners wear socks; others don't. One tireless theoretician of our sport, Charles Steinmetz, thinks running sockless is better because of the weight it saves when your feet get wet, but you should do whatever is most comfortable. For what it's worth, I like the feeling of having my feet in direct touch with my shoes, although the advantage may all be in my mind. Whatever, I've run dozens of marathons sockless and haven't had any trouble. The only exception is in warm, sunny weather when dark pavements become blisteringly hot. If the heat is intense enough, it comes right through the soles of your shoes and makes you uncomfortable. (In such a situation, running through a stream or puddle, if you're lucky enough to find one, helps.)

If you decide to wear socks, choose cotton or wool ones. Nylon, some runners say, can tear your skin up. If you want to keep weight to a minimum, tennis anklets, which are made of cotton, are a good idea.

SHORTS

Nylon shorts, the kind that are slit up the side, are best in hot weather. They're light and cool, and they dry quickly when they get wet. In weather that's cool but not brisk enough for long pants, cotton shorts will give you a touch of warmth. But compared to nylon shorts, they seem to me both stiff and heavy. Incidentally, some runners sew a little three-by-three-inch pocket on the front of their shorts for carrying candy, toilet paper and so forth.

LONG PANTS

When it gets really cold, you need something to protect your legs. You'll be surprised, though, at how cold it can get before you have to switch from shorts to long pants. I run in shorts until it gets close to the freezing point. Then I wear a pair of black leotard pants under my cotton shorts. These cut the force of the wind and keep out some of the cold; furthermore, their dark color helps soak up any available sunshine. Except when it's extremely windy you won't have to put on sweat pants unless it gets below –7 degrees C. (20 degrees F.) It's a good idea to avoid sweat pants whenever you can. They're heavy, bulky and floppy and will do nothing for your running, especially if they get wet. Wear them only as a last resort in the worst weather. I practically never take them out of the drawer.

JOCKS

If you're a woman you don't have this problem, but if you're a man you have to decide whether to wear a jock or jockey shorts. Try jockey shorts first. If they don't give enough support, switch to a jock. If you decide on a jock, pick one with as narrow a waistband as possible to prevent curling—an inch is about right—and choose nylon; it dries faster than cotton.

SHIRTS

When the temperature is above 21 degrees C. (70 degrees F.) the shirt question is simple for men: don't wear one. If you're racing, an Amateur Athletic Union rule says you're supposed to wear some sort of shirt, but officials are increasingly relaxed about this in these liberated times. You'll keep cooler and feel more comfortable without a shirt. (There's nothing like a soaked T-shirt clinging to your skin to make you wish you were doing something else.) If you don't feel right going out in public with no shirt on, try wearing a loosely woven net vest, the kind with just straps instead of sleeves. High-quality ones are available at sporting goods stores, but you can find perfectly good ones in the underwear departments of dime stores. To make them cooler, some people cut lots of holes in their running shirts or snip off the bottom part.

As the temperature gets cooler, you'll want to put more on your upper body. First add a T-shirt, then a sweatshirt and finally a sweatshirt over a T-shirt. When it gets really cold, a light jacket will keep you warm no matter what the weather outside. I have an old wool sweater that I put on over my T-shirt when it gets really cold. With a sweatshirt on top and my nylon outershirt over that, I have on four layers, each with its cushion of warm air. Some runners recommend turtleneck sweaters because they minimize heat loss from the carotid arteries.

When it's cold you'll see a lot of warm-up suits. They look nice, but they seem to me an unconscionably expensive way to keep warm when there are so many cheaper ways.

Incidentally, don't ever buy a plastic sweatsuit. Especially in warm weather such suits get so hot inside that they're dangerous. Furthermore, whatever loss of weight they produce is just water loss, and therefore merely temporary.

GLOVES

During my first winter of running I bought a pair of leather ski mittens, figuring to put an impermeable barrier between my hands and the cold air. My idea didn't work. After a few minutes of running my hands were swimming in sweat because there was no way for moisture to get out. What I needed was something that would breathe. Wool gloves or mittens are fine, but I like white cotton gardening gloves best; they still cost less than a dollar a pair. When they're dirty toss them into the washing machine along with your other clothes.* Some people are convinced that mittens or old socks keep you warmer than gloves, but I haven't noticed any difference.

HATS

Forty percent of lost body heat escapes through your head, so what you wear there matters. In the summer some runners wear a painter's cap for protection. This may be a good idea if you're bald or your hair is thin, but if you have plenty of hair I think it's better not to wear anything. After all, you want to let the heat escape from your head as easily as possible, and a cap doesn't help. The only exception might be a race where plenty of ice is available, as it was in the sweltering 1976 Boston Marathon. Then you can pop ice cubes into your cap as you run and let the cold water drip down your face and neck to cool you.

When it's sunny some runners wear plain visors, the kind that are held on by a headband. To me, they don't seem necessary, though they do keep the sun out of your eyes and prevent long hair from flopping around.

In the winter, hats serve a different purpose; they help keep your body heat in. Then they're essential, especially if you're going to be running for a long time. Some people like to wear a sweatshirt hood instead, but it bothers me to have my ears covered—maybe because I like to hear approaching cars. What I've found best is a simple wool hat, the kind sailors call a watch cap. If it's not very cold you can wear it turned up and let your ears stick out. When it's really freezing, you just roll it down and feel snug. If it isn't too cold, a simple wool headband is fine.

MASKS

I once met a runner who insisted we all ought to wear special breathing masks to filter dirt particles out of the air. He wore one

* Wash all your running clothes often and thoroughly. Nothing will chap you faster than dirty, salt-soaked clothes.

whenever he ran, and he used to delight in showing people how dirty it got. What was caught by the mask, he pointed out, didn't get into his lungs. Somehow the idea has never caught on, but if you run in a particularly polluted area or are especially fastidious, you might consider it.

One kind of mask you occasionally do see when the weather is bitter is a ski mask. There are two reasons for wearing one—one good and one bad. A ski mask will keep your face from getting frostbitten, and even if it isn't cold enough to produce frostbite the mask will make you feel comfortable if you don't mind looking a bit bizarre. What a ski mask won't do is warm the air you breathe. Some people are worried about "burning" their lungs in cold weather, and many beginners won't go out at all when it gets much below freezing. Their fear is groundless. Your mouth, windpipe and lungs can tolerate extremely cold air. In a decade of running I've never heard of anyone whose breathing was at all bothered by the cold.* I've seen top athletes run five-minute miles when the temperature was well below zero. At that pace you can be sure they're doing some deep breathing.

NIGHT RUNNING

If you run at night it's important to be seen easily, so don't wear dark clothes. After you're dressed, put a white T-shirt on over

* The one exception is angina patients, who may experience pain when it's very cold.

everything else, or get a reflective vest; they cost less than $10 and are available from sporting-goods stores that deal in running equipment.

Some runners attach strips of reflective tape to their shoes to attract the attention of motorists. As you try different techniques to make yourself more visible, you'll quickly learn which works best. Cars will swerve the moment drivers spot you, and how early they swerve indicates how clearly you are being seen. If they don't swerve until they're five yards away, you need a different wardrobe—and paid-up insurance. But whatever you wear, run facing traffic so you'll be able to see cars coming and take evasive action.

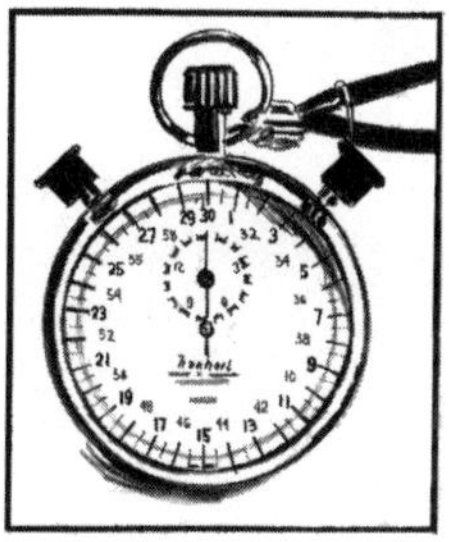

OTHER EQUIPMENT

One of the few other things you may eventually want is a stopwatch. Every once in a while it's interesting to time yourself over a familiar course. You don't have to run at top speed; simply run the course a bit harder than usual. With training, your times will come down.

A watch is also useful if you do a lot of running in unfamiliar places—on business trips, say, or while you're on vacation. With a watch, you'll have some idea of how far you've gone.

You can, of course, use an ordinary wristwatch, but if you're racing it's helpful to have what's known as a chronograph. A chronograph has a regular watch dial and two or three smaller ones that together keep track of elapsed time. It's the only practical way of computing your pace accurately at mile checkpoints. Figuring becomes increasingly difficult as you get tired, as you will in a long race, but with a little practice you'll be able to multiply 17 by 7½ right up to the moment of exhaustion.

Some runners always take along a few sheets of toilet paper for emergency use. And it's a good idea, too, to have a dime in case you pull a muscle and have to call home.

There's one other category of equipment you'll need from time to time: medical gear such as Band-Aids, Vaseline, skin toughener and liniment. But there's no need to buy them in advance; wait till you need them.

13 Coping

What to Do About Rain, Hail, Snow, Dogs and Other Vexations

In the high reaches of certain mountain ranges, where the air is so cold that few animals can survive, specially adapted species of insects live in a microenvironment, a thin layer of sun-warmed air that covers their rocky dwelling place like a skin. A quarter-inch above those balmy rocks they would perish, but within that warmed skin they live as contentedly as tourists in the Bahamas. Some of the special pleasures of running come when we too are in microenvironments. There is a joy in braving cold, wind, snow, rain and hazardous terrain in comfort. Some of the pleasure comes from being out in weather that drives more faint-hearted people indoors. Part also comes from learning how to create a microenvironment in foul weather that makes conditions next to your skin no more blustery than those in your living room.

Running is most fun when you do it every day. There is a feeling of self-mastery in setting forth no matter what the weather; one's spirits receive a particular lift when ingenuity has been required.

Some people are easily dissuaded from running; nightfall, cold, heat, rain or a few snowflakes dissolve their will power. Yet there are few conditions under which it is impossible to run in comfort. Connecticut's winters are harsh. Once I ran in a blizzard so severe I could hardly push my door open against the wind. I was nearly blown off my feet on the icy roads. Yet within a few minutes, despite icicles on my eyebrows, I was sweating pleasantly and feeling fine. It was fun knowing that though an improperly dressed person would quickly have developed frostbite, my sweatsuit, wool hat, gloves and nylon jacket turned the air next to my skin into a balmy summer day.

HEAT

Of all the circumstances under which you'll run, hot weather is the most hazardous. Even in cool weather a runner generates enormous quantities of heat as a by-product of his metabolism—up to thirty times the amount produced at rest. It is easily dissipated through the skin when the surrounding air is cool, so this heat does not build up in the body. But running in hot weather is different. Because heat does not leave the body as easily when the surrounding air is hot, body temperature increases, and there is the possibility, especially if you persist in running hard, that it will rise to the danger point—104 degrees F. or so.

Fortunately, because the body operates best within a narrow temperature range, it goes to great lengths to maintain the correct balance of heat and cold. For example, it opens its damper at the slightest sign of overheating. Experiments have shown that an unclothed person who is relaxing feels most comfortable at a temperature of eighty-five degrees F. or so. If the temperature rises three or four degrees above this, the body activates its heat-regulating mechanisms. First the skin's blood vessels enlarge in order to bring warmed blood from the interior and thus let heat escape into the air. (This accounts for the flushed look some people get in warm weather.) Second, the heart rate and blood flow increase, turning the skin's blood vessels into more effective radiators.

If those mechanisms are enough to keep body temperature stable, nothing more happens. But assume that the air temperature continues to rise. Now the body calls upon its reserves: sweat. The sweat glands wet the body with as much as three quarts an hour in extreme heat, and under most circumstances this evaporation is enough to keep body temperature within its proper range.

But not always. A person exercising heavily, as in running, has special problems in hot weather because he or she produces considerably more heat than someone at rest. If the body's thermoregulatory mechanisms can't keep the temperature low enough, three conditions may result. In order of seriousness they are:

1. *Heat cramps.* These occur in the voluntary muscles, such as the calf, and are usually the first sign of trouble. Some authorities say extra salt, taken either in pills or as part of your diet, helps prevent heat cramps. Others, however, insist that extra salt isn't necessary. They say we get plenty in a normal diet, citing as evidence the fact that runners—even those who don't salt their food at all—often finish a long race crusted with sweated-out salt crystals. Apparently, they argue, we get plenty of salt without trying. For what it's worth, I don't eat much salt and I've never felt a need to increase my intake. I suspect that the best answer to the salt question lies in individual experimentation.

2. *Heat exhaustion.* This is brought on partly by fluid loss (the result of sweating), and partly by the fact that the body's cooling system has sent so much of its blood supply to the skin. The correspondingly decreased flow of blood to the brain can produce confusion or even unconsciousness. Heat exhaustion thus acts much like a circuit-breaker, usually preventing the third, more serious stage.

3. *Heat stroke.* In heat stroke the body's temperature is extremely high—110 degrees F. is common—and the skin is usually (though not always) hot and dry. Other symptoms are dizziness, vomiting, diarrhea and confusion. Immediate attention by a doctor is extremely important.

If you see a runner with heat cramps, or if you yourself develop them, massage usually helps relieve them, and salt water—half a glass every fifteen minutes for an hour or so—restores the body's chemical balance. For heat exhaustion, administer salt water as above; have the victim lie down and raise his feet eight to twelve inches; loosen his clothing; and cool his body with wet cloths and by fanning. In the event of heat stroke, body temperature must immediately be lowered with cool water or rubbing alcohol, or by putting the victim into a tub of cold water. Prompt medical care is imperative.

A second heat-related problem, dehydration, is dangerous because the body is so dependent on water. Its many chemical reactions take place in water. The substances bound for the body's various parts are water-borne, and water is crucial in keeping body temperature stable in hot weather. If exercise doesn't last long, ordinarily dehydration isn't a problem. If exercise continues, however, it can cause 1) a loss of water from the bloodstream; 2) a disturbance in the concentration of certain substances in the blood and cells; 3) heat exhaustion.

There are however, several steps you can take to minimize the likelihood of developing all the foregoing problems.

First, wait until you're used to the heat before working out hard. It takes from seven to ten days to become acclimated to hot weather. During this time the heart rate decreases, sweat production increases, and sweating starts earlier. The most effective way to acclimate yourself to heat is to work out more intensely each day. Once you're used to running in the heat, acclimatization lasts about two weeks.

Drink lots of water while you're exercising. It used to be considered unwise to drink while working out. Recent studies have shown, however, that athletes, including runners, function best when allowed to drink whenever they want to. A 5 percent drop in body weight can reduce efficiency by 15 percent, and 6 percent is about the maximum you can comfortably tolerate. To compensate in advance for fluid losses, some authorities even recommend drinking *before* you work out.* The reason is that our bodies can absorb liquids only half as fast as we sweat them out on a hot day.

Dress lightly. (Even a T-shirt covers some 40 percent of the body.) Wear light-colored clothes to reflect the sun.

Help your sweating mechanism by dousing yourself with cool water—the cooler the better—whenever you can. On warm days I often run along the Mianus River. If I feel hot I stop and wet myself down. (I don't, however, recommend drinking river water.) In a race, if you're handed more water than you can drink at once, drink all you can and then pour the rest on your body. (Dr. R. P. Clark of the National Institute for Medical Research in London has found that of all parts of a runner's body, the thighs heat up most.) If you do, you'll notice an immediate improvement in your running ability, although some runners find that if their feet get wet they are more likely to blister.

Warm up as briefly as possible. As pointed out earlier, warming up increases the body's heat, and extra heat is certainly not what you need. (A study at Western Kentucky University showed, incidentally, that long hair, even as long as shoulder-length, doesn't affect an athlete's ability either to withstand heat or to recover from its effects.)

A brief but comprehensive summary of these suggestions is sent to Boston Marathon competitors. Part of a sheet entitled "Medical Facts You Should Know" reads as follows:

* Dr. Richard L. Westerman and Charles Martin, specialists in the subject, call it "prehydration." Less elegantly but more graphically, researcher David L. Costill calls it "cameling up."

Heat Problems: These occur when it is hot or muggy or both and result from dehydration, loss of salt, and rise in body temperature to dangerous levels. To prevent, try to work out for a week in warm weather; on the day of the race salt your breakfast heavily and/or have a cup or two of very salty broth *no later than 10 a.m.* (salt tablets prior to competition can induce nausea). Drink about two or three ounces of water at every refreshment station along the race course. *Don't* wait until you're thirsty because then may be too late.

Not all people are equally troubled by heat. Some runners seem to have a sort of immunity to it and run well even in midsummer, while others are slowed appreciably on the first warm day. Your ability to tolerate heat depends partly on your size. A heavy person is at a disadvantage in heat because, pound for pound, the skin has less heat-dissipating surface. Furthermore, fat inhibits heat's escape. But some of the differences in people's ability to run in heat are mysteries; the best explanation may be simply that we're not all alike.

HUMIDITY

Humidity is not a problem in itself. It becomes one only because it compounds the difficulties runners experience in heat. When the relative humidity is 100 percent, not much sweat evaporation occurs unless it is windy. Under such circumstances the body may heat up badly. You can use a wet-bulb thermometer to tell how severe a problem humidity is; a reading above 70 degrees means that competition will be difficult. A wet-bulb temperature of 80 degrees is pretty much the upper limit for athletic activity, however light.

COLD

Although it may sometimes seem unpleasant, even extreme cold isn't much of a problem. With a little experience and some attention to the suggestions in Chapter 12 you'll find it easy to dress comfortably in any weather. In fact, the chief problem is to avoid *over*dressing. When a blizzard is howling it's hard to restrain yourself from putting on an extra sweatshirt or a pair of heavy ski mittens. If you dress lightly you may, it's true, feel chilly when you first step outdoors, but within a few minutes you'll find yourself sweating as if you were in a tropical rain forest. Experiments by Canada's National Research Council show that the amount of clothing needed to keep a resting person comfortably warm at 70 degrees F. will keep a runner warm at –5 degrees.

The key to winter dressing, therefore, is to wear as little as you can—just enough to keep you pleasantly warm. After a while you'll

be surprised to discover how few clothes you need—a good thing, too, because extra clothes weigh you down and make running more difficult. But be careful on days when the weather may worsen during your run. If it turns cold when you're a long way from home you may be in for some real discomfort. Stephen Richardson suggests that in changeable weather you take along a nylon jacket. Such garments are light enough to be stowed in a pocket or tied around your waist, yet give a lot of protection.

To minimize the effect of evaporative cooling, plan your run so that you're running to windward as you start and downwind as you finish. Even in extremely cold weather it's astonishing how pleasantly warm you can feel while running downwind, and—see the table on page 151—how cold you can feel when you're running into the wind.

Dressing for winter running is easy if you understand how the body protects itself from the cold. The first priority of its regulating mechanisms is keeping your head and torso warm enough. If excessive cooling there becomes a problem, your body sends these parts of your anatomy extra heat, even at the expense of your fingers and toes. If, on the other hand, all's well with your head and torso, any leftover heat is available to be sent elsewhere. The lesson is clear: always dress so that your head and torso are warm. Wear a heavy wool hat and enough clothes to protect your chest, stomach and back.

Dr. William C. Kaufman of the University of Wisconsin conducted an experiment that neatly demonstrates the body's system of priorities. When he exposed volunteers to cold he found that as long as their torsos were warm enough, no matter how cold their fingers and toes became, they didn't shiver. But when he kept their fingers and toes warm and let their torsos get cold, they started shivering—the body's way of forcing itself to work, burn calories, and thereby create heat.

An incidental cold-weather hazard—though not, I am happy to say, a common one if you dress properly—was described not long ago in the *New England Journal of Medicine* by Dr. Melvin Hershkowitz of Jersey City, New Jersey. It is frostbite of the penis, and it was incurred by a fifty-three-year-old physician during a thirty-minute run in below-freezing weather. Fortunately, symptoms disappeared within a few minutes. The patient, according to the report, has instituted rigorous precautionary measures.

HIGH ALTITUDES

Altitude isn't usually a problem. It takes only about a week to become fairly well acclimated to a 3,000-foot increase, and once your body has adjusted, you can work just about as hard as someone who has lived there all his life. If you should ever go to a high altitude, take things easy for a few days, then start working out, a little harder each day. Before long your body will have manufactured extra hemoglobin—the substance in the blood that carries oxygen—as well as increased its total blood volume and breathing efficiency. When that happens you're as fit as a mountain goat.

RAIN

One day while I was running it began to pour. It was a warm day, and even though I was quickly soaked I was happy and comfortable. A car pulled alongside me and the driver rolled a window down. "Want a lift?" he called. I thanked him and waved him on. "You'll get soaked!" he insisted. When I finally explained that I enjoyed the rain, he shook his head and drove off.

Like altitude, rain is usually not a difficulty. On a hot day you'll be grateful for it. It's only when the temperature drops below 13 degrees C. (55 degrees F.) or so that you'll want to protect yourself from it. A light rain jacket is usually enough.

SNOW

Running in the snow is a wonderful experience. When there's a thin sprinkling on the ground you'll feel as if you're running in a Christmas card. It's only when the snow gets deeper that it will bother you, and then only because you won't be able to maintain your usual pace. Don't try; accept conditions as they are. Because you'll be working harder you'll get just as much exercise going slowly. Instead of counting miles, count minutes. If you ordinarily run for half an hour, do that and no more. What does it matter if you don't cover as much ground?

ICE

Running on ice is tricky. Especially on wet ice, it's easy to slip and pull a muscle. Avoid it if you can. If there's ice on the roads in the morning, wait for cars to wear it away; it may be gone by later in the day. Better still, find a place that isn't icy—perhaps a snowy path or field. I've never tried it myself, but I've heard of people running along the covered walkways of shopping centers. I recently talked with a runner who sometimes wore crampons of the type used by mountain climbers, and I once met a woman who said she used spiked running shoes when it was icy. The trouble with such devices is that when you come to bare roadway they jar your legs and set up an annoying clatter. Probably the best solution is to use an indoor track until the weather eases up.

HAIL

If it begins to hail while you're running, common sense is the most reliable guide. When hailstones are small and don't threaten your life, health or equanimity, press on. When they get big enough to hurt you, take shelter. Fortunately, hailstones of that size are rare. I've been in perhaps a dozen hailstorms and have never had to stop running—though I've come close to it.

WIND

You'll be aware of wind whenever it's blowing at eight to ten miles an hour. If you're running against it, it will slow you down and make you feel sluggish. Don't let it bother you. Act exactly as you do when you're slowed by snow; simply accept the fact that you can't move as fast as usual. Put your head down, lean into it, work your arms energetically and make the best of it. But watch out for sudden gusts; they can be dangerous. If you're in a race, you can console yourself with the thought that everyone else is running under the same handicap.*

If the wind is at your back, enjoy it. It will make running easier, lengthen your stride and feel like a friendly hand pushing you along. The 1975 Boston Marathon was run in a blustery tailwind, and all of us, including the winner, Bill Rodgers, were cheered on by it.

Wind is a problem only in low temperatures. Because of the wind-chill factor, a given temperature feels colder than in still

* But for a way to minimize the effect of wind, see Chapter 17.

RUNNING WHEN IT'S COLD AND WINDY

When it's windy, the severity of cold increases more than you might imagine. This table, adapted from U.S. government sources, shows how winds of various speeds lower the apparent temperature.

Temperature (°F.)	*Wind Speed* 10 MPH	20 MPH	30 MPH	40 MPH
+50°	40°	32°	28°	26°
+30°	18°	4°	− 2°	− 6°
+20°	4°	−10°	−18°	−21°
+10°	− 9°	−25°	−33°	−37°
0°	−21°	−30°	−48°	−53°
−10°	−33°	−53°	−63°	−69°
−20°	−46°	−67°	−79°	−85°

weather. (See the table on page 151.) In a twenty-mile-an-hour wind, for example, a temperature of 50 degrees F. feels like 32. Because the effect becomes more pronounced as the wind blows harder, use caution.

LIGHTNING

Once in a while you'll get caught in a thunderstorm. If you can, get inside a building or a car. If you can't, stay away from water, ridges and solitary trees, and don't touch metal. Get into a hollow or ditch and crouch down, under brush if possible—unless it's wet there. If your hair stands on end, an electrical charge is building up nearby and there's imminent danger of a lightning strike. The best thing to do, according to the latest word from the Geneva-based International Commission on Atmospheric Electricity, is to kneel down, press your knees and feet together, put your hands on your knees, and bend far forward to make your body as unlike a lightning rod as possible.

And, perhaps the commission should have added, pray. Once, near the summit of Mount Madison in New Hampshire, my wife and children and I were caught in a thunderstorm as we hiked on a trail that snaked its way along a ridge. At one point our hair stood on end and Saint Elmo's fire danced on the metal frames of our backpacks. We got off the ridge in a hurry.

SAND, SLUSH AND MUD

All three will slow you down. Since there's not much you can do about them, be philosophical.

Sand is annoying when it gets into your shoes. If you're running on a beach, you may be more comfortable running barefoot; it's no trouble to carry your shoes, one in each hand. Whenever you can, land on patches of seaweed (watching out for jellyfish); you'll sink in less and have more secure traction.

As for slush, it's chiefly a nuisance, not a danger. When you run, your feet keep working so hard that even severe cold usually won't hurt them. They may feel numb for a while after you're back home, but soon they'll come tingling back to life, ready to take you dancing all night. The chief problem with slush is the cars that splash it all over your body. There's nothing like a faceful of the stuff to take the fun out of a winter's day.

I find it hard to say anything good about mud. It makes you slip, gets your clothes dirty, and, should you fall down in it, subjects you to the merry laughter of your companions. Stay out of it if you can, and be careful if you can't.

ROUGH TERRAIN

Uneven ground—forest trails and rocky paths, for example—are no problem if you don't run on them for too long at a time. If, however, you put in a lot of mileage on uneven ground, the stabilizing muscles of your legs tire, and this increases the chances that you'll twist an ankle or fall. Take rough terrain in small doses. Be particularly careful not to step in a hole, trip on a fallen limb, stub your toe against a rock, or slip on wet leaves. And if you have any Achilles tendon pain, however slight, stay away from rough terrain altogether.

HILLS

When I first started running I considered hills my enemy. They were hard to run on, made me slow down and shorten my stride, and left me winded. But it finally occurred to me that if hills were hard to run on, they might be doing me some good. And so they were. Running uphill strengthens the quadriceps, increases cardiorespiratory capacity and makes it easier to run uphill next time. You can't, of course, run uphill as fast as you can downhill; that's simply one of the things runners learn to accept.

When you come to a hill, start climbing at a pace you think you can sustain. (It's discouraging to start out fast, then have to fade to a walk.) Lean forward, shorten your steps and swing your arms parallel to your direction of movement as if you were a steam locomotive, rather than across your body. Think of uphill running as shifting gears. You want to cultivate an efficient style, one that gives plenty of power for overcoming gravity; speed can wait until you reach the top. Then you can celebrate by letting yourself fly.*

* In a race, however, don't go downhill at an all-out pace. You'll tire more than you think, and be half dead when you reach the bottom.

DARKNESS

Most of us do at least some of our running in the dark, either in early morning or at the end of the day. There's nothing to it if you observe a few simple rules:

1. Run facing traffic and stay close to the edge of the road. If a car should look threatening, simply step off the road. Of course, there are hazards in leaving the pavement for the dark unknown—ankles have been broken this way—but it's an easy choice, considering the alternative.

2. Wear a reflective vest or at least light clothing. If you forget and go out in a dark-blue sweatsuit, you'll notice a distinct and disturbing difference in how soon the cars veer away.

3. Run on roads you know well. Before you venture onto a road in the dark, survey it carefully to make sure it has no potholes or other booby traps.

4. Don't look directly at headlights; bright light temporarily blinds you. If, as frequently happens, a driver forgets to lower his beams, try to catch a glimpse of the road ahead and memorize its contours. Looking slightly away from light also helps to bring into play your less light-sensitive peripheral vision.

FOG

Running in fog is much like running in the dark, except that it rarely gets so thick you have trouble seeing the road ahead. But remember that in fog motorists can't see as well as usual, even in daylight. Further, because they're concentrating on driving, they may not be ready for the sudden materialization of a runner. Try to run on roads without much traffic, or on paths or sidewalks.

Don't wear gray in fog; you'll blend right in and be invisible. Red and orange contrast well with fog.

CARS

Night or day, cars deserve caution. Few drivers will go out of their way to maim you—though it's not unknown*—but some seem to have only a vague sense of where they are on the road. As mentioned a moment ago, it's always important to face traffic but there is one exception to this: a sharp curve. On the inside of such a

* One theory, enunciated persuasively by George Sheehan, is that runners are seen as a threat to society's prevailing values. Once you've had a beer can or two tossed in your direction, it's difficult not to suspect that Sheehan is on to something.

curve drivers can't see far ahead, so always run on the outside of the bend. The risk from traffic on the blind curve is greater than the risk from traffic behind you. Both dangers are minimized if you stay away from narrow roads.

Another automotive risk is breathing exhaust fumes. I had always known carbon monoxide was bad for you, but I never realized how bad until I read an article in *Runner's World* by Dr. Harry Daniell. Daniell pointed out that carbon monoxide attaches itself to the blood's hemoglobin even more tightly than oxygen, and that, unlike carbon dioxide, it does not readily disappear but circulates in the bloodstream for some time. If, therefore, you run in an atmosphere heavy with carbon monoxide, the concentration in your blood increases. Furthermore, during a full eight hours of sleep only half the carbon monoxide in your body disappears.

The moral is clear: run where there are as few exhaust fumes as possible. Even in the city you can usually find lightly traveled streets.

DOGS

Every runner has at least one dog story. Frances Goulart tells of a dog that bit her while she was running. The owner laughed and remarked, "He only nipped you." "Nipped me!" said Mrs. Goulart. "Look at my stomach! I'm bleeding." Whereupon the owner laughed again. "He was just playing," he said.

Mrs. Goulart's story illustrates a peculiarity of dog owners—their belief that a dog, no matter how murderous, is incapable of doing wrong. A few years ago I had some bad moments with a Great Dane in a public park near my house. In alarm, I picked up a stick in order to hold the beast at bay. Its owner rushed over and ordered me to drop the stick.

"You're frightening my dog," he said.

"Your dog is frightening me," I replied, none too pleasantly. I was not at my cheerful best.

"Well, do your practicing somewhere else," he said. "Tiny has as much right to be here as you have."

In short, you can expect little sympathy from dog owners. Instead, you must learn to fend for yourself. There are several theories about how to do it. Over the years I have probably tried them all, and have discussed the subject with innumerable other runners and even with a running veterinarian who offered some insights into canine psychology. Here, then, are the principal ways runners customarily deal with dogs:

The "nice doggie" gambit. In the belief that love really does conquer all, some runners try Christian charity by attempting to make friends with dogs. All that Christian charity does, I am sorry to say, is make an animal wonder what's wrong with you.

The Richardson riposte. Stephen Richardson, a dog owner and close student of dogs, relies on an authoritative "No!" or "Go home!" He says this always works, but then he's six-foot-three. I suspect that just about anything works when you look like Richardson.

The no-doggie ploy. This one consists of simply ignoring the beast, and it doesn't work well. When a dog goes to the trouble of barking at you, it wants attention. It will only become more menacing until it gets the audience reaction it feels it deserves.

The mad runner caper. To execute this one, wait until a dog is close to you. Until this strategic moment, run as usual. When the dog is nearly upon you, turn, make a blood-curdling noise and flail your arms as if demented. Even a dog seriously bent on mischief will think twice about pursuing a relationship with so unpredictable a soul.

The bluff. Dogs naturally don't like to have things thrown at them. If, therefore, you bend down as if to pick up a rock—there doesn't actually have to be one handy—all but the boldest animals will retreat. If the menacing dog is one you pass often, tossing a real rock in its direction from time to time, or squirting a one-to-three solution of ammonia and water at it, will suggest who's boss. It may continue to bark at you but will probably keep its distance. Incidentally, try not to get caught at this by the dog's owner.

None of these techniques is foolproof. Still, the last two, as indicated, seem to work best. My veterinarian consultant was able to shed some light on the reason. Dogs, he explained, are assiduous defenders of turf. They quickly learn their territorial limits and zealously guard their borders. If a passing runner shows no sign of threatening these borders, a dog will usually content itself with some harmless warning barks. Therefore, upon sighting a dog, the prudent runner crosses the street in order to avoid hallowed ground. But try not to act afraid. Dogs are extremely responsive to fear and only become more aggressive.

PEOPLE (HARMLESS)

Especially on weekends, when sightseeing motorists are out, you'll occasionally be asked for directions. When the inquirer is going the same way you are, it's no problem; if you have the information he wants, have him drive along with you as you tell him what he needs to know. When the car is going in the opposite direction, though, you face a hard choice. Do you obligingly answer questions, and therefore interrupt your run, or simply run on? I've never solved this one. Sometimes, especially when the person in the car looks particularly helpless, I stop. At other times, I confess, I feign a trance and run right by.

When people ask questions, try not to be impatient with them. Providing information to passers-by is, I've finally concluded, the runner's public trust and an inseparable part of our lot.

Among the other people (harmless variety) you'll encounter are those who urge you on with an upraised thumb or such encouraging words as "You're looking great" or "Way to go." These accolades are to be welcomed, encouraged and acknowledged with an appreciative wave.

PEOPLE (HELL-BENT)

For reasons best known to themselves, some people can't stand the sight of a runner. There aren't many of them, but when one comes along you know it. They shout abuse at you from passing cars, fling objects at you and sometimes drive so erratically that you fear for your life. Others gather in ugly little clots on streetcorners and mutter about your manhood and the shape of your legs.

There are essentially three schools of thought about how to handle this problem. One school counsels stoicism. Ignore them, its adherents say, and they'll go away.

A second school advocates fighting back. Shout obscenities, they suggest; make vulgar gestures; in extreme cases hurl lethal objects.

The third school urges you to catch curmudgeons off guard by smiling disarmingly and saying something friendly. "Even the hard-core hecklers are often softened a bit by a runner's unsolicited friendliness," a runner named Pete Hanrahan wrote in *Runner's World.*

One of these techniques may consistently work better than the others, but I don't know which it is. Still, I have no doubt which is most satisfying to a runner's soul. At a recent meeting attended by several hundred specialists interested in scientific aspects of the sport (many of them runners themselves), a psychiatrist told of an incident in which a solitary runner was heckled by a carful of teenagers. The runner overtook the car at a traffic light. Holding a steady pace, he took one heavy step on the car's trunk, another on the roof, and a third on the hood—leaving three great dents to mark his passage. The assembled specialists gave the story a standing ovation.

14
Eating to Run
Good News If You Really Love Food

A *few years* ago, soon after I had started running, I yielded to temptation one day and ate an enormous lunch: two hamburgers, French fries, a milk shake. On the way home from work I cursed my will power. I felt leaden and dreaded the terrible, plodding run I was sure I would have that evening. If I got through it at all, it would be on sheer doggedness; I was sure there would be no joy in it. Instead, it turned out to be one of the best runs I've ever had. I floated, my shoes barely kissing the earth. My feet were feathers, in swift and subtle communion with asphalt, sand and grass.

Now consider another run. This time I was starved. I was training for a marathon and wanted to be light and lean. Even before setting out, I felt weak. Furthermore, the day was hot—in the nineties—and I remembered with no relish my last two runs in the same heat. Yet as I dogtrotted down my driveway searching for rhythm, I suddenly knew that this too was to be an extraordinary day.

Unbothered by the heat, I moved easily along the sticky asphalt roads, feeling light, powerful, tireless. At Greenwich Point, a wooded seaside park three miles from my home in Riverside, Connecticut, I stopped for a drink of water, then went on, enjoying the sight of geese, rabbits and pheasants, and keeping an eye on the progress of a sailboat making its way down Long Island Sound. In the hills at the end of the run I finally tired a bit but felt no need to slow down.

One lesson to be drawn from these two almost identical runs in which my nutritional preparation was so different is that our bodies move in mysterious ways. Another is that nutrition isn't everything. You can try to improve your running by eating sensibly, and in the long run you'll probably have some success, but eating right is no guarantee that any particular run or race is going to be a good one. There are too many other variables in the equation.

Even professional nutritionists find it hard to agree on matters you might suppose would surely be beyond debate. For example, is fasting a good idea for a runner? This would seem to be a fairly fundamental question, one long since answered, yet in *Food for*

Sport, Dr. Nathan J. Smith says: "Now and then a question arises regarding the advantages of periodic fasting. Fasting limited to 24 or 48 hours need not be damaging to a healthy individual, but an athlete cannot expect to compete effectively if he is deprived of energy sources for such periods during his training. There is no evidence to suggest that periodic fasting provides any competitive advantage." In contrast, *Food for Fitness,* published by the editors of *Runner's World,* gives a quite different view: "Many people undertaking fasts of several weeks or more mention feeling 'strong as steel,' even increasing in strength during the late stages of not eating."

Two individuals may even respond differently to the same regimen, so each of us must discover how his or her own body works. Roger Bannister, who ought to know, once said, "What applies to one person doesn't necessarily apply to another. It's easy to build a whole mystique about diet and the pharmaceutical side of sport. There's no proof that special foods or extra vitamin supplements are necessary as long as people eat a normal, balanced diet. I think the essence of good performance is doing it the natural way."

Yet in spite of all these caveats, there do seem to be a few general principles worth heeding, particularly in view of the fact that, according to recent studies, dietary deficiencies are surprisingly common.

Eating and drinking can be made into enterprises of incredible complexity, and this is particularly true of sports nutrition. Not long ago a group of researchers gathered in Leningrad for an international symposium on the nutrition of athletes. They came from Eastern Europe, Japan, Brazil, Cuba, England, and the United States and many other countries. On the dais and off, they argued endlessly about nutritional matters so minute that you and I would consider them insignificant. As George V. Mann, a physician who attended the conference, explained in *The Physician and Sportsmedicine,* "When many competitors are very good and almost equal, attention turns to training factors that will give some small advantage."

Average runners, and even most runners who are better than average, need no such knowledge of nutritional minutiae. We simply want some general information about how to eat sensibly. Since we're going to make so many deliberate mistakes anyway—a glass of beer or a piece of cake—it hardly makes sense to become fanatical about the subject. Hence, this chapter will only examine some of the generally accepted principles of athletic nutrition. It is written on the assumption that you have already been exposed to, or can easily find out about, garden-variety nutritional rules. After all, you got this far on your own.

To start with, one notion should be cleared out of the way. Some people persist in thinking there are certain "miracle foods." There aren't. *Nutrition and Physical Fitness,* by L. Jean Bogert and other authorities, a classic in the field, puts it this way: "A good diet—one based on meat, milk, fish, poultry and eggs, whole grain cereals, legumes and nuts, leafy green vegetables, and other vegetables and fruits—will meet all the nutritional requirements of athletes. Vitamin pills and special supplements are not needed and should not be relied upon because they may lull the individual into thinking he has met his nutritional needs when in reality he may still be lacking in protein and minerals." Similarly, the same Dr. Thomas Bassler who was quoted earlier, enunciating the American Medical Joggers Association point of view, says, "We do not endorse the use of any specific foods or diet supplements. Avoiding highly refined foods is recommended: sucrose, starch, saturated fats, and distilled alcohol." Otherwise, Bassler says, a normal, well-balanced diet containing fresh fruit, raw vegetables and not too much meat is best.

Nor, for that matter, are there really any "health foods," even though we label some foods thus. A container of fruit-flavored yogurt, for example, often considered a health food, contains some 250 calories, as many as you'd find in the same amount of ice cream. Still, if it makes you feel better to buy food at so-called health-food stores, there's no reason not to. There's probably something to be said for avoiding the pesticides, herbicides and fungicides that go into so much of what we eat nowadays. But in a nutritional sense health foods and ordinary foods work in exactly the same way. (Two notable exceptions are refined sugar and white flour, neither of which do us any good and, in the case of sugar, may do us considerable harm.)

For many years it was thought that athletes needed more protein than other people. Nutritionists now agree that they don't. What you *do* need more of, particularly before a run of more than an hour, is carbohydrates. The reason lies in the body's way of converting the chemical energy in food into mechanical energy. The process is somewhat complicated—complicated enough, in fact, that if you think about its details while running you're likely to worry yourself into an inert heap by the side of the road. Whole books have been written on the subject. (One of the briefest and best is E. C. Frederick's *The Running Body;* see the bibliography.) For practical purposes you'll know enough if you simply remember that protein, important as it is for other reasons, doesn't count much in energy production. Studies have shown that diets low in carbohydrates and high in fats markedly reduce energy, while the opposite diet—high carbohydrate, low fat—increases energy. One reason is that about 10 percent less oxygen is needed to metabolize a given unit of carbohydrate energy. Another is that a high-carbohydrate diet can pack the muscles with more than their customary amount of glycogen, the substance which, once the body converts it into glucose, is oxidized and turned to energy.

All this doesn't mean that you will gain anything but weight by *over*eating carbohydrates. It does mean, however, that when you're choosing food, it's better to lean toward carbohydrates than fats. One day I stopped by Bob Glover's office to say hello. It was a Wednesday, and on Saturday Glover was planning to run a fifty-mile race. As we sat talking, he broke pieces off of a succession of raisin cookies and popped them into his mouth. To a nonathlete, such a diet would have looked insane, but Glover knew what he was up to. (He came in fifth in the race and felt fine practically all the way.)

What Glover was doing is exactly what most top athletes do before a long race. The process goes by the name of carbohydrate loading or, in more scientific terminology, supercompensation. Researchers have discovered that if the body is deprived of carbohydrates for a few days, then fed large amounts, the energy-producing glycogen in muscles can be increased by as much as 300 percent. The results are twofold: first, you have more energy; second, you may postpone—and perhaps avoid altogether—the dread moment known as "hitting the wall," when one's energy stores are exhausted. Men, as mentioned earlier, seem to be more susceptible to hitting the wall than women are. Because they have larger natural sources of fat, women can stave off exhaustion considerably longer.

Carbohydrate loading is a fairly recent development. "Only ten years ago, we all ate a steak the night before a race," says Paul Fetscher, a marathoner from Long Island. "Now we're busy packing away pasta." Carbohydrate loading was developed by a Swedish physiologist named Eric Hultman. The process takes exactly a week, though the optimum time varies from person to person. On the first day you take a long, exhausting run. Then for three days you train normally while eating a diet extremely low in carbohydrates and high in protein. During the last three days you eat more carbohydrates than usual—bread, spaghetti, cake and so forth—and cut down on protein. Thus nourished, the muscles soak up all the glycogen they can hold. ("Loading" is a slightly misleading term. It doesn't mean stuffing yourself. You should eat about the same amount you ordinarily do but alter the proportions.)

Studies of marathoners have shown that those who observe this routine do measurably better than those who don't. Still, not every marathoner is a party-line carbohydrate loader. Frank Shorter follows the second part (high carbohydrates) but not the first (low carbohydrates), in the belief that when he's training hard every run is glycogen-depleting. He doesn't feel there's any need to rid his body of glycogen; it's already gone.

Not all nutritional researchers think carbohydrate loading is a sound idea. Even Eric Hultman says it may not always be a good idea. Since every gram of glycogen is chemically associated with three grams of water, he notes, the additional weight in the muscles may interfere with performance.

Many excellent runners have developed similar reservations. Don Dixon, a documentary film-maker who ran his fastest marathon, a 2:41, at the age of forty-nine, skips the first phase, just as Shorter does. But he does take a depletion run and then for three days goes heavy on the carbohydrates.

Aside from carbohydrate loading, most runners eat much as other people do. You don't even need extra vitamins, no matter how hard you're working out. But you should be careful to eat green and yellow vegetables and fresh fruits; they're important sources of the vitamins needed to metabolize carbohydrates and fats. As few as 1,200 to 1,500 calories, so long as they are selected from a variety of wholesome foods, will give you all the vitamins you need. Some vitamins are simply excreted if you take too much of them. Others—the fat-soluble ones like A and D—are stored in the body and may produce adverse effects as they build up over a period of time. A few years ago, after Linus Pauling began praising vitamin C's role in preventing colds, I took it regularly during an entire winter. I caught one cold, so mild it didn't cost me even a day's running. As an experiment, the next winter I didn't take any vitamin C at all, and again I had one mild cold. Admittedly my one-man experiment doesn't prove much, and I suspect that running ten or so miles a day in heat, cold, ice, snow, slush and rain simply has a toughening effect. Nonetheless, many runners, including one physician I talked with, swear by vitamin C.

There's one other exception to the generalization that runners should follow fairly ordinary diets, and this is immediately before a race or a long training run, when food—the quantity of it, at any rate—really counts. It's a good idea, for example, to stay away from filling foods like eggs, bacon and sausages; instead, choose toast or muffins with jam or honey. Some runners can put away enormous stacks of pancakes—something of a traditional meal before the Boston Marathon—or bowls of oatmeal, but such foods make many of us feel uncomfortably heavy, especially if they're eaten less than five or six hours before a race. Remember that what you eat on the day of a race isn't going to contribute much to your energy; it's too late for that. All it's going to do is keep you from feeling hungry.

This may seem to go against common sense, but a study conducted at Oklahoma State University showed it to be true. Sixty-eight of the university's football players were divided into four groups. One group ate a steak breakfast, another pancakes, a third oatmeal, and the fourth no breakfast at all. Later in the day the football players ran two miles, and there was no difference in their performance. In other words it doesn't matter what you eat before you run, or even whether you eat at all.

People have long thought it unwise to try to store up extra energy by eating sugar before or during a run. Sugar can produce cramps, nausea, and in some cases an overreaction that leaves you with a lower blood sugar level than normal. At a recent medical conference, however, a Stockholm physician and researcher named John Wahren presented evidence indicating that taking sugar *during* a run may increase energy. But there's no point in trying to eat anything else in the middle of a race; you won't be able to digest it. Your body is too busy moving blood and oxygen and attending to complex chemical reactions to digest food. No matter how hungry you feel (and the chances are you won't feel hungry at all), you're not going to starve, not even during a marathon.

What you *do* need to be concerned about is liquids. A loss of as little as a quart can slow you down, and losing twice this amount can do real damage. It's important, therefore, to replace fluids promptly. Coaches, as noted earlier, used to think it was good to sweat but bad to drink during a workout; the discomfort of thirst was thought to toughen up an athlete. Research has shown this to be untrue. The body works best when fluids are replaced, preferably with something cool (but not ice-cold), as soon as they are lost.

After a race you won't feel hungry for a while. Your body is busy getting itself back to normal. If you eat too soon, you may feel nauseated or crampy. A reliable guide, I've found, is to wait until your body tells you it's ready. Trust it. It *knows.* Until then, just sip liquids. Rudy Oehm, a Massachusetts cardiologist and marathoner, suggests drinking a variety—soup, water, fruit juices, soft drinks, perhaps some beer. Because the body loses various kinds of fluids when you run, he explains, no single drink is exactly right for making up the loss. Give your body a cafeterialike choice, he says, and it will find what it needs.

What about alcohol? Many serious runners enjoy an occasional beer. Few of them are heavy drinkers, though one runner, a man of considerable distinction, is said to drink nine or ten bottles of beer every day, and one of our nation's top marathoners drinks a case or more a week. (I don't know how they manage it; both of them remain elfin in size.) As for me, after a long, hot run I find that there is nothing like the taste of a cold beer. (It cancels out the calories lost during the whole mile of running, but that's a small price to pay.) The inventive Dr. Bassler has even come up with a sound medical reason for drinking beer: the dehydration of long-distance running, he points out, may cause kidney stones, especially if you are training in a hot, dry climate. Water, he says, quenches your thirst before you've drunk enough for your kidneys. Beer doesn't work that way, since, as every beer drinker knows, it goes more directly to the kidneys.

Bassler's recommendation is not universally approved, and has drawn a sharply worded rebuke from Dr. Harold W. Moody, chairman of the South Carolina Commission on Alcohol and Drug Abuse. Bassler points out, however, that alcohol is responsible for fewer deaths than such everyday foods as sugar, starch and saturated fats. "Runners who maintain adequate mileage—3,000 to 6,000 miles per year—are also taking adequate nutrients and need not be concerned over their beer intake," he writes.

Still, if you want to become really serious about running, you may decide to stay away from alcohol altogether. After all, it does add weight—it's pure calories—and in addition to impairing coordination, decreasing your ability to process oxygen and reducing muscle strength, it has, as noted earlier, an adverse effect on your tolerance to heat. Indeed, studies have shown even a single bottle of beer can affect your ability to run in hot weather, and that the effect lasts for as much as two days.

Nevertheless, if it were a question of deciding whether to give up drinking or smoking, I'd unhesitatingly stay with the drinking. As little as fifteen puffs of a cigarette can cause a 31 percent decrease in the body's oxygen-handling ability. In fact, I don't know of a single even semiserious runner who smokes, and I suspect that there are none. One of the special pleasures of postrace banquets is being in a roomful or two or three hundred people and realizing that not one of them is smoking. It's a rare experience in these oversmogged times.

What about coffee and tea? Caffeine, which is found in both, stimulates the central nervous system, promoting wakefulness, increased mental activity and the release of the stimulant epinephrine, the natural form of adrenaline. There has been a great deal of controversy over whether it should be considered a drug in athletic competition. (It was once on the International Olympic Committee's doping list, but was withdrawn.) I like coffee and tea and suffer no discernible ill effects from them, so I'll probably go right on drinking them. Most runners do.

Because of a symptom called "cotton mouth," runners sometimes worry about drinking milk. I've never suffered from it, but one source describes it as "a condition of dryness and discomfort in the mouth." Supposedly it is caused by milk, but this isn't so, researchers at the University of Connecticut's Physical Efficiency Laboratory have found. Cotton mouth, they say, isn't caused by too much milk, but by too little fluid.

Spurred on by a growing interest in running, you may want to dig more deeply into nutritional lore, and certainly there is much to be learned. But whatever regimen you decide on, no matter how standard or bizarre, be wary of simply adopting it unquestioningly. Remember that your body isn't exactly like anyone else's. Don't be afraid to try something different, for sooner or later in their search for energy most good runners adopt one or another odd eating habit. When I talked one afternoon with Ted Corbitt, the former Olympic marathoner, I was startled to notice that he was munching on a large, raw sweet potato. Bob Glover eats baby food during long races. Don Dixon keeps a suppy of canned sardines in his office. Each is convinced, perhaps rightly, that his special food confers some peculiar benefit.

It is impossible to explore every one of the nutritional enthusiasms of runners. Each April 3,000 and more people run in the Boston Marathon, and each of them, I'd be willing to bet, has trained on a slightly different diet.

However, there is one way of eating that claims enough support among runners to make it worth close scrutiny, and that is vegetarianism. I remember lying on a cool patch of grass after a long, hot race in Meriden, Connecticut, and listening as Amby Burfoot, a lean, bearded schoolteacher who won the Boston Marathon in 1968, quietly explained his vegetarian regimen to several other runners. But I had been running for a long time before I realized how many vegetarian brethren Burfoot had, or why.

One reason the discovery was so slow in coming is that the typical vegetarian runner is not a proselytizer. I had, I confess, always thought of vegetarians as part of the vast lunatic fringe, and I assumed that they would tend to be as wild-eyed and vocal as other true believers. But they go their own gastronomical way, living quietly on fruits, vegetables and nuts, and not caring whether you or I join them. Like Corbitt and Burfoot, many of them are very good runners indeed.

Vegetarians do claim that their way of eating gives them more energy. They like to cite the case of the swimmer Murray Rose, who won two Olympic gold medals in 1956, of the distinguished Australian runners Herb Elliott and John Landy, and of Johnny

Weismuller, who became a vegetarian and went on to set six world swimming records.

Of course these people could simply be flukes who did well in spite of bad diets. Apparently, however, they are nothing of the kind, if the scientific research cited by vegetarians is to be believed. One of their favorite studies, undertaken as long ago as 1907, compared the physical endurance of fifteen meat-eaters and thirty-four vegetarians. When asked to stretch their arms out horizontally for as long as they could, only two of the meat-eaters were able to do so for fifteen minutes, and none could do it for thirty minutes. Of the vegetarians, twenty-two did it for fifteen minutes and fifteen for thirty minutes or more (one is said to have held the pose for three hours).

Still, the case for vegetarianism is not based only on the energy factor. It rests on a number of others, too, some of which seem to be fairly persuasive.

There is, for example, the physiological argument. Mankind, vegetarians say, was simply never designed to eat meat, which is the reason people sometimes choke on it and die—the so-called café coronary. Unlike the wolf, which uses spikelike teeth to tear meat into large chunks and then swallows it whole, human beings have teeth that were meant first to cut and then to grind—ideal for eating a banana, squash or carrot, but not at all right for filet mignon. At a medical conference not long ago Dr. W. S. Collens of Maimonides Hospital in Brooklyn said, "The dental structure of herbivorous animals consists of sharp cutting incisors, while the molars have a flat or nodular surface used for crushing and grinding food. This presupposes that such animals are phylogenetically constructed to live on vegetables, leaves, roots, fruits, nuts, and berries. . . . Examination of the dental structure of modern man reveals that he possesses all of the features of a strictly herbivorous animal." This, vegetarians say, is why we tolerate cholesterol so poorly, and why, according to one study, strict vegetarians have only one-sixth as many heart attacks as the rest of us. We were never intended to eat so much cholesterol in the first place—if indeed any at all.

Meat itself, vegetarians and many others say, isn't good for you in any case. It's high in fats and contributes to heart disease and—in animals, at any rate—to cancer. It is a breeding ground for bacteria, and it isn't digested as easily as plant foods. Furthermore, aged meat, the kind most of us like, is really partly putrefied. (Just reading some of the more vividly couched vegetarian tracts is enough to turn you away from the stuff, the validity of their arguments aside.)

Finally, vegetarians tell us, the history of their movement is almost as old as mankind itself, and therefore has been thoroughly validated over the centuries. In fact, no less a person than Pythagoras is considered to be its founder. Other advocates of this diet have included such diverse figures as Socrates, Plato, Aristotle, Milton, Newton, Voltaire, Rousseau, Thoreau, Tolstoy and the animal-loving St. Francis of Assisi.

Hoping to find out more about athlete vegetarians, I paid a call one day on a remarkable woman named Frances Goulart (who, you will recall, was earlier cited for being bitten by a dog). Mrs. Goulart, who is in her late thirties and weighs all of eighty-five pounds, is an author of three books on vegetarianism. The first, *Bum Steers,* is an impressively varied collection of nonmeat recipes, with considerable discussion of the nutritional justification for them. *The Ecological Eclair* is about nonsugar desserts, and *Bone Appétit!* examines—I swear I'm not making this up—natural foods you can serve your pets.

Mrs. Goulart lives at the end of a narrow dirt road in rural Connecticut, with her husband, Ron, a prolific writer of science fiction, and their two sons. She runs nine or ten miles a day and also bicycles, swims and plays tennis.

"The things I eat might be repellent to some people," Mrs. Goulart said. "For one thing, meat has stimulants in it, and you miss them when you first stop eating meat. It takes a while to get used to being a vegetarian."

There are, Mrs. Goulart explained, three kinds of vegetarians: the 100 percent vegetarian, sometimes called a vegan; the lacto-vegetarian, who uses milk, as well as products made from it; and the lacto-ovo-vegetarian, who consumes both milk and eggs. Mrs. Goulart is a lacto-ovo-vegetarian.

"You kind of drift into these things little by little," she said. "Ron was doing some writing about food, and I decided I'd try going without meat for a while. I felt better right away. I didn't seem to require it. For one thing, your body doesn't have to work as hard to digest fruits and grains, so you run better. It stands to reason that you've got more energy for running if your body isn't busy doing something else."

Mrs. Goulart smiled at my next question; she had heard it before. "No," she said, "vegetarianism isn't simply *different.* It's *better,* especially as you get older. When you're young you tolerate meat a lot more easily, and it really counts as you get older."

Mrs. Goulart believes that there is something of a conspiracy in the country's schools of nutrition to keep the merits of vegetarianism quiet. "The schools are very conservative," she said. "They have the information, all right, but they're a half-century behind the times."

Mrs. Goulart is a racer as well as a runner. She has set a number of course records for women and has a good-sized collection of trophies. Since she attributes much of her running success to what she eats, she is eager to share her knowledge. As I was leaving, she thrust a brown paper bag into my hand, with instructions to heat it before I ate it. "It's wheat loaf," she said, "just the thing for carbohydrate loading before a marathon."

Since Mrs. Goulart recommends this food so highly and regards it as a runner's ideal food, I asked her for the recipe. Here it is:

WHEAT LOAF

4 tablespoons minced onion *or* scallion
1 garlic clove, peeled and chopped
2 tablespoons walnut oil
½ cup parched cracked wheat
½ cup salted walnuts
1 egg, slightly beaten
¼ cup soy granules
1 teaspoon (or more) poultry seasoning
1 teaspoon vegebutcher salt*
pepper to taste
½ teaspoon hickory-smoked salt
¼ cup freshly grated Romano or Parmesan cheese
½ large potato (organically grown, if possible) scrubbed and with skin on, grated

1. Sauté the minced onion and the garlic in a skillet with the walnut oil. Stir in the cracked wheat and coat it with the oil; cover tightly. Steam-cook for fifteen minutes.
2. Grind the walnuts to a gritty meal and blend with egg. Put in a bowl with the soy granules, seasonings and cheese.
3. Add the cooked cracked wheat and the potato to the bowl and combine well, using your fingers. If more moisture is needed, add a little milk or broth. Bake for thirty minutes at 325 degrees.

Mrs. Goulart also gave me a number of books, articles and pamphlets on vegetarianism. Reading them during the next several days, I came to see that vegetarianism means more than the simple avoidance of meat; it also involves the search for pure and whole-

* Vegebutcher salt, available at health-food stores, consists of spices, herbs, dried vegetables, sea salt and brewer's yeast.

some foods in general. For example, although it is not a requirement of vegetarianism, most vegetarians are not keen about either white sugar or white flour. Sugar has been suspected as a factor in atherosclerosis, gout, vitamin B deficiencies and even cancer, and of course its role in tooth decay has been thoroughly documented. "You can undo a week of training in just five minutes," says Bob Hoffman, a former Olympic weightlifter, speaking of the effects of sugar. As for refined flour, one source says it is so lacking in nourishment that even insects stay away from it.

Vegetarians also tend to cook less than other people because, they say, heat destroys enzymes, minerals and amino acids. One night when my wife and I had dinner with the Goularts, the hors d'oeuvres consisted of celery, tomatoes and cheese, while dessert was simply fresh fruit. (The main course, perhaps out of deference to us and to Mrs. Goulart's husband, a nonvegetarian, was cooked.)

If you decide you'd like to try vegetarianism, how do you begin? Most vegetarian authorities urge you to proceed slowly in order to give your body—and your mind—a chance to adjust. One way to do this is to plan a changeover period of a week or two. During this time eat progressively smaller amounts of meat and larger amounts of plant protein. Vegetarians recommend using different kinds of beans in combination. This improves their protein value, since they tend to complement one another.

Many people think that without meat they won't get enough protein, but plants provide plenty. Cereals are 10 percent protein. Common varieties of bean are 25 percent, and soybeans 40 percent protein. There's only one essential nutrient you can't get from plants: vitamin B_{12}. For it you need some sort of supplement.

All of which would seem to be a small price to pay for being as fit as Mexico's renowned Tarahumara Indians, who not only live extremely long lives but also routinely run 200 miles at a time in mountainous terrain. They do this on corn, beans, squash and practically no milk, meat or eggs—a diet much like the one our own vegetarians advocate.

15

Preventive Maintenance

How to Keep Everything Working Right

By itself, a good diet won't guarantee you trouble-free running. As noted previously, running can jar the body, tire it, change its structure and some of its functions, and alter its chemical behavior. If it becomes severe, any one of these effects can interrupt or curtail your running. Most interruptions, however, need not occur, for all but a few injuries are preventable. Perhaps the most convincing evidence is the fact that runners who have been at it for several years hurt themselves far less than beginners do. One reason is that with time the body toughens up, but a far more important one is that runners learn what to do and what not to do. When I first started running I had one problem after another—blackened and broken toenails, shin splints, sore muscles, Achilles tendinitis. Now, even though I run faster, harder and longer, I rarely get hurt. Most runners would confirm this.

The typical runner learns mainly by experience—sometimes bitter. A few cautionary tales do, it is true, come our way from friends

and from *Runner's World,* but it's hard to take much interest in some awful-sounding malady like chondromalacia patellae until we're suffering from it ourselves. Hence we muddle along, learning chiefly by trial and error how to avoid or treat injuries. Perhaps it would violate human nature to learn in any other way, but it is at least theoretically possible. The suggestions and warnings in this chapter, if heeded, may save you years of having to discover them the hard—and painful—way.

DON'T STRAIN

After you've been running for a while it's tempting to imagine that you've become indestructible. Day after day you put more effort into your running, and a sort of continuing miracle occurs: nothing falls apart. So you take this as a license to run faster and longer. Sooner or later something *does* break down—a muscle, a tendon, a bone or your good disposition—because you simply can't continually run harder unless you do so in extremely small increments.

How small? Much depends on how fast your body recovers from a workout. Some people can put in two days of hard training and then, after only one easy day, feel rested. Most of us, however, need more rest—perhaps two or even three easy days between the hard ones. The main point is to give your body time to repair through rest what you've torn down through exercise.*

If you don't take it easy occasionally, you won't improve. You can easily tell how much rest you need if you pay attention to how you feel. Sometimes, for no apparent reason, you'll feel sluggish or lazy. On those days, once you start running you'll discover that you're not really tired at all. You'll feel springy, and in no time your laziness will vanish. Sometimes, though, even after a thorough warm-up your legs will feel heavy and you just won't want to run; if so, don't push yourself. Run slowly and patiently, keeping in mind that better days will come.

Fatigue isn't the result of speed and distance in themselves, but of running at a speed and over a distance greater than you can comfortably handle. I may tire after a half-mile; you may be able to run twenty easily. If you tire yourself day after day, fatigue accumulates. One of the first signs of the fatigue-on-fatigue effect is an out-of-sorts feeling. For no good reason you're cranky, ill-tempered and impatient. Routine tasks seem formidably difficult. Among other signs of cumulative fatigue are these:

1. Pain in the joints, muscles or tendons, especially if it's more severe than usual.
2. Trouble falling asleep or staying asleep.
3. More colds, fever blisters and runny noses than usual.
4. Continual thirst (a result of dehydration).

* Among other things, fatigue results from too little blood sugar, too much lactic acid, too little water, too few electrolytes, too little glycogen, too much heat, and too many metabolic wastes. Recovery from all this can't be instantaneous.

5. A tired feeling, especially if you still have it after a night's sleep.

If you have only one of these symptoms, it's nothing to worry about, but if you have two or more, it's an almost certain sign you're overtired. The remedy is to ease up for a while. Skip a day's running, or cut your mileage in half for two or three days. Above all, don't do any fast running. Wait for your energy and zest to come back, and only then resume normal running.

If you race, particularly long distances, you'll have residual fatigue for several days after competition. You may think you feel fine, but the tiredness is lurking inside you, waiting to fell you with a cold, a muscle pull or worse.

Probably the chief enemy of sound training is dogmatism. Once we have planned our regimen, we're reluctant to change, feeling weak-minded if, for example, we set out on a two-mile run and end up doing only a mile. It may not, however, be lack of will power, but the smartest thing to do.

Holding the arms too high produces an ungainly style

RUN EFFICIENTLY

Chapter 19 describes a run with Bill Rodgers, one of the world's top marathoners. Watching him run is like seeing an artfully designed piece of machinery; every component is synchronized and in harmony. Although this is a wonderful way to run, for you or me to try to imitate Rodgers would be silly. We're not built the way he is, our bones aren't articulated with each other in the same way, and our various centers of gravity are in different places. If we were to try to imitate Rodgers's style or anyone else's, we'd be working against our own bodies and increasing the risk of injury. The only sensible way to run is your own, no matter how much it deviates from textbook style. Above all, don't try to land on the balls of your feet like a sprinter. If you do, you'll almost certainly hurt your Achilles tendons. Instead, land on your heels and roll forward, pushing off with your toes.

Most beginners hold their arms too high. When they finally try positioning them lower, with the forearms roughly parallel to the ground, they usually find that they feel more coordinated. Try various arm positions until you find the one that seems most natural. Once you discover the right spot, there's no need for any more experimenting. Like your voice and fingerprints, your style is something you can't do much about. Fortunately, there isn't any need to, since a natural and relaxed style—the one that comes most easily—is the best way to minimize injuries.

WEAR GOOD SHOES

Don't try to save money on shoes. Stay away from the second-rate shoes put out by chain stores trying to capitalize on the current interest in running.

Good shoes do at least three things that inadequate ones don't. Because they fit right, they minimize blisters. Because they're properly padded, they cushion shocks. Because they have a stable heel, they keep lateral sway to a minimum and reduce wear and tear on leg muscles.

If you must save money, do so by wearing cut-off blue jeans instead of running shorts, or a worn-out shirt with the sleeves cut off instead of a T-shirt. But *please* don't try to save money on shoes.

TAKE CARE OF YOUR FEET

The sole of each of your running shoes has some thirty square inches of surface, but only a few of these touch the ground at one time. Thus the repeated impact of your weight is concentrated on an area not much larger than a puppy's paw. It's no wonder feet give runners trouble—blisters, blackened toenails, aches, pains and occasionally even broken bones. Happily, many if not most of these injuries are preventable, primarily by wearing proper shoes, with inserts custom-designed by a podiatrist if necessary (see

Chapter 16). A couple of other routine maintenance procedures are also imporant.

Keep your toenails closely trimmed. When your foot lands, it tends to keep moving inside its shoe. The result is that the toes move toward the front. If the nails are too long, they take the brunt of the impact, become painful, turn black and eventually fall off. It doesn't feel as bad as it sounds, but when your feet are in this condition they'll never win a beauty contest.

Take care of blisters as they develop, and try to catch them while they're small. They need not keep you from running, but they do require attention. Cover small ones with first-aid cream and tape, and leave the tape there for five or six days; they'll usually heal with no further trouble. Once you've discovered the spots where you usually get blisters, toughen the skin there with tincture of benzoin, and before you run, lubricate each spot with a good-sized glob of Vaseline. Using different running shoes on alternate days helps, too.

The longer you run, the fewer blisters you'll get. But when the pavement is hot or you're wearing a new pair of shoes, they are always a danger, so be alert for the first sign of them.

STRETCH BEFORE YOU RUN

Chapter 5 described some simple warm-up exercises for beginners. After you've been running for a few weeks, strengthened muscles need a more comprehensive set of exercises. The reason is twofold. First, as noted in Chapter 3, running doesn't rate high on the flexibility scale; runners therefore require such exercises more than most athletes do. Second, running strengthens some muscles but leaves their antagonists—the muscles that oppose their efforts—weak. To prevent imbalances that can cause injury, these antagonists must be strengthened.

The best all-around set of stretching exercises are six that have been popularized by Dr. George Sheehan. He recommends the following:

1. To stretch your calf muscles and Achilles tendons, stand about three feet from a wall or tree. With your feet flat on the ground, lean in until your legs hurt slightly. Hold this position for ten seconds, then relax. Repeat five or six times. If you're suffering from chondromalacia patellae, a knee condition described in the next chapter, this exercise may be painful. In that case, a useful variation is to lie flat on your back on the floor, put a couple of pillows under the affected knee, weight the foot and straighten the leg. The pressure on the knee joint is considerably lessened this way.

2. To stretch your hamstrings—the muscles at the back of your upper leg—keep both legs straight and put one foot up on a waist-high table, or something lower if you can't reach that high. Bend your head toward your knee until you feel strain. Hold this position for ten seconds, gripping your leg or foot to steady yourself if you like, then relax. Repeat the exercise five or six times with each leg. (Ted Corbitt, who is a physical therapist, says he thinks this is more effective: keeping your knees bent, bend over and touch the floor. Then, with your fingers on the floor, push upward until you feel your hamstrings pulling hard. After a few seconds, bring your hands up off the floor and slowly straighten up, vertebra by vertebra, until you are standing upright. Repeat this procedure five or six times.)

3. To stretch the lower back and also the hamstrings, lie on your back, arms down by your sides, and bring your legs, with the knees straight, over your head. Lower them as far as you can, touching the floor behind you if possible. Stay in this position for ten seconds, relax, and repeat five or six times.

4. To strengthen your shin muscles, sit on the edge of a table and hang a five-pound weight on the lower part of the foot just above the toes. (A paint can with rocks in it works fine.) Raise your toes slowly, keep them up for a few seconds, and repeat the exercise until you're tired.

5. To strengthen your quadriceps (usually referred to simply as "the quads"), sit on the table again and hang the weight over the toes of one foot. This time, however, raise the weight by straightening your knee. Hold it up for a few seconds, lower and repeat the exercise five or six times with each leg.

6. Finally, to strengthen your stomach muscles, the antagonists of the powerful back muscles, do twenty or so sit-ups with your knees bent as before. Your hands can be either locked behind your head (the hardest way) or extended over your head (the easiest way). Whatever way you do them, however, sit-ups should be begun by tucking in the chin and curling the body up from the floor in order to maximize use of the stomach muscles.

A growing number of runners stretch by using yoga exercises. The Salute to the Sun, described in most books on yoga, is a particularly good all-around routine. Even if yoga exercises are used for stretching, however, the last three routines described above should accompany them in order to increase strength where it's needed.

GET ENOUGH SLEEP

Runners need plenty of sleep. Fatigue tends to accumulate quickly if you don't sleep enough, leaving you listless, unenthusiastic and susceptible to colds. Sometimes, job and family responsibilities, late-night television and a daily running regimen make it hard to find time for enough sleep. If you can bring yourself to do it, turning the set off a half-hour earlier works wonders.

EAT PROPERLY

For scientific guidelines, see the preceding chapter. Some rules, though, are just good common sense. For example, don't eat for several hours before a run. If you do, you'll only feel heavy, and your digestive processes will steal energy from your running. Don't load up on junk foods. They may fill you up, but they don't give a fair return in energy. Use fat sparingly; fats are digested more slowly than proteins or carbohydrates. Don't eat too many fresh fruits, prunes and the like; they'll force you to interrupt your run when you least want to. Above all,

STAY THIN

There are two reasons for becoming as thin as possible. First, you'll run better that way. The less weight you carry around, the faster you'll go. Second, the lighter you are, the less strain there is on the body's cartilage, joints and muscles. A simple calculation will show why. Your feet strike the ground about 1,600 times per mile. If you weigh 175 pounds, that's a cumulative impact of 280,000 pounds. But if you reduce your weight to 150 pounds, the cumulative impact has been pared to 240,000 pounds—a saving of twenty tons per mile.

AVOID CHAPPING

A runner quickly learns where chapping usually occurs. The most common sites are the lips, nipples, crotch and underarms. A few good-sized smears of Vaseline before starting out will usually prevent chapping. Putting Band-Aids on your nipples—especially before a long run like a marathon, where rubbing is going to be sustained—will prevent painful wear. (Incidentally, chapping is equally common in summer and winter; a damp sweatsuit almost precisely duplicates the environment of a humid summer day.)

PREVENT FROSTBITE

Suggestions for cold-weather dressing are found in Chapter 12. If they are scrupulously followed, cold should be no problem. However, since your face is usually exposed no matter how cold it is, be on guard against frostbite when it's windy and severe. Coat your face with Vaseline. Some runners carry a ski mask for use when running upwind in frigid weather. When the wind is coming from behind you, the mask can be stowed in a pocket or tucked into your waistband.

If you encounter trouble in spite of the foregoing precautions, see the next chapter for some words of advice—and, should you need them, of consolation.

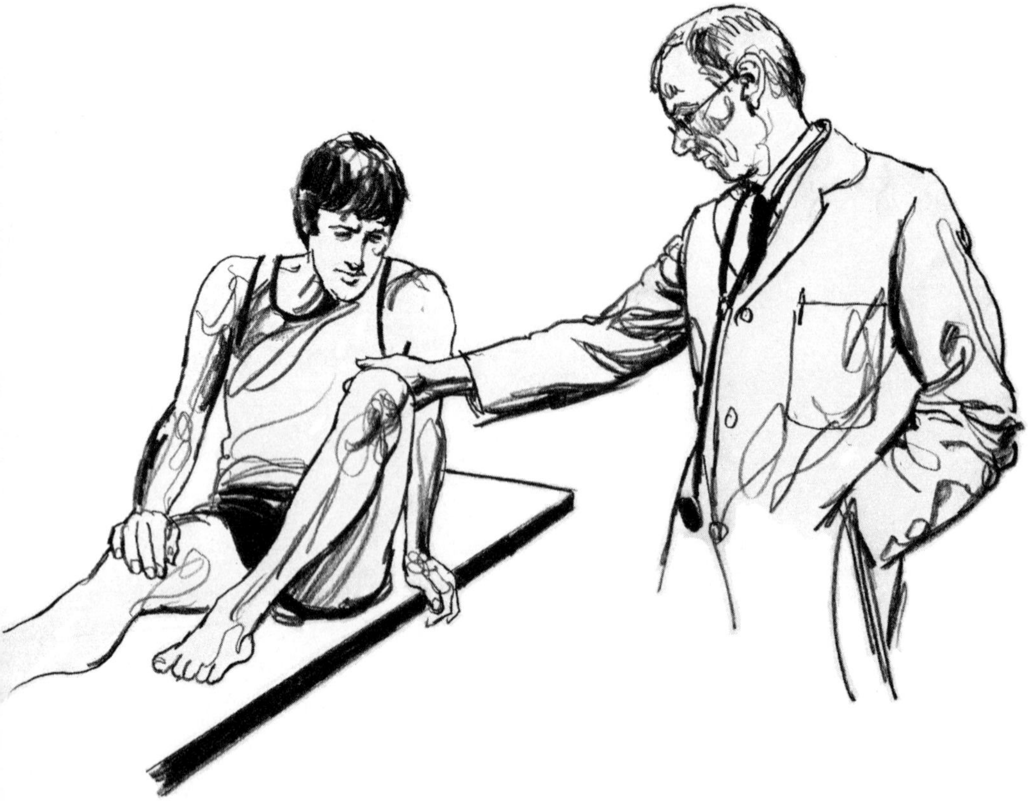

16

If, Despite Everything, Something Goes Wrong

A Medical Paradox and What to Do About It

Running is a curious medical paradox. The very activity that improves our hearts and lungs, protecting us from heart attack, stroke and other ailments common to our times, brings its own special maladies—what Dr. Sheehan has called the diseases of excellence. These come chiefly in the form of sore feet and legs, but they sometimes include other problems as well. When these injuries appear, another curious phenomenon is the inability of most doctors to do much about them.

A brief but telling scene occurred not long ago at a Manhattan cocktail party. A physician new to running fell into conversation with an executive who has been running for ten years. For several weeks the doctor had had a sore Achilles tendon that had not yielded to any treatment he had been able to devise. The executive told the physician he had once had the same problem. Galvanized, the physician removed a shoe and sock and offered the offending tendon for examination. The executive probed gently, inquiring as he did so whether the tendon hurt here or here or here, then offered the physician his diagnosis and recommended a certain treatment: heat, taping and a reduced running schedule. Within a few days the doctor reported that the executive's prescription had brought the relief he had so long been seeking.

This story is not as odd as it may seem. Most doctors are taught to treat disease, not health. They tend to feel most comfortable with a person who is plainly sick—with a broken bone, cough, headache, or something identifiable as a bona fide medical problem. They are uneasy when confronted with anyone who is searching for physical excellence. Dr. Gabe Mirkin of Silver Spring, Maryland, once wrote a regular column on sportsmedicine for the *Washington Post* and has taught a course on the same subject at the University of Maryland. Recently he wrote me:

> My feeling is that physicians abuse athletes by operating when they shouldn't and by injecting cortisone and Xylocaine. After all, physicians are paid to do something. This is why, when most runners are injured, they expect the physician to act. Actually, however, there is very little a physician can do after a runner is injured. His main job is to prevent injuries. He can, for example, examine and treat a runner for the factors that predispose him or her to injury—lack of flexibility, muscle imbalance, and structural abnormalities. By asking the right questions he can determine whether an injury was caused by overtraining. Finally, he can advise the runner on the need for rest.

Mirkin's observation about the medical profession's fondness for surgery was borne out when I consulted a Park Avenue orthopedic surgeon about a foot infection. After examining me, he said that he could prescribe some pills to clear up the infection but that they wouldn't do anything for the underlying cause. I asked him what, if anything, he could do about that. "Cut," he replied crisply. I took the pills, got rid of the infection and in two weeks was running again. Since then I have had several years of trouble-free running. Of course, it's possible that the problem will someday recur and that surgery will be needed, but in the meantime I've had those good years.

Mirkin reports a similar experience: "One orthopedist suggested knee surgery. As I was afraid of surgery on myself, I elected to do nothing. As Benjamin Franklin, who must have known about overly ambitious physicians, said, 'God heals and the doctor sends the bill.' Eventually my knee healed."

It is interesting and perhaps significant that doctors themselves are so suspicious of the role their associates play in the lives of runners. If this were nothing but an intramural squabble, you and I would have little reason for taking an interest in it, but it is not. On the contrary, it is indicative of a medical phenomenon that sooner or later affects practically every runner.* What it boils down to is that it is difficult for anyone to find knowledgeable treatment for athletic injuries. Aside from a few team doctors and specialists, most physicians simply don't know much about them. Notice what happens whenever a doctor hurts himself while running; the chances are he is as baffled about what to do as the rankest layman would be. And no wonder. Recently I looked through a number of standard medical textbooks of the sort used in our best medical schools. Aside from brief references to the slowing of the heartbeat as a result of endurance exercise, these books had practically nothing to say about athletics. A doctor I met while running confirmed that in all the time he spent in medical school, he could recall only part of one day that was devoted to athletes' problems.

Of course there are some doctors who are knowledgeable about athletic injuries, but there are far too few of them, and they are not always available where most needed. This is why the typical runner ends up serving as his own doctor, patiently ferreting out information through trial and error and the accumulated experience of other runners.

What follows is a catalogue of the runner's most common ailments, with some remedies.

RUNNER'S KNEE

This is more properly known as chondromalacia patellae, a linguistic hybrid from the Greek words for "cartilage" and "softness" and the Latin word for "a small plate" (i.e., the kneecap). It is the most common injury among runners. Although its precise cause is obscure, it is associated with excessive wear between the kneecap and the end of the femur, the upper leg bone. When the bones mesh properly, the kneecap moves smoothly within an indentation at the lower end of the femur. Occasionally, however, alignment is incorrect, and instead of staying in the hollow where it belongs, the kneecap grinds against one of the slopes in the indentation. If the grinding is prolonged, some of the kneecap's cartilage becomes worn. Pain, stiffness and swelling result.

To cure chondromalacia, many doctors recommend that you

* A closely related issue, particularly for those who are in excellent physical condition, erupted a while back in the letters-to-the-editor column of the *New York Times Magazine* after a doctor named Richard Spark wrote an article questioning the usefulness of regular physical examinations. One doctor, Stephen B. Yohalem of New York City, wrote: "It is surely ironic that in this country a patient requires a doctor's statement that he or she is feeling well."

stop running.* Usually, however, that's not necessary. Runner's knee is often relieved simply by cutting down temporarily on mileage, doing strengthening exercises for the quadriceps muscles and running on a surface that slopes downward toward the injured side—a road with a high crown, for example. (For chondromalacia of the right knee, run with traffic; for chrondromalacia of the left knee, against it.) However, many doctors feel that despite its name runner's knee is not really a knee problem at all but a foot problem, caused by faulty weight-bearing characteristics. This is borne out by the fact that chondromalacia often disappears after a runner starts wearing inserts—sometimes called orthotics—that change the foot's support patterns and thus shift the relationship of the kneecap and femur. Therefore, if your runner's knee is stubborn, see a podiatrist, preferably one who regularly treats athletes.†

FOOT PROBLEMS

Since the feet contain 214 ligaments, 38 muscles and 52 bones (a fourth of all the bones in the body), it's hardly surprising when something goes wrong with them. The foot problems of runners fall mainly into the following five categories.

Blisters

Prevention, as noted in the preceding chapter, is the best cure. When a blister does form, however, there are several remedies. If it's small simply treat it as described earlier. If, on the other hand, it's so big that it hurts, puncture it with a sterilized needle and squeeze out the fluid, then cover it with Vaseline and a gauze pad and tape it. Or, better still, use ⅛-inch adhesive foam rubber like that included in an Alpine Aid blister-care kit. Usually you'll find

* Runners who are prone to injury, and who are not lucky enough to have a doctor sympathetic to their problems, frequently encounter this all-purpose advice. Tom Talbott, a runner in his mid-forties, went to a doctor for a back problem. On being questioned, he said that the injury hurt most after running. Not surprisingly, the doctor then recommended that his patient stop running. Talbott, who has been running—and competing—for a quarter of a century, replied, "You don't understand. I don't consider myself well unless I'm able to run." The doctor replied, "That puts an entirely different light on things"—and set about finding an acceptable alternative.

† According to some doctors, one of the causes of chondromalacia is Morton's toe. Named after Dr. Dudley Morton, author of a 1935 study called *The Human Foot: Its Evolution, Physiology and Functional Disorders,* Morton's toe is nothing more than a condition in which the first toe is shorter than the second (although an unusually mobile first toe often has the same effect). Because the first toe normally absorbs twice the stress borne by the other four toes combined, problems can develop in the heel, the leg, the knee and even the back when it fails to do its job. Whatever the role of Morton's toe in chondromalacia and other maladies, there is no invariable cause-and-effect relationship. Many people with Morton's toe never develop any trouble.

that you can go right on running with no trouble. It's only if an infection develops that you may need to see a doctor.

Stress fractures

A stress fracture is a minor change in a bone's structure caused by strain or jolting. Generally these don't require casts or taping and will disappear with rest, but they are frequently mistaken for shin splints or bruised feet. (Diagnosis is tricky, even for a doctor who knows what to look for, because they don't always show up on an X ray.) Stress fractures occur most often in the longest toebones (the metatarsals) and the two bones of the lower leg (the tibia and fibula). As a result of the current trend toward high-mileage training, some authorities say that they are more common today than they once were. Stress fractures almost always disappear in six weeks or so if training is reduced to the point where you can run in comfort. Staying on a soft, yielding surface also helps.

Bone bruises

To the layman's ear, the medical name for this condition—calcaneal periostitis—suggests some dread disease. Actually, it's nothing more than an inflammation of the heel caused by repeated pounding. Heel cups, available at sporting-goods stores that deal in running equipment, relieve the pain while the injury heals.

Plantar fasciitis

This is an inflammation that occurs where ligaments in the sole of the foot join the heel, and its chief symptom is pain in the heel. Like a bone bruise, plantar fasciitis can often be relieved by heel cups or other padding.

Heel spur

Without an X ray, it is difficult to distinguish this, a bony growth on the heelbone, from plantar fasciitis. Nor is there usually any need to, since it too is often relieved by heel cups. Only in stubborn cases will a doctor recommend surgical removal of the growth.

ANKLE PROBLEMS

Ankles sometimes become sore either from too much wear or from too much running on uneven surfaces. As I write this, my friend Charles Steinmetz has had a sore ankle for two weeks as a result of having run hard enough in the Philadelphia Marathon to break his own record. But Steinmetz, a specialist in preventive medicine, says he isn't discouraged. He knows that minor injuries are occa-

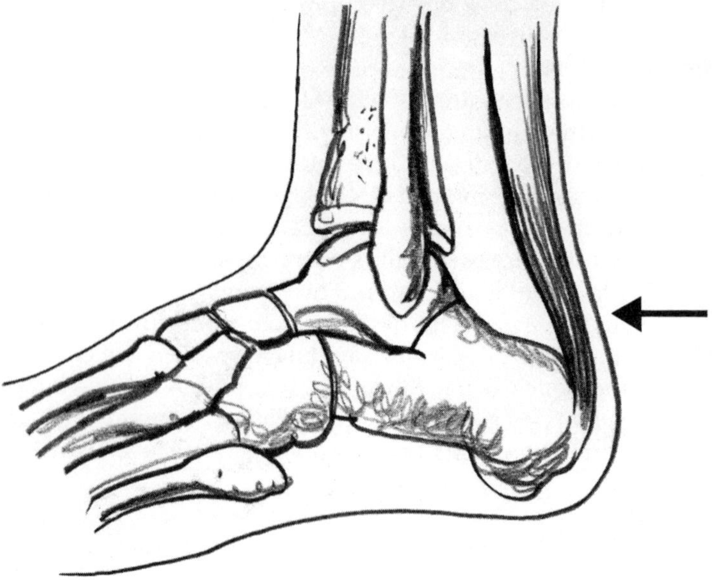

Inflammation of the Achilles Tendon

sionally the price of athletic accomplishment. Besides, the ankle is healing steadily. Such injuries are easy to accept and deal with.

What is less easy to bear, and certainly less easy to cure, is the most vexing ankle injury runners are subject to: Achilles tendinitis. (It's spelled with an *i* because the Latin root is spelled that way.) This is an inflammation of the sheath within which the tendon at the back of the ankle slides. When it becomes inflamed, it enlarges, creating too tight a fit, and friction and pain result. Hundreds of thousands of words have been written about the treatment of Achilles tendinitis, and the recommendations from both lay people and doctors range from exercise to surgery. However, there is something of a consensus about several points.

Since Achilles tendinitis feels worse when the tendon is stretched, shoes with good heels (and an added heel lift if necessary) usually relieve the pain. Some authorities also recommend soaking the sore tendon in hot water frequently and applying ice to it after running. Taping with an elastic bandage sometimes helps.

It is essential to curtail your fast running until the inflammation disappears. Confining your workouts to flat, unyielding surfaces (so that the heel can't rock or sink in) also helps. So does avoiding uphill running, which stretches the tendon.

If you should get Achilles tendinitis, you'll probably conclude that it's worth avoiding a recurrence no matter how much trouble it is. Stretching the calf muscles and tendons as described in the preceding chapter, both before and after running, is the key preventive measure.*

Don't treat Achilles tendinitis casually. Once you've got it, don't try to prove how tough you are. If you run too far or too fast, it can develop into a partial or complete tear of the tendon, and when this happens, you've got real trouble.

SHIN SPLINTS

Shin splints are simply inflamed muscles and tendons. Although they most often occur in beginners, they sometimes develop in advanced runners after an increase in training intensity. Shin splints range greatly in severity; sometimes they are nothing but a dull ache, while at others they make running impossible. They are caused mainly by jolts, by running too high on your toes, and by working out in shoes that are too stiff. Wearing flexible, well-padded shoes and landing on your heels usually helps.

MUSCLE SORENESS

Avoiding sore muscles altogether isn't possible or even desirable, since training necessarily overworks the muscles, but you can minimize the pain. Sore muscles result from metabolic waste products cast off during exercise, as well as from infinitesimal tears. Soreness is lessened if you continue to exercise mildly for a few minutes after a workout; this will flush the waste products from your muscles. Increasing the intensity of exercise gradually over a period of weeks rather than suddenly also helps. Once you have sore muscles, there isn't much you can do about them except take a sauna and wait for the pain to go away. If you can find somebody to give you a good massage in the places that hurt, you'll feel better. You may still be sore, but at least you won't feel friendless.

CRAMPS

When you decide to contract a voluntary muscle—a calf muscle, say—your brain sends a message through your body's nerve network. Once the message reaches the nerve ends, it releases a chemical conductor for the electrical impulse that contracts the muscle. When contraction is complete, the brain sends a second

* Another preventive measure, some runners say, is occasionally to wear negative-heel shoes. A few years ago, when negative-heel shoes were at the height of their vogue, I bought a pair. Although I find it almost impossible to walk any distance in them, I often wear them to stretch my calf muscles after running.

message that orders the release of a chemical that neutralizes its effect and thereby prevents electricity from reaching the muscle. According to one theory, cramping occurs either when the first chemical—it is called acetylcholine—reaches the muscle in the absence of a message from the brain, or when the second—cholinesterase—fails to arrive on time. A simpler, though not contradictory theory is that cramps are the result of a salt, calcium, potassium, magnesium or vitamin B deficiency. Some authorities even say that cramps are caused simply by fatigue, but of course this begs the question of the biochemical mechanism that produces them. Whatever, cramps can usually be relieved by stretching, kneading and walking. (If you sit down, they may come right back.) Runners who frequently get cramps might first try increasing the salt in their diets and then, one by one, the other chemicals.

SIDE STITCH

A side stitch almost always occurs while you're running hard enough to require deep breathing for a long time, and it will quickly disappear when you run more slowly. Some runners seem to be more susceptible than others, but everyone is helped by training. It is in fact rare to get a stitch when you're in good condition. Thus the symptom can be minimized, and perhaps eliminated altogether, by increasing your fitness. If you do get a stitch, breathe deeply using your stomach muscles, and run more slowly. If you're in a race at the time, the second suggestion won't seem a very reasonable one; then it's just a question of how much discomfort you're willing to tolerate. No one has ever died of side stitch.

BLOODY URINE

Blood is occasionally seen in the urine after an exhausting workout, especially by the best competitive runners (Frank Shorter, among others). It can result from several causes—the destruction of minute amounts of muscle, for example—and doesn't usually indicate any problem. Still, if it recurs, it's a good idea to consult a doctor, preferably one who regularly sees athletes.

RUNNER'S BLAHS

Sometimes, for no clear reason, a runner will feel lackadaisical, uninterested in life around him and depressed. When this happens, the cause is almost always overtraining—working out too hard and too often for full recovery to occur. Easing up on running and getting enough sleep is the cure.

17

Racing

Notes on the Competitive Spirit

Some runners never race. I know people who faithfully put in ten miles or more every day but never go near a starting line. Some, perhaps influenced by the noncompetitive ethos of the Frisbee culture, don't like the idea of winning at someone else's expense; others simply don't enjoy all that hard breathing and discomfort. Some runners avoid racing because they remember their driven feelings during Little League games or their anxiety before high school tennis matches.

But for many of us a race is a chance to compete primarily against ourselves, to see how much faster we can go than we have before. It's fine if we happen to pass someone or surprise a rival inches from the finish line, but those aren't the main pleasures. That's why there's such camaraderie at races. Other racers aren't your chief competitors; you are.

Still, there's no rule that every runner must race, so don't feel obligated to. If you're not interested in competing, skip this chap-

134
332

ter for now, but remember that it's here. Maybe later, as your running improves and you find yourself occasionally reaching a state of buoyant and tireless strength, you'll want to try some racing.

How do you find and enter a race? If you live where there are lots of runners, watch the sports pages for announcements of races or running-club activities. When you find one, call the person in charge and ask him or her about racing. Stop in at a sporting-goods store that deals in running equipment and ask a salesperson how to get in touch with someone who can tell you about races. If you live near a college or university, call the physical-education department and talk with the track coach. Look for announcements in *Runner's World.* Send an inquiry to the Road Runners Club of America, including a stamped self-addressed envelope.* Finally, when you come across other runners ask them if they know of any forthcoming races. Before long you'll probably have enough competition lined up to keep you as busy as you want to be. In my area, it's possible during the summer to race on Thursday nights, twice on Saturday mornings and again on Sundays. Four races in four days seem excessive, but they're available if anyone wants to run in them—and some hardy and indestructible souls do. In the winter, races are only slightly less frequent.

Of course, following the advice in this chapter is no guarantee that you'll do well in competition. One of the deepest mysteries in athletics is what causes good and bad days. There are times when you feel wonderful, yet run dreadfully, other days when you feel terrible, yet unaccountably have a fine run. A doctor with whom I discussed this told me he thinks the phenomenon has to do with the body's biological tides and rhythms, as well as with the sometimes subtle interactions of factors like diet and training. When you run poorly it's also possible that you are harboring a cold or other infection, one not severe enough to produce detectable symptoms but enough to lower your strength.†

There's not much that can be done about such imponderables, but there are many things we can control, and it is these that we must pay close attention to in racing. It's one thing to finish badly because your body won't move any faster, quite another to do so because you're wearing the wrong clothes or because someone passed you while you were daydreaming.

* For its address see Appendix A.

† A top runner faces a different competitive problem. As soon as a champion has set a record or won an Olympic medal, he or she has less incentive to improve. Writing in *Scientific American,* Henry W. Ryder, Harry Jay Carr and Paul Herget point out that the chief restraints on world-class athletes are not physical but psychological.

There are two aspects to racing, the physical and the mental, but they are inseparable. No matter how fit you are, you won't run a good race unless your mind is on what you're doing. That's why this chapter is concerned not just with tactics but with psychology. Let's examine briefly how your mind can help and hurt you in a race.

A race starts long before the gun goes off, sometimes months or even years before. As you read this, runners are readying themselves for the next Olympics. By the time they compete they will have spent many hours thinking about what they intend to do.

Such mental rehearsals will toughen their minds just as training strengthens their muscles. An opponent's move will call forth precisely the response they have prepared for. Pain will produce the instruction not to slow down. Being passed will call forth a counterburst of acceleration.*

Most people don't want to spend months or years getting ready for a race, but you'll race better and have more fun doing it if you give some thought to what you plan to do with your mind while you're running. Then you'll be ready to cope with such things as pain, fatigue and the efforts of your opponents.

Pain and fatigue are different in practice from what they are in theory. Before a race it's easy to tell yourself you'll continue to run hard even after you've started to hurt. In the race itself, however, it's a hard resolution to keep; pain and fatigue erode the will as the mind tires along with the body. No matter how much you race, you'll never entirely surmount this problem. You can, however, become cleverer at dealing with it.

The examples of top runners are instructive. Dr. William P. Morgan of the University of Wisconsin reported recently on a psychological comparison of world-class distance runners and ordinary ones. The two groups differed most in what he called "their perceptual processing of sensory information during running." What caught Morgan's attention was the ability of the best runners to tolerate pain. Ordinary athletes, he found, characteristically try to escape the pain of running by thinking about other things. Before a marathon, for example, one man he interviewed customarily put an imaginary stack of Beethoven records on an imaginary turntable and listened to them as he ran. Another, a Ph.D. candidate, reviewed his schooling year by year. In contrast, the world-class runners thought only about the race. They monitored their bodies, urged themselves to relax, assessed the degree of pain they were experiencing, and asked themselves how much more they could tolerate. Try to follow their example. After all, it doesn't make much sense to enter a race and then try to forget you're in it.

Top runners have also come to grips with what it means to win or lose. Competition is a complicated matter. In *The Madness in Sports* Arnold R. Beisser writes of a tennis champion who never had an easy match and who always won by a narrow margin. By doing so, according to Beisser's analysis, he was implying that there were only slight differences between himself and his opponents, thereby protecting himself from the guilt—and the conse-

* To strengthen such responses, some athletes have recently been experimenting with transcendental meditation. TM first came to the attention of runners after certain researchers claimed it improved cardiovascular efficiency. Since then, a number of other athletic benefits have been attributed to it. A physician with whom I discussed the matter told me that in his opinion the principles outlined in *The Relaxation Response,* by Herbert Benson, achieve much the same result as TM. A number of his patients, he said, have benefited from them. Another physician told me, however, that this research shows TM doesn't do any good at all.

quent punishment—that would result from defeating someone too one-sidedly.

Such fear is not as far-fetched as it may seem. I had run four or five marathons, all badly, before I finally finished one fast enough to qualify for the Boston Marathon. In the final fifteen or twenty minutes, when I knew I had a good chance of success, I experienced distinct feelings of anxiety. When I passed other runners, I felt there was something unseemly about what I was doing; it seemed wrong to succeed when they were going to fail. Perhaps you'll never have such feelings, but before a race it's a good idea to acknowledge the possibility you might, so you won't be caught off guard by them if they appear.

Of course there is more to getting ready for a race than psychological preparation. If the race is important to you, try to arrive early enough so that the carbon monoxide your system has absorbed while driving to it will have a chance to dissipate.

Also be careful about what you eat and drink before a race. Although it increases endurance, the common practice of carbohydrate loading (see Chapter 14) can be overdone, particularly if it results in your gaining a couple of unneeded pounds. And even a small amount of alcohol the night before a race will diminish your ability to run well in hot weather. Try to develop the habit of eating and drinking wisely and sparingly; then before a race you need only stick to your routine.

Take along everything you need. Few distractions are more frustrating than getting to a race and discovering that you've forgotten something. Some runners make a check list of what to take—everything from extra shoelaces* to rain gear. Although I'm not that organized, it's unquestionably a good idea. Whatever you do, don't forget that the weather, especially during the spring and fall, can be changeable. For example, at the Boston Marathon, which takes place in mid-April, you must be ready for everything from an inferno (1976) to chilly blasts (1975).

If you can, study the course before a race, either by taking a slow run on it as a warm-up or else by driving over it. It's good to know where any hills or sharp turns come, and, in the case of a cross-country race over difficult terrain, where the path is too narrow for passing. It's helpful, too, in the final stages of a race, to know exactly how far away the finish line is. Few things are more discouraging than to expect a finish line that never seems to come.

Finally, just before the start, make a final visit to a bathroom—or, if there isn't one, to an out-of-the-way bush. Forgetting this rule can produce highly distracting thoughts during a race.

* In regard to shoelaces, always tie them in double knots. It's the only way to be sure you won't have to stop to tie them during a race.

As you hear runners talking before a race, you'll notice that few of them sound in good health. There is always much conversation about ailments and symptoms, and to hear them tell it, practically none of the contestants have been able to take more than a half-dozen halting steps during the past month. This is a tradition of long standing, a reflection of the runner's superstition that to admit you're feeling fine is to guarantee that you'll run poorly. Don't waste sympathy on your sickly rivals; starting guns have produced more miraculous cures than Our Lady of Lourdes.

Even if you yourself don't exactly imply that you've just risen from a sickbed, it's smart to understate your expectations. If, for example, you think that with luck you'll run five miles in thirty-five minutes, tell anyone who asks, "I'm hoping to break thirty-eight." Then if you do succeed in breaking thirty-five, the accolades will be more enthusiastic. A New York City runner named Gerry Miller is a master at this. "I was out partying until four this morning," he'll say, "and I haven't run in the last six weeks because of leg trouble. I'm just going to run this one slowly, as a workout." A moment later he's off, bright as a bird, matching the leaders step for step.

Another preparation before the race starts is the warm-up. If it's a hot day, keep it to a minimum in order to avoid raising your body temperature unnecessarily. Otherwise, run slowly for eight to ten minutes, do some stretches and finish with a couple of brief sprints to get your heart, lungs and muscles ready for hard work. As mentioned earlier, there's controversy about how much good a warm-up does. Nonetheless, one respected Swedish researcher, Per-Olaf Åstrand, has reported a 5 percent increase in oxygen-processing ability after warming up. Since oxygen use and running speed are closely related, the warm-up seems to be a tradition worth adhering to.

Now for the race itself. The strategy and tactics of racing are complex,* and depend on such factors as distance, rain, weather, opponents, and your own strengths and weaknesses. Millions of words have been written on the subject. Your first decision is where in the pack to start. If you're too far forward, the runners behind you may jostle you or even knock you down as they pass. Too far back and you'll have to snake your way forward through the crowd. When you're new at the sport, you'll find it easiest to start toward the rear. You can always pass other runners later on. As you gain experience, you'll be able to pick the right spot by looking for runners of approximately your own ability.

Once underway, your most important task is to find the right

* Unless, that is, you adhere to the practice of an Olympic marathoner from England who told me his secret strategy: "I start at a brisk pace and run at ever-increasing speeds."

pace and stick to it. Starting too fast is a common mistake. At the beginning you should feel as if you're going a bit too slowly. If your pace is too quick, fatigue will force you to slow down later. The body is parsimonious with its energy supply; there's only so much available.

As you search for the right pace, also establish a comfortable rhythm. Most runners can settle into an efficient rhythm only by giving full attention to it; when their minds wander they run jerkily. So keep your mind on your running: remind yourself to relax, stay loose and run easily. Since excess motion consumes oxygen and energy, try not to flail your arms, bounce up and down, or let your head bob any more than it must.

If it's a hot day or a long race, drink a cup or so of water just before you start. At the water stations along the way, take water early and often. Even if you don't feel thirsty, you're already sweating. By the time thirst signals you that it's time to drink, it's too late to catch up.

When you've found your proper place in the pack, your main job thereafter is to make the most of your advantages. To do this you must acknowledge your strengths and weaknesses. Some runners are best downhill, others uphill and still others on the flat. Put extra effort into your strength; the advantage you'll gain will discourage opponents.

Running uphill is hardest, of course, and this is why many runners, anticipating a respite, slow down as they approach the crest of a hill. Don't; that's the time to push harder. If you run powerfully over the crest onto the downhill portion, and only then relax, you'll find you've gained a lot of yardage over many of your opponents.

Downhill portions of a course also have their hazards—the chief being that you'll run too fast and tire yourself. Unless it's close to the finish line, don't go all out in downhill running. Occasionally you'll be passed by a runner as he sprints downhill. Don't worry; you'll probably catch him soon after you reach the bottom—a sure sign he was going too fast.

Physiologically, the most efficient way to run a race is at an even pace, with a fast finish. However, you'll find that for tactical reasons you'll sometimes want to vary your pace. For example, if

you're approaching a cramped trail in a cross-country race, get ahead of as many opponents as you reasonably can. As soon as you hit the narrow place you'll get strung out, and afterward it's better to be toward the front.

The same applies to sharp turns. If you're able to pass someone before a turn, sprint a few yards while you're out of sight. When he next sees you, he'll be downhearted to see how far ahead you suddenly are.

When an opponent threatens to pass you, a brief show of strength may discourage him. Don't simply let someone go by unchallenged, for you may discover that *his* show of strength was only bravado. Tom Talbott used this tactic on me with good effect in a five-mile race in Connecticut. I had been trying to beat him for five or six years, and finally thought I had him. On a steep uphill portion of the race I passed him. He struggled back, passing me. I passed him twice more, but each time he fought back. Finally, discouraged by his tenacity, I let him go. He beat me by several seconds.

In overtaking someone, surprise him if you can and pass with a show of authority. If he speeds up, don't let it discourage you.

It also makes sense to vary your speed in order to take advantage of an opponent's wind shadow. About 7 percent of a runner's energy goes into moving air molecules out of the way. If, therefore, you can run in the lee of another runner, where the air has been broken into nonresistant burbles or where you can escape the wind's full force, you'll save significant amounts of energy. You'll also put the runner you're following under psychological pressure. It's harder to lead than to follow, since the leader must constantly wonder whether the runner following him is going to make a move.

How can you tell how well you're doing in a race? One way is to wear a stopwatch and watch for mile markers. (In some races someone will call out your time at them.) The only problem, as mentioned in Chapter 12, is doing the math in your head as you run, particularly as you tire, but it's not impossible. Assume that your time at the three-mile mark is 19:57. A 7-minute pace would give you exactly 21 minutes. You're 63 seconds under that. That's 21 seconds a mile. Your pace, therefore, is 7 minutes minus 21 seconds, or 6:39 a mile. Some runners simplify things for themselves by writing down their projected timetable and carrying it with them.

There's also a way to tell whether you're gaining on a runner ahead of you. Start counting your footsteps when he passes a particular point, then count how many steps it takes you to reach that point. After a while do this again. If it takes you fewer steps, you're gaining on him; if more, you're losing ground.

Strategy in a race depends partly on conditions. On a hot day run more slowly than usual at the start, even if you feel you could go faster. Heat wears runners out, and toward the end you'll be glad you saved some energy. On hot, sunny days, run in shade whenever you can. If spectators are offering cold water, drink some and douse yourself with the rest. Never pass up a chance to run through spray from a hose.

In road races you won't vary your stride much except in going up and down hills. Cross-country races are different. Here it's important to adapt to varying terrain—to take short, choppy steps in mud and sand, or to lengthen your stride during flat stretches.

In races on tracks, if you're like me your chief enemy will be boredom. As I've already said, I stay away from them as much as possible. On a track your main task is to concentrate on what you're doing; if you let your attention wander you're sure to slow down.

Because of the turns and cramped conditions, strategy is tricky in track running. You have to choose precisely the right place to pass—usually as you come out of a turn (though the element of surprise is greater if you pass unexpectedly as you enter one). And you have to time your finishing kick, or final burst of speed, so it comes at just the right moment—neither so soon that you'll tire and slow down, nor so late that you'll fail to catch your opponent.

Finishing is equally tricky in a road race. You need to know exactly what you're capable of. If you have a weak kick, you'll want to put lots of distance between yourself and your competition. With a strong one, you can afford to wait until later. Once you begin your kick, however, don't slow it. Often another runner, seeing you begin it, will try to stay with you. If you relax, no matter how slightly, he's likely to beat you.

Finally, as you approach the finish line, keep pushing. Resist the supplications of your aching muscles; run at top speed across the line. More than one race has been lost a foot from the finish line.

18 Boston and/or Bust

How to Get There Blisterless and Beatified

Each Patriots' Day, a Monday in mid-April, several thousand lithe, hollow-cheeked men and women in running shoes gather near an undistinguished byway called Hayden Rowe Street in the hamlet of Hopkinton, Massachusetts, exactly 26.21875 tortuous miles west of the Prudential Center in downtown Boston. There they take a last drink of water, Gatorade or some dreadful-tasting fluid of their own devising, smear a final gob of Vaseline wherever their clothing can rub, tie their shoelaces into double knots and empty their bladders on the vegetable gardens and flowerbeds of the imperturbable residents of Hopkinton's big old frame houses. Overhead, three helicopters from the Boston television stations prowl the heavens, waiting, and children perch in the leafless trees. Friends and families say goodbye as if their loved ones were bound for the moon, never to be heard from again. At precisely noon, when an official points a pistol toward the skies and fires a shot, a bobbing mass of lean, gristled humanity heads past

Hayden Rowe and the First Congregational Church and begins a purposeful ooze down Route 135 toward the towers of Boston far to the east.

Just over two hours later one of the participants, having traversed the hilly, winding road at some five minutes a mile, and in the process suffered the agonies of the damned, crosses the finish line. Thereafter his slower fellows arrive. The first come into view swiftly, with determination; the last run haltingly and wear gaunt and haggard expressions. Some limp or are bleeding where their skin has worn raw or, because they are past caring what anyone thinks, are crying and clutching each other like soldiers after a dreadful retreat. Hal Higdon, an accomplished runner as well as an entertaining writer on the subject, summed up the mystique of the race when he wrote, "The difference between the mile and the marathon is the difference between burning your fingers with a match and being slowly roasted over hot coals." Later, however, as the tortures of the race subside, something like a miracle occurs. A mood of beatific calm settles in, a certitude that no matter what terrible tortures were endured out there on that lonely road, running the Boston Marathon was worth every ache, cramp and anguished moan.

Not all marathons are like Boston; each has its own idiosyncrasies. The mid-winter Atlantic City Marathon is a simple out-and-back course, flat as a billiard table and seemingly almost no challenge—except that it must be negotiated not once but three times. The old New York City Marathon, before the inventive Fred Lebow and his fellow officials devised a course that snakes its way through all five boroughs, consisted of tedious repetitions of a villainously hilly roadway through Central Park. Such marathons dull the spirit. Boston is different. Curiously, it is not the world's most prestigious race at that distance (the quadrennial Olympic marathon is), nor its most difficult (the course is more downhill than up), nor even its most scenic (unless you have a liking for freight yards, trolley tracks and urban sprawl). Nevertheless, it is the single race that captures and summarizes most of what is excellent in marathoning.

This has been particularly true since 1972, when for the first time women were permitted to compete officially. Until then they ran by various ruses—false names, disguises and other subterfuges—because officials were convinced that they couldn't bear up under the punishment. In 1976, when a twenty-year-old college student named Kim Merritt won the women's division in 2:47:10, faster than all but 145 of the male entrants, her record pace must have laid such anxieties to rest forever.

Boston's mystique persists despite the fact that in recent years it has, perhaps unavoidably, turned elitist. Until only a few years ago it was open to anyone; then, as entries became so numerous as to be unmanageable, officials reluctantly instituted a qualifying standard: three hours or better in a previous marathon unless you're a woman or over forty, in which case three and a half hours qualifies you.

Part of Boston's appeal is attributable to its history, which is traceable all the way back to 490 B.C. In that year a messenger, one Phidippides, ran from Marathon to Athens to carry word of a Greek victory over 30,000 Persians. ("Rejoice," he declared. "We conquer." Then, the story goes, he died.) However, it was another two and a half millennia until the marathon took root here. Inspired by the 1896 Olympics in Athens, a group of Bostonians decided to stage one in 1897 from Metcalfe's Mill in Ashland to downtown Boston. The course, just under twenty-five miles long, was laid out mainly on dirt roads, and the contestants were mostly local men—machinists, milkmen, farmers—who made their own running shoes, trained without coaching and ran largely on will power. First across the line that year was John J. McDermott of New York City, with a time of 2:55:10, more than 45 minutes slower than today's record over a longer distance.

Marathon courses varied greatly in length in the early days, but the standard distance finally emerged at the 1908 Olympics in England, when officials added a few yards in order to stretch the starting line to the walls of Windsor Castle, the better to afford the royal family a view. Slow to tamper with tradition, Boston finally adopted the official distance in 1927. (The longer course didn't faze the tireless Clarence DeMar, who that year won for the fifth time in 2:40:22.) Even as the marathon came to maturity, however, it remained a race of long shots, many of the winners apparently coming out of nowhere. In 1926, for example, it was thought to be a toss-up between DeMar and Finland's Albin Stenroos, the 1924 Olympic winner. No one paid much attention to a nineteen-year-old delivery boy from Sydney Mines, Nova Scotia, named John C. Miles, who wore swimming trunks and white sneakers and had never run more than ten miles. But it was Miles who, running with Stenroos and DeMar until they weakened, finally passed both and won in 2:25:40. A decade later an equally improbable winner was a Narragansett Indian named Ellison M. "Tarzan" Brown, one of history's great marathoners. Brown lived in Alton, Rhode Island, and, in addition to all the running he did, had an unusual wrinkle in his training: he chopped wood. One day he ran a 4:24 mile on a cinder track in bare feet, and on another occasion ran two marathons in twenty-four hours, winning both despite a double hernia. In our own time, one thinks of Bill Rodgers, as unheralded an athlete as ever took the lead, and a runner who, despite having stopped several times to drink water and tie his shoe, currently holds the course record.

Part of Boston's appeal also is due to the fact that its spectators are like no others. A Bostonian will get a faraway look in his eyes as

he tells you of sitting on his grandfather's shoulder to watch the race. As you run along roads lined with these wonderfully appreciative onlookers, you know that they really understand what you're going through. There are perhaps half a million of them each year, yet no one taunts you or jeers at your knobby knees. Where else would a policeman stationed on Heartbreak Hill address a runner through his public-address system with these words: "When you reach the crest of the hill you have six miles to go, and it's all downhill. Your achievement has been superb, and you have my fullest admiration"? Where else would children line the course with outstretched hands in the hope of touching an athlete, even if it is only you or me? If you're going to feel terrible, what better place to do it than in plain view of people capable of understanding the scope and meaning of your suffering?

The Boston Marathon begins weeks before the event itself, with long runs on winter's icy roads.* By New Year's Day the race begins to tug at your mind. You may be out on a wind-blasted Ohio plain, the snow howling in your ears, yet in your imagination you are bobbing past the cheering crowds of Boston. One day in Central Park, as I was circling the 1.6-mile path around the reservoir, a runner confided that during the rigors of training he kept his spirits up by imagining that he had reached various points along the Boston course. For such people the race has an almost mystical power.

Two or three years ago, arriving in Boston a day early, I detoured off the Massachusetts Turnpike to see what Hopkinton looked like without the crowds. The town was quiet, a New England village with a silent, tree-filled square, and for the first time I saw that it was really quite an ordinary place. Number 4 Hayden Rowe, the last house on the left, was trimmed with old-fashioned fish-scale shingles and an incongruously decorative turret. The First Congregational Church at the end of the street had a gold weathervane and a tower capped with copper long since turned green with oxidation. It was much like any of a hundred towns you've seen, except for one detail: in the street near the square were painted two broad white lines, between which the best runners, and for some reason the women, start in a sort of seeding system. Near those lines, to my surprise, stood a half-dozen people, obviously runners, who like me had come for no other reason than to pay sentimental homage. (The starting line has since been changed.)

There is a curious uneasiness in finally arriving in Boston. Your preparations are finished; whatever training you failed to do will never be done now. Furthermore, the night before the race you will sleep badly, have restless dreams and awake too early. One runner I know, sharing a hotel room with a friend, awoke at three A.M. on the day of the race to discover his roommate working off nervous energy by doing push-ups. Another participant, half crazed with nerves before 1976's Bicentennial marathon, went out on Boston Common and by the dawn's early light ran six miles. Eventually,

* Unless, of course, you live where it's warm. Comparatively few Boston Marathon participants do, however. In the 1975 race, out of a total of 2,121 starters, 340 came from New York, 307 from Massachusetts, 190 from Canada, 110 from Pennsylvania, 97 from Connecticut and 95 from New Jersey. California had only 77, Texas 48 and Florida 28.

however, morning finally comes, and then Boston restaurants do a land-office business serving pancakes to runners hoping to pack in one last morsel of carbohydrate. At 8:30 the buses leave for Hopkinton. There, in the old days, you used to undergo the world's most perfunctory physical examination, a practice abandoned in 1976. Now you merely report to the high school gym and are handed your number, along with four safety pins to fasten it to your shirt, and a perforated tag, one end of which reads "Retain This Check," to affix to whatever gear you want to have waiting for you at the finish line. The gym is noisy and smells of wintergreen. Runners, who work out much of the time in old gray tatters, are wearing their finery—shorts imprinted with stars and stripes, bright headbands and crisp nylon jerseys bearing the names of their running clubs (the Kettering, Ohio, Striders, the Enfield, England, Harriers, the Richmond, Canada, Kajaks, the Beverly Hills Striders, the Sugarloaf Mountain Athletic Club, and the Ondekoza, Japan, Drummers, the last an impressively indefatigable percussion orchestra that first participates in the race, and then, hardly pausing for breath, starts entertaining the crowd with its huge $20,000 drums).

Toward noon, feigning calmness, you wander toward the growing crowd at the starting line on Route 135. Now is the moment to take one last drink and to head one last time into those backyard gardens. The helicopters are in place overhead, their rotors flailing at the April skies. At the foot of Hayden Rowe Street the press photographer's truck waits, its tiers of wooden seats bristling with long lenses. Near the starting line stand the best runners—the likes of Rodgers, New Jersey's two-time runner-up, Tom Fleming, and Connecticut's perennial dark horse John Vitale. Farther back is the vast mass of ordinary mortals, and behind them the former cardiac patients seeking unassailable confirmation of their cures, the unofficial participants bent on a lark, and those who simply like to start slowly and work their way up through the crowd, picking off their rivals one by one.

The starting gun sounds. Unless you're up front with the top athletes, in the beginning you have trouble finding room to run until the crowd thins, so you bounce in place or simply walk until you can finally break into a run. At last you're on your way in earnest, feeling good and moving with an easy, relaxed gait. This feeling is deceptive; it will not last more than an hour or so, and that will leave another ninety minutes or more during which the race will be, to one degree or another, a struggle. How much of a struggle depends upon 1) what kind of shape you're in; 2) what the weather is like; 3) what kind of day you're having; and 4) how intelligently you pace yourself.

At least some of these factors are controllable, so if you know what to expect at each stage of the race, your chances of running well are considerably improved. To that end, here is a mile-by-mile gazetteer of the Boston course.

0 TO .8 MILES: GETTING STARTED

This first part of the Boston Marathon is entirely downhill, but now is no time to press hard and tire yourself. Anyway, at this point the course is so clogged that passing requires an inefficient, weaving path. Simply hold your position and try to stay out of harm's way in the crush. More than one runner has been knocked down in the first few hundred yards, especially in the squeeze of rounding the corner from Hayden Rowe Street onto Route 135.

.8 TO 3 MILES: A TIME FOR CAUTION

The hills flatten out at exactly .8 mile, where there's a house on the right with a swimming pool in its yard, and soon a gentle uphill begins. At the 1-mile mark you'll see a Christmas-tree nursery and a sign reading "Liberty Mutual Research Center." The next half-mile takes you past rocky pastureland on the right. At 2.1 miles a sign announces "Entering Ashland," and at 2.7 miles another sign indi-

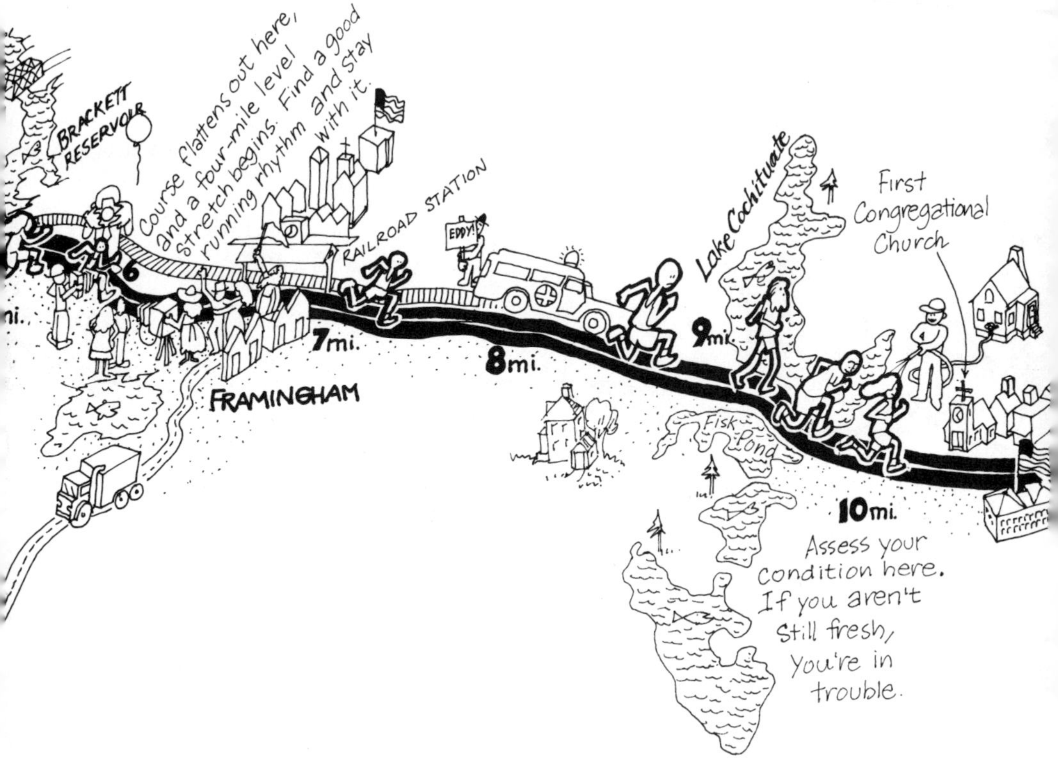

BRACKETT RESERVOIR
Course flattens out here, and a four-mile level stretch begins. Find a good running rhythm and stay with it.
RAILROAD STATION
EDDY!
Lake Cochituate
First Congregational Church
6
7mi.
8mi.
9mi.
10mi.
FRAMINGHAM
Fisk Pond
Assess your condition here. If you aren't still fresh, you're in trouble.

cates "Laborers' Training Center." At 3 miles a gentle downhill ends.

Thus far the course, though gently rolling, has been mainly downhill. The chief danger, therefore, is that you'll run this segment too fast. Jerry Nason, who has covered more than forty of the annual marathons for the *Boston Globe,* believes that the most common error is a failure to realize how fast you're going in the first part of the race. "Too many people," he says, "run a fast first half, then have to slow down. An even pace almost always works best."

3 TO 6.5 MILES: ASHLAND TO FRAMINGHAM

You're settling in now. You've calmed down and started to sweat. You're breathing easier and your legs are loose. If you're the sort of runner who likes conversation, now is the time, while your body still feels right. At 3.5 miles you swing sharply right past Romeo's Supermarket, and .3 mile later you cross Main Street in Ashland. This is a good place to start drinking fluids, whether you're thirsty or not. In another half-mile you pass Brackett Reservoir and start climbing a gentle hill. The numeral 5 on a pole to the right indicates the five-mile mark. (Farther on you'll notice that many of the miles are marked—though sometimes confusingly, at two or three widely

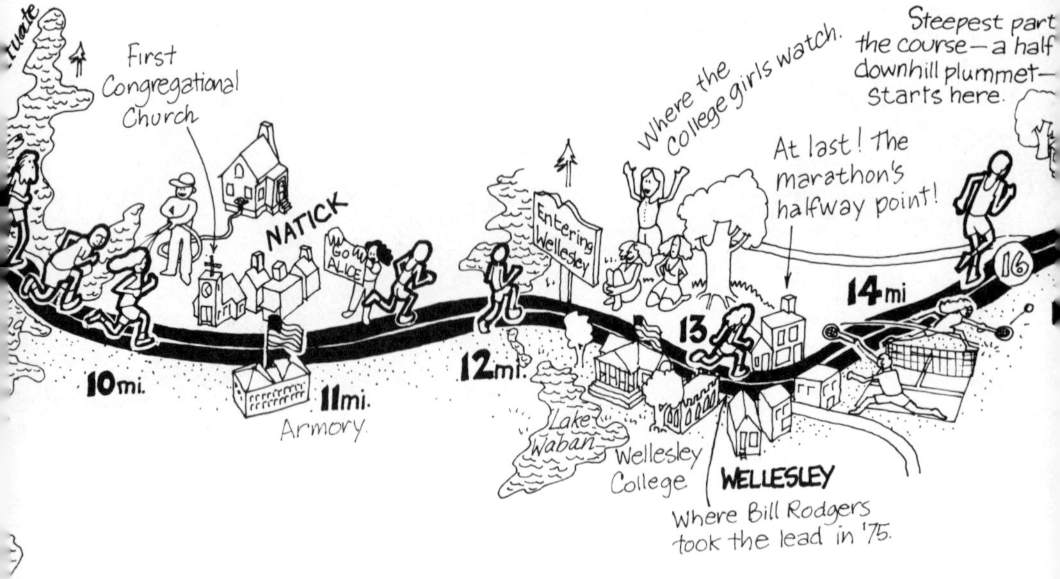

separated places.) At 5.7 miles you pass La Cantina Pizza and the Werby Industries building on the left, and at 6.7 miles are running past the Framingham railroad station. (For marathoners, probably the fittest group of people in the world, an incidental point of interest about Framingham is that it was the scene of the famous Framingham heart-disease study.)

6.7 TO 10.5 MILES: FRAMINGHAM TO NATICK

Moving out of Framingham you encounter a restful level stretch. Should you want to check your running style, you can catch a glimpse of your reflection at 7.8 miles in the long front window of the Hansen Electrical Supply Company. A tenth of a mile later the road begins to slope uphill again. A mile farther on, Lake Cochituate comes into view on your left and Fisk Pond on your right. You pass a dense stand of pines and finally you're in the pleasant town of Natick with its big nineteenth-century houses, each one on a rectangle of green lawn and with great shade trees to shield you momentarily from sunshine. When you reach the intersection of Main Street and West Central Street you've run just about 10.5 miles, and the clock on the tower of the First Congregational Church gives you a chance to check your pace.

At this point you should still feel fresh and springy. A marathoner who is tiring at ten miles is in trouble.

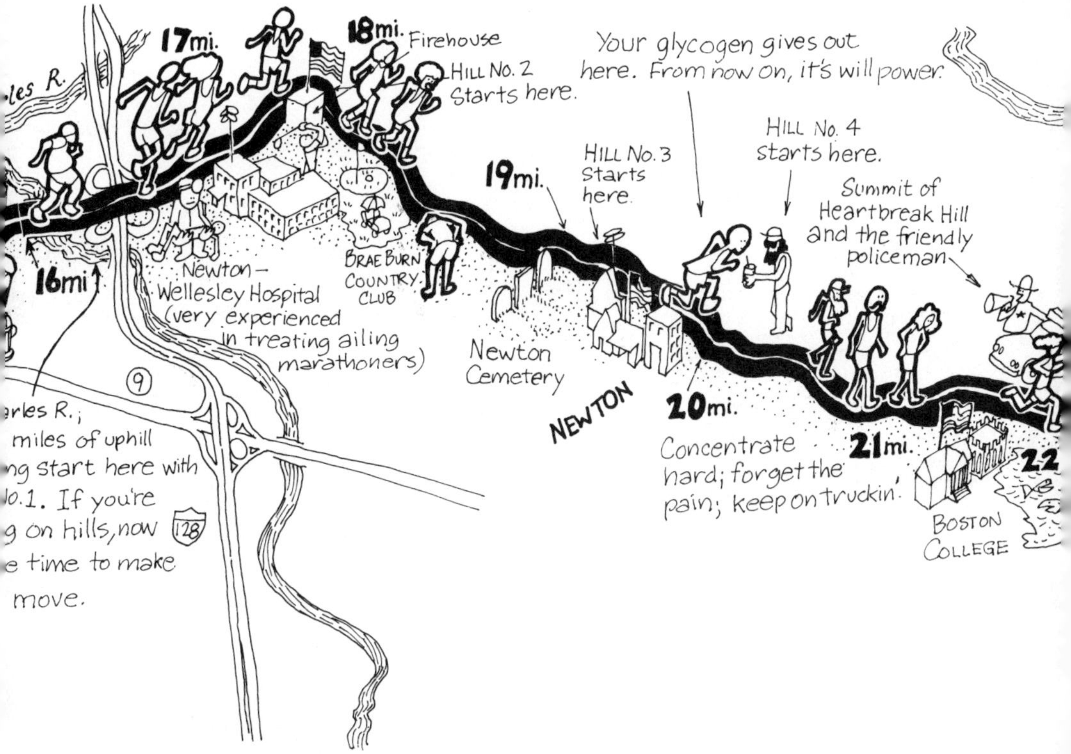

10.5 TO 13.1 MILES: NATICK TO WELLESLEY

Moving eastward out of Natick you pass St. Patrick's Hall and, a bit farther along, the 726th Maintenance Battalion armory. At 11.4 miles a long, gentle downhill stretch begins, and at 12 miles you pass a sign: "Entering Wellesley." Four-tenths of a mile farther along you pass the courts of the Wellesley Tennis Association, and in another .3 miles the modern world's most appreciative marathon fans, the girls of Wellesley College. In another half-mile you're in the town. The halfway point is here, not far from the Marco Polo Gift and Garden Center and the Idiot's Delight Clothing Store.

13.1 TO 16.3 MILES: WELLESLEY TO THE CHARLES

Now, before fatigue and hills wear you down, assess your running style. Concentrate on staying relaxed and minimizing bounce and needless arm movements. From this point on, you'll be grateful for whatever energy you can find.

Half a mile past the marathon's midpoint you leave Route 135 and swing onto Route 16, headed for Wellesley Hills. At 14.2 miles you pass some grassy playing fields, seven tennis courts, and soon, in Wellesley Hills itself, the yellow canopy of the Berkeley Restaurant (14.8 miles). A long flat stretch carries you across Route 9 and, at 15.7 miles, to the brink of the steepest section of the course, a

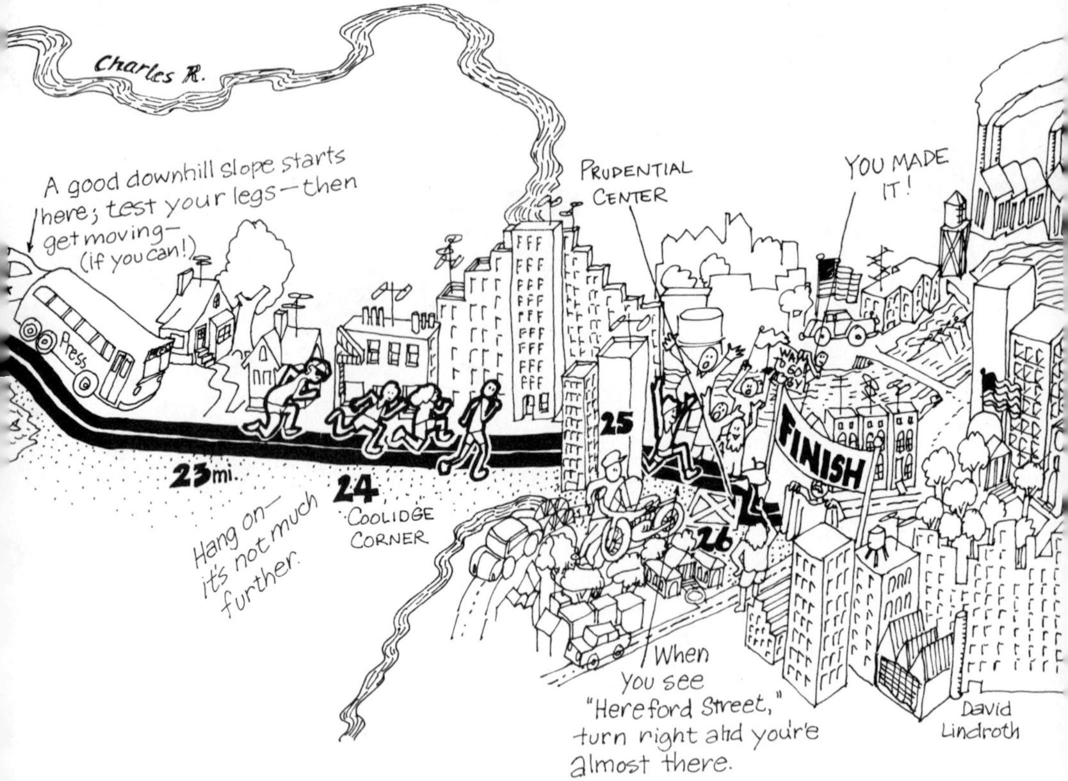

long downhill that is a harbinger of the torture to come. The hills are always the race's big test. Two runners can be matching each other stride for stride when the hills begin, but when they end, one runner has almost always established a decisive lead.

The downhill stretch ends at the Continentale Barber Shop in Newton Lower Falls. At 16.2 miles you cross the Charles River, and now, exactly when your body least craves uphill running, you start climbing.

16.2 TO 21.4 MILES: THE HILLS

There's no question about it; this is the toughest part of the course. You can reach the 16.3-mile mark feeling fit and optimistic, and five miles later you may be a ruin. This is the beginning of what is known collectively as Heartbreak Hill, a series of either three or four hills (depending on how you count them) that wear down the toughest athlete. No single hill is particularly steep or long; it is simply that they come at the wrong part of the race and in combination are more than anyone but a masochist would wish for.

The first hill starts at precisely 16.2 miles, the second at 17.8, the third at 19.5 and the fourth at 20.6. While you're climbing them you cross Route 128, pass the Newton-Wellesley Hospital, make a ninety-degree right turn at the Newton fire station, and in the process pass the race's most drama-conscious spectators—a silent and attentive throng with a finely honed taste for the sight of suffering. Why else would they choose to do their watching on Heartbreak Hill?

There are many theories about how to handle hills. Whatever yours, this section of the race will put it to the test. What seems to work best for me is to take the first couple of hills fairly slowly, remembering that there are more to come. It also helps if you keep your mind off the distance still to be traveled.

21.4 TO 26.2 MILES: HEARTBREAK HILL TO THE PRU

When you reach the top of Heartbreak Hill you'll know it, for the crowds will tell you. They'll also shout that from here on it's all downhill, a statement so palpably false that it could come only from someone who has never run the race. It's true that there are many downhill portions, in particular as you run past the Boston College Alumni Hall and the Baptist Home of Massachusetts, but the course quickly flattens out at 21.9 miles, as you start running alongside trolley tracks. Finally, however, starting at 22.8 miles, you reach a good downhill stretch. The crowds here are denser. People jam the course and hang from windows, so if you're not dazed with fatigue you feel like a hero. Suddenly, at 25.4 miles, you catch a glimpse of the Prudential Center, looking reachable for the first time. You pass the Korean Karate School (25.8 miles), the Bull Restaurant (26 miles) and the Harvard Club of Boston (26.1 miles). Finally you turn right onto Hereford Street, negotiate a long, shallow hill, swing left at the Prudential Center and coast down a ramp toward a yellow banner that reads FINISH. There is no experience quite like reaching that banner. In the 1976 Boston Marathon I arrived only a step or two ahead of a runner from Japan. We threw our arms around each other in a sweaty embrace. Neither of us spoke the other's language, but it didn't matter; there was nothing that needed saying.

To the right of the finish line, toward the Pru Center, is a fountain. It's a good place to cool your feet. Wait for me. With luck I'll be along in a while.

For all its fame, the Boston Marathon course is not an unusually grueling one. Using Geodetic Survey maps and a precision altimeter, a runner named Larry Berman discovered that the descent from start to finish is 425 feet, not 225 as had generally been thought. As you run it, however, you'd never guess it.

GREATER

19

A Run with a Champion

An Olympic Marathoner with a Thought or Two About His Craft

I am on a road a few miles north of Boston, running with Bill Rodgers of Melrose, Massachusetts, an Olympic marathoner and one of the world's fastest runners at 26.2 miles. My feet make their customary *slapslapslap* sound on the pavement. Rodgers moves without a sound, gliding smooth as a cat along the left-hand edge of the road. In the past three weeks he has won two marathons, first defeating 2,001 other runners (Frank Shorter among them) in New York City and then, ten days later, flying to Japan to leave a five-man Japanese relay team in ruins. He is still feeling the jet lag, he tells me, and his stomach is upset.

His problems don't show. He bobs along rhythmically, and is cheerful and talkative. He is wearing a green and orange warm-up suit that flops loosely on his thin, bony body. It is late afternoon and it is turning cold, the way he likes it. It was on a day like this, in April 1975, that he covered the Boston Marathon course so decisively that he not only won the race, a handsome achievement in itself, but set a course record of 2:09:55. ("It can't be true," he said afterward. "I can't run that fast.")

Rodgers is in his late twenties, just the age when marathoners ripen, but he could easily be taken for five or six years younger. He is, as mentioned in Chapter 6, five feet eight and a half inches tall and weighs 125 pounds, exactly what he weighed in junior high school. His hair is sandy blond, his teeth are small and startlingly regular. As he runs, he suggests an extraordinary mechanical harmony, every part working in diligent concert with every other. His arms rock like pendulums. His feet strike the ground softly, at the heel, then roll forward until only a spot of toe links his body to the earth. Then he floats through the air for an unbelievably long time until another heel finally sinks gently to the pavement. As he moves, his head neither rises nor falls but acts as if it were gyroscopically stabilized.

"If I ever stopped running I'd feel terrible," he says, "as if I were slowly decomposing. I enjoy being fit. There's a feeling of independence about it. If I get a flat tire and am ten miles from a gas station I can just run there, instead of sitting for three hours and freezing."

Rodgers grew up in a town called Newington, in the center of Connecticut. In that part of the state the vowels come out pinched, the way they do here and there in the Midwest (or at least the way they did before television made us all alike). When he says the word *marathon*, the first syllable rhymes with *care*. Somehow the accent makes him sound more rural then he really is.

I am running with Rodgers because I hope to find out how a world-class runner looks on his craft and what he thinks about during a race. But I am also interested in Rodgers as a phenomenon. He is, I believe, a particularly interesting runner—one with an unusual ability to push himself when no rivals are around. (His best marathons have been his loneliest.) Most runners run hardest when they can see the tormented faces of their opponents and hear their labored breathing. What is it, I wonder, that makes Rodgers different?

We had started our run accompanied by Rodgers's wife, Ellen. It was she who, before they were married, encouraged him to train hard for the 1975 Boston Marathon. (Recalling that he looked droopy at the halfway mark in Wellesley, she remarked later, "I was ready to kill him.") Ellen has wavy brown hair, a nice smile and a gentle manner. For a mile or so she chatted with us; then, explaining that two miles is her limit, she turned back. Rodgers said goodbye and picked up the pace.

We are running beside a small muddy pasture. The trees are

bare, and a horse stares at us as we pass. "There's not much room for the poor horses around here any more," Rodgers says.

I ask him how he felt when he won the Boston Marathon.

"I was very nervous before it started," he replies. "The year before, I was in fourth place for eighteen or twenty miles. Then I faded and came in fourteenth. I knew I could be up there even farther, so I was psyched up. I knew the top runners were there, but I felt very strong mentally. When the gun went off we took off fairly quickly. I was a little bit back at first, but after a mile or two I caught up with the leaders. The pace was pretty even. Then after about eight miles Mario Quevas, a Mexican runner, went out ahead. Jerome Drayton went with him and I decided what the heck, I'd go after them. Drayton and I ran together for about three miles. Then he moved out."

I ask Rodgers whether he had known who Drayton was. Rodgers gives a quick, nervous laugh and says, "Oh, I knew who he was, and I knew he had run a 2:11. What happened was that people were cheering for him, and it irritated me. Why would they cheer for him, from Canada, more than for me, from Boston? I got furious. I ran really hard for a while, and he fell back. That was the race right there."

Rodgers set his record in that marathon despite the fact that he stopped once to tie his shoe and four times to gulp some water. "I can't run and drink at the same time," he maintains. He laughs again and then goes on: "I guess tying my shoe freaked a lot of people out. The lace was loose, and I remember thinking, *Maybe I'll trip on it.* It was a good chance to stop and relax. So I stopped, tied it, took a deep breath and started in again. It was really no big deal, but it freaked out a lot of people. Some of the runners, too, I guess."

Rodgers and I are running along a road that parallels Interstate 93, a north-south route just west of where Rodgers lives. Two runners, a boy of ten or so and a man, approach us. We all wave. The boy looks up at Rodgers, recognizes him and says, "Hi, Bill." Rodgers says, "Hi, son." For a few seconds we can hear the sound of running shoes on the pavement behind us. Then it is quiet again.

Rodgers talks about his childhood. "I was okay at most sports," he tells me, "but not at baseball. I was pretty inefficient at it. In the first place, I have poor eyesight. I remember I was trying out for Little League, and a guy hit a fly ball. I had glasses on and was staring up at the sun. The ball went right through my hands and hit the ground. *Gloom!* But even in elementary school I was faster than most kids. I always loved to run. They would time me around a baseball diamond and I was fast. I forget what my time was, but it

Bill Rodgers stops during the 1975 Boston Marathon

was good. When I was sixteen I ran my first race, a mile—a super distance to me then. My time was good but not earth-shattering. During sophomore year in high school I used to go out on the track and try to run a mile as fast as I could. I was trying to break five minutes, but I never could do it."

It was during this year that Rodgers began to suspect that he had some unusual abilities. "They had a distance run," he tells me, "and all the gym classes at Newington High School ran it. It was a mile and a tenth, I think. I was the fastest in the school. During my last two years at Newington we had a coach who was pretty good. He had about the loudest voice in all of Connecticut. I improved quite a bit."

Rodgers is feeling better now and running harder. I have to work to keep up. He makes a left turn into an underpass that leads from the west to the east side of Route 93. In the underpass my footsteps echo noisily off the walls, but Rodger's are silent, as if he were moving through cotton batting. In a few minutes we reach a reservoir. The late-afternoon sun has turned the water to gold. "If we go around the reservoir," Rodgers says, "it will be exactly nine miles."

As we run along the water's edge Rodgers says, "Four years ago I had never thought of entering a marathon. After I graduated from college I worked for the post office for a few months. Then I got my conscientious objector's classification and found a job at Peter Bent Brigham Hospital in Boston. For two or three years I watched the Boston Marathon. I was smoking a pack a day at the time—*bad news!* Then I joined a Y and started running again. I ran indoors on this dingy little track. I couldn't even remember what it was like to run outdoors. Finally one day I went out to a park. I started feeling strength coming back, and I remember saying: *This is great. I've got to do more of this.* So in '73 I ran in the Boston Marathon. I bombed out. It was hot and I had a cold and I remember cramping and being on the side of the road. I quit running for two months. I thought, *I will never be a really top-level runner.* I was sure I could never force myself to run hard in the heat."

Although Rodgers has been talking steadily ever since we started, he has showed no signs of breathlessness, not even on the hills. Furthermore, he has demonstrated a continual concern for my safety. "This is a bad part," he'll say. "We'd better go single file here. . . . Don't cross now, wait for these cars. . . . We've got a nice sidewalk to run on just ahead. . . . Watch out for those rocks."

He starts talking about racing tactics. "In the '76 New York Marathon," he says, "Chris Stewart caught up with me. I had been in the lead for a while and suddenly there he was. So I said to myself, okay, I'm not going to try to break away from him immediately. I'll run with him for a while and see what he's like. I try to assess each runner. Are they really strong? I look at their running style; I listen to them breathe. Maybe I even talk to them to see what they have to say. That's what I did with Stewart. I didn't know who he was, so I asked him his name and he told me. Then I knew who he was, and that he had a fast marathon time. So after a while I said to myself, okay, now I'm going to run a little bit harder and see what happens. Fortunately he began to have some difficulty and fell back."

We are nearly around the reservoir now. It is dusk, and in the west the sky is streaked with red. Rodgers looks at it and says, "Wow! Look at that!" He is still running without a sound. I am feeling ragged.

A track writer once told me that Rodgers had never reached his potential because he isn't tough enough mentally. The writer claimed that Rodgers is intimidated when he looks around before a race and sees all those world-class runners. I ask Rodgers what he thinks of the criticism. "I've heard that," he replies thoughtfully. "I know I have that reputation, but I don't think I'm that way any more. If I'm psyched up for a race I'm ready to run with anybody. The top runners in the world can be there, but I'm not intimidated at all; I'm looking forward to it. It's only if it's humid that I worry. At the Montreal Olympics I had this feeling of doom because it was so humid. As a result I overreacted. Whenever anyone made a push, I went with him. I wanted a world-record pace. Then I felt this weakness coming on, and I knew there was nothing I could do. It was"—he uses the word again, with feeling—*"doom."* Rodgers finished way back in the pack.

Ordinarily, he continues, he feels fine during a marathon. "If I don't lose a lot through perspiration," he tells me, "I won't cramp and it won't be too strenuous. I try to run efficiently. I have certain ways of holding my arms. I'll try not to bounce up and down too much, to concentrate on running forward. If my legs are cramping a little I'll position my feet in different ways, maybe land a little differently. Or maybe lean forward a little, or stretch my back if it's tight. A marathon is a forcing—trying to maintain equilibrium, smoothness and efficiency all the way to the end. It's especially tough in the last miles—that's what makes the marathon unique. If you're well trained, then you can hold up in those last miles. If you're not . . ."

During our run Rodgers has mentioned the mental aspects of running, a subject that interests him, several times. He returns to it again now. "In a marathon," he says, "I never let myself think, *I've got twenty-six miles ahead of me.* You have to think of your race as it is right then and there. At the same time you keep in mind the prospects for the future. For example, if someone is three hundred yards ahead, it's nice to know who he is and how he's running. If he's running at the same pace you are, you can sit back, nice and cool, and say, *I'll catch him later.* But you don't say to yourself, *I've got fifteen miles left to go.* Never! I just take it in little segments at a time. In a marathon I like to start easy, run hard for a while in the middle to try to shake the others, and then coast home. I'm able to

do some pretty hard running in the middle because I don't worry too much about the next part."

Now, suddenly, I understand how Rodgers races. He does his best running not when he is alone, but when he is pressed. But his best is so good that very often after a while there is simply no one left for him to run with. Running alone in the later part of a race is his reward for running so well earlier.

Rodgers begins to talk about his future. "I'd like to get myself really up for some marathon where there might be ideal conditions," he says, "and maybe get under 2:09.* Then, someday, I'd like to knock off a 2:07. I'd like to push things down a little bit."

We are running along a country road not far from Rodgers's house. It is nearly dark, and on impulse I ask him if he'll show me the way he runs in a marathon. I want to know what a world-record pace feels like. "Okay," he says. "We'll go a little faster when we get to that next telephone pole." When we reach the pole Rodgers rises onto his toes and accelerates with sinuous smoothness until he is floating along at just under five minutes a mile. It is a

* The record is 2:08:34, set by Derek Clayton of Australia in 1969.

pace he knows well. With considerable ungainly effort I manage to stay with him. The road is smooth, and I am able to turn my head and watch him as he runs. His arms rock back and forth effortlessly, his gloved hands as loose as laundry on a clothesline. With each step his legs cover so much pavement that I take three steps for every two of his. Now, for the first time, his shoes make a faint sound, a feathery *whooshwhoosh.* "I guess I'd be running about like this in a race," he says. "It's hard to tell exactly." I feel a stitch forming an ugly knot in my rib cage.

"Maybe I'd be going a little bit slower," he says. "It could be faster, though. It would depend on who was there." I notice that he is not breathing hard, and it occurs to me that I am running a foot or so from one of the most perfect cardiovascular systems on earth. If you were to ask a particularly cunning engineer to invent a two-legged machine expressly for running, he would no doubt come up with something very much like Rodgers.

Mercifully Rodgers slows down, and once again we move at a bearable pace until we reach Rockland Street, where he lives.

Rodgers and his wife, who are both schoolteachers, rent the top floor of an old house at the far end of a horseshoe-shaped street. To get to their apartment, you climb an outside flight of wooden steps. Their living quarters consist of four or five small rooms. It is a pleasant place. Bright green plants hang in the windows, and in the kitchen Ellen is fixing macaroni and cheese and baking chocolate-chip cookies. Rodgers opens the refrigerator and, ignoring three bottles of Michelob, gets out a quart of ginger ale. He pours some of it into a glass and drinks it. On the kitchen table are bottles of vitamin C, Thermotabs and something called Body Ammo 2.

I take a shower. Later, while Rodgers showers, I talk with Ellen and look around. On a table next to a medium-size television set is a silver platter, his first-place trophy from the 1976 New York Marathon. On the wall of one room mementos are hung: a "Bill Rodgers Day" proclamation from the mayor of Melrose, awarded after he won the Boston Marathon; a photograph of Rodgers and Shorter finishing a race together; an enormous plaque won at a marathon in Japan; a poster advertising the Montreal Olympics.

His hair wet, Rodgers returns, and I ask him whether any of his training techniques are applicable to beginners. "Sure," he says. "Run whenever you feel like it. If you want to run, just take off and go. I do that all the time. I'm uncomfortable when I walk. I have a very awkward kind of walk, so I don't feel very good doing it. One of my legs is an inch longer than the other; a podiatrist told me that. So I'd rather run. The truth is, I hate walking."

20

The World's Sickest Running Club

Sometimes a Heart Attack Is the Best Thing That Ever Happened

One day in 1965 Mort Hirschfield, a tall, athletic-looking New York City insurance agent, was sitting in his living room watching television when suddenly his chest began to feel peculiar. At first, he said later, it was as if someone were tightening a steel band with a thumbscrew. It was a heart attack, a bad one, but Hirschfield was lucky: he did not die, as two out of every three heart-attack victims do.

Hirschfield had always worked and played hard, skied in the winter, and done pretty much what he wanted to do. Now, suddenly he was an invalid, so when, a few weeks later, his doctor prescribed exercises, Hirschfield was startled. "How can I exercise?" he said. "I've had a heart attack!"

"That's right," said the doctor, "but that's in the past. You can't sit on your ass for the rest of your life."

Following instructions, Hirschfield reported to the West Side YMCA, just off Central Park, and under his doctor's vigilant eye began working out, something he had thought he would never do again. "He'd have me try a little of this and a little of that, very moderate stuff," Hirschfield remembers. "I'd run around the track once or twice and he'd take my pulse. I'd exercise for maybe fifteen minutes, then have to quit and take a shower." Still, he stuck at it, and in time began to notice some improvement. To his astonishment, before long he felt as good as he ever had. "Now I can work out for forty-five minutes easily and feel great," he says. "I don't know where I'd be without running."

By studying the electrical signature of Hirschfield's heart on a cardiogram, a specialist can see that he once had a heart attack, but it is equally plain that his heart is now functioning efficiently.

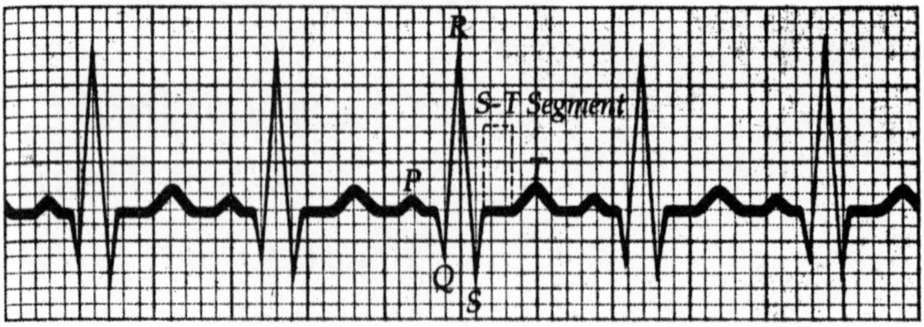

An electrocardiogram; abnormalities in the S-T segment and T wave may indicate heart disease

Hirschfield, who is in his late sixties, works a full schedule, does whatever he wants to in his leisure time, and three nights a week goes to the Y for exercise classes designed especially for heart patients.

I visited one of these classes recently, and if I hadn't been told that the participants had once been seriously ill, I would never have guessed it. Two or three were only in their thirties; the rest were an even sprinkling of men in their forties, fifties and sixties. (Most heart-attack victims are men, although, as noted in Chapter 8, women after menopause begin to catch up as they lose their mysterious natural immunity.) Everyone in the class was running, chatting and laughing, and there was a lot of good-natured kidding, much of it directed at the imperturbable instructor.

A generation ago people like Hirschfield and his associates would have been told to avoid exercise, relax and make the best of a bad situation. Within a few years many of them would have been dead. My father had a heart attack when he was thirty-five, and until he died eight years later he lived the life of an invalid. Once—just once—in those eight years I remember seeing him toss a football. The rest of the time he sat quietly, read, listened to music and (as I came to realize much later) put his affairs in order.

In the years since then, cardiologists have learned that it isn't necessary for their patients to go gently into that good night. They've learned how to help them fight back, and in that battle one of their most effective weapons has been running. Even the scarred heart has remarkable adaptive abilities. Under the rigors of exercise it does not weaken but becomes significantly stronger—strong enough, in many cases, to withstand easily the strain of running a marathon (recently described by Dr. Loring B. Rowell of the University of Washington as "one of the major insults a person can voluntarily give his cardiovascular system"). The psychological benefits of such a return to physical fitness are enormous. People feel less fear, more confidence and less depression.* Furthermore, in practically every case their sex lives improve.

All this would be of little general interest if only an occasional person fell victim to a heart attack, but we are currently experiencing an epidemic of them. (To estimate your chances of being affected, see the chart on page 229.) In 1975, the most recent year for which figures have been assembled, approximately 1,000,000 Americans had heart attacks. Their average age was only thirty-five years and nine months, and this average is dropping precipitously. If the trend continues, by 1980 it will have dipped below thirty, and by 1985 it will be only twenty-eight. Of the heart patients who survive an initial attack, 4 to 6 percent die each year. However, if they start a medically supervised program of running and other exercises, the rate drops to well under 2 percent. Furthermore, says the director of one of the most highly regarded cardiac rehabilitation programs, Dr. Terence Kavanagh, "In terms of the quality of life there are even more grounds for optimism. One study showed that one-third of a sample of our patients had neurotic-type personality and developed excessive depression after a heart attack. In most cases, patients became less depressed as they became more fit."

As noted in Chapter 4, doctors are cautious about asserting that running guarantees a longer and better life. Kavanagh, a long-time champion of exercise and the author of a provocative book entitled *Heart Attack? Counterattack!,* reports that even though his program is a decade old it has not yet been in operation long enough to permit proper statistical evaluation. He says, "A more thorough analysis of our figures is needed before these results can be accepted as anything more than encouraging." Some doctors are even more wary. Dr. Herman K. Hellerstein, a professor of medicine at Case Western Reserve University and an authority on the

* Depression is a classic postcardiac sympton. It is especially difficult to combat because most patients deny that they are depressed.

RATE YOUR HEART-ATTACK RISK

This chart, adapted with permission from one prepared by the Cardio-Metrics organization in New York City and based on factors that the American Heart Association has singled out as most decisive in determining a person's risk of heart attack, will give you a reliable estimate of the danger you yourself face. Although of course it is not an infallible predictor of health, it reflects current scientific research and is therefore a useful guide. You will notice that some factors, such as heredity, are beyond an individual's control, while others, such as exercise, weight and smoking, are in most cases well within our power to change. The important point is not to worry about factors you can't affect, but to work on those you can do something about. To score yourself, check the appropriate description for each risk factor; then, using the indicator numbers at the left of each row, add up your total number of points. Ten to twenty points indicates low risk; twenty-one to forty, moderate risk; forty-one to sixty, high risk.

---

rehabilitation of heart patients, told a group of colleagues at a recent conference that distance running is potentially hazardous and has aroused unrealistic expectations; he said that even when it undeniably benefits a patient, it doesn't necessarily benefit him in the best possible way.

It is no surprise that medical authorities disagree with one another. Running is such a new therapeutic technique that its effects have not yet been fully measured. Still, whenever any interim evidence has emerged, it has invariably supported the probability that running is enormously beneficial. This is why Kavanagh insists, even in the face of his incomplete statistics, "You've got to play the odds."

An explanation of what a heart attack is will help us understand how exercise helps a heart patient. When it occurs, it seems like a sudden event, but it is not. The conditions that predispose one to a heart attack have usually begun decades earlier with the build-up of cholesterol and other materials that have narrowed the heart's own arteries and thus limited its blood supply. In civilized countries atherosclerosis, as this narrowing is called, is common. It was found in a significant number of Americans killed in the Korean War—their average age was twenty-two—and is frequently detected in schoolchildren. Sometimes an early warning comes in the form of angina pectoris (commonly referred to simply as angina)—a chest pain, usually short-lived, indicating that the heart isn't getting enough oxygen. Ordinarily this occurs during exertion, and

	Heredity	Blood Pressure	Diabetes	Smoking	Weight	Cholesterol	Exercise	Emotional Stress	Age	Sex and Build
6	Three or more relatives who had heart attacks before age 60 (parents & siblings only)	High blood pressure not controlled by medication	Diabetic with complications (circulation, kidneys, eyes)	More than 40 cigarettes daily	More than 50 lbs. overweight	Over 281	Complete lack of exercise	Intense problems, can't cope, see a psychiatrist	Over 60	Male, very stocky
5	Two relatives who had heart attacks before age 60	High blood pressure partly controlled by medication	Diabetic on insulin—no complications	21–39 cigarettes daily	36–50 lbs. overweight	256–280	Sedentary job, light recreational exercise	Constantly need pills or drink for stress	51–60	Male, fairly stocky
4	One relative who had a heart attack before age 60	Persistent mild high blood pressure, untreated	High sugar controlled by tablets	6–20 cigarettes daily	21–35 lbs. overweight	231–255	Sedentary job, moderately active recreation	Take pills or drink for stress on occasion	41–50	Male, average build
3	Two or more relatives who had heart attacks after age 60	High blood pressure only when upset	High sugar controlled by diet	Fewer than 5 cigarettes daily	6–20 lbs. overweight	206–230 (or don't know)	Sedentary job, very active in recreation	Moderate business or personal pressures	31–40	Female after menopause
2	One relative who had a heart attack after age 60	Normal blood pressure (or don't know)	Normal blood sugar (or don't know)	Cigars or pipe only	Up to 5 lbs. overweight	181–205	Moderately active in job and recreation	Rare business or personal pressure	21–30	Male, thin build
1	No heart disease in family	Low blood pressure	Low blood sugar	Nonuser or stopped permanently	More than 5 lbs. underweight	180 or below	Very active physically in job and recreation	No real business or personal pressures	10–20	Female still menstruating
Your Score										
									Total	

disappears when the activity stops. Some angina patients live for years without having a heart attack, but if the narrowing of the arteries continues, the likelihood increases that a clump of debris will one day produce a blockage. When this happens, the supply of blood to part of the heart muscle is cut off. For a while the muscle aches, and it is this that a victim feels. Finally, as the oxygen-deprived muscle fibers stop contracting, the pain subsides and the attack ends, leaving in its wake a partially dead heart. The severity of an attack is determined by how much of the heart dies.

If the victim lives, no matter how much of the heart's blood supply has been affected by the attack–myocardial infarction is the medical term–the heart promptly begins to heal. In the recovery process, white blood cells arrive to remove the heart's spent muscle fibers, and new blood vessels, replacements for those damaged by the attack, begin to snake their way through the muscle. Finally, within a month or two, scar tissue forms. At this point, exercise can begin to work its miracle of recovery.

It has already been noted that aerobic exercise has a number of beneficial effects on a normal heart. Among other things, it slows the heartbeat, increases the amount of blood pumped with each contraction, lowers blood pressure and blood fats, and increases the ability of working muscles to remove oxygen from the blood. Exactly the same processes take place in the heart of a person who has had a myocardial infarction. Something else of prodigious significance also occurs: under the influence of exercise, the heart vastly increases its density of back-up blood vessels (or, as doctors call them, collaterals). This remarkable adaptive mechanism first came to scientific notice some two decades ago when a researcher named R. W. Eckstein, experimenting with dogs, tied off various coronary arteries to induce artificial heart attacks. After a time he began to exercise some of these dogs, while the others were left in cages to lead sedentary lives, much like those of corporation executives. The results constituted a landmark in physiological research. To compensate for the loss of the tied-off vessels, the exercised dogs grew new coronary arteries, while the sedentary dogs didn't. Exercise was able to do what rest could not: overcome the damage done by these artificially induced heart attacks.

It is precisely this phenomenon that lies behind today's proliferation of postcardiac exercise classes. A few years ago at Myrtle Beach, South Carolina, a group of medical specialists, assembled at the National Workshop on Exercise, wrote: "Epidemiologic and other studies have demonstrated that regular physical activity is associated with a better state of well being, enhanced quality of living, and apparently reduced morbidity and mortality from ischemic heart disease [i.e., disease caused by an inadequate blood supply]. For these reasons, comprehensive patient care should include enhancement of physical fitness."

Many physicians have rallied around this and similar endorsements of exercise for heart patients. At Barnes Hospital in St. Louis, for example, Dr. Jon Cooksey, a cardiologist, has organized a running program for cardiac patients. "We've measured a 35 percent improvement," he says. "Heart rate is lower by an average of seventeen beats, and the blood pressure is lower." The case of Howard Pattiz, a patient in his early fifties, is typical. When he began the program not long after his heart attack, he could shuffle through only seven short laps around the track, but within six weeks he was doing thirty-four.

In Greenwich, Connecticut, the hospital and the Health Association sponsor a medically supervised program for heart patients. They recently reported on one patient who could hardly walk two blocks when he joined the program, but who eventually ran a mile nonstop in eleven minutes.

In La Crosse, Wisconsin, the La Crosse Cardiac Rehabilitation Program has been in operation since 1971. When I talked recently with its executive director, Phillip K. Wilson, he said that several hundred patients had participated since classes started and that their results had paralleled those achieved elsewhere. The La Crosse program is one of the few that puts out its own newspaper, the *Cardio-Gram* (see Appendix A), a publication that includes articles on everything from foot trouble to heat stroke to sex after a heart attack.

One of the nation's most ambitious and successful postcardiac programs is found in Hawaii. There Dr. Jack H. Scaff, Jr., an internist and cardiologist in his early forties, has long conducted a thrice-weekly program for heart patients. In 1974 Scaff and a cardiologist colleague, Dr. John O. Wagner, got the idea of expanding the program to include people who had not had attacks but who, because of sedentary lives, were in danger. Accordingly, they started a Sunday-morning clinic to teach nonrunners how to complete a marathon. "The Honolulu Marathon Clinic," Wagner says, "has made it possible for middle-aged, sedentary, nonrunning people to learn how to compete in a marathon without being intimidated by the elite, young, skinny runners they see running around town all the time." The Honolulu program has spawned similar clinics in San Diego, Los Angeles and Reno. Nonetheless, it will probably be some time before those cities threaten Hawaii's supremacy: while the average national density of distance runners is 9 per 100,000 people, Hawaii's is 82. (Second-place Oregon's is only 19 per 100,000.)

One of the best-known rehabilitative efforts is in Toronto. There,

Dr. Terence Kavanagh, right, with heart patients

Terence Kavanagh, a pixieish transplanted Dubliner who serves as medical director of the Toronto Rehabilitation Center, conducts a program that has attracted interest and envy the world over. More than a decade ago Kavanagh's background as physician, athlete and athletic official (he is much involved in Canadian amateur sport) prompted him to start looking into endurance exercise as a rehabilitative measure for heart patients. Within five years seven of his patients, three of whom had had not just one attack but two, were able to run in and complete the Boston Marathon. Interestingly, the idea for attempting the 26.2-mile run didn't come from Kavanagh himself, but from one of his patients. In his book the doctor describes how it developed:

> One day, while we were changing after a five-mile run, someone half jokingly remarked how great an achievement it would be to finish a marathon. For a second or two there was complete silence, a few questioning glances, an uneasy grin, and finally one or two doubtful laughs. Then the moment was gone. Gradually, week by week, the idea grew in our minds. What at first seemed to be a preposterous joke became a serious consideration and then a firm resolve. For me it was, in a way, the moment of truth. I had motivated these men to run; as far as I was concerned they were rehabilitated, and I had

> made no bones in telling them so. They had trusted me. To put it succinctly, the time had come to put up or shut up! I decided that we would make the attempt.

Kavanagh was criticized by colleagues and accused of "showboating," as one put it. Nonetheless, all seven patients finished the marathon in good condition. It is hardly surprising that they presented him with his own special trophy inscribed to "Dr. T. Kavanagh, Supercoach, the World's Sickest Track Club."

Kavanagh's rehabilitation program is not as dangerous or foolhardy as it might seem. For one thing, it is based on a careful assessment of each patient's condition; for another, it consists of a carefully graduated regimen, beginning in some cases with as little as a thirty-minute one-mile walk—scarcely more than a crawl. Finally, even after a patient has graduated to running Kavanagh does not recommend a pace faster than a ten-minute mile. (His program is outlined in detail in his book.)

Though cardiologists shudder at the thought, some heart patients simply prescribe their own programs. Tex Maule, author of *Running Scarred,* was a *Sports Illustrated* writer when he had a heart attack a few years ago. Maule not only spent much of his time with athletes, but had always been energetic himself; hence it seemed natural to start running as soon as he was able to. Working out every morning at a track not far from his office, he finally developed enough endurance to run the first several miles of the Boston Marathon without mishap.

Al Martin, a Houston physical therapist interested in cardiovascular rehabilitation, also prescribed his own program against medical advice. Thirty-one when he had his heart attack, he followed standard medical textbooks and started alternately running and walking specific distances with a stopwatch. Whenever he felt pains in his chest he slowed down. Martin says, "I emphasized long periods of low intensity rather than intense short runs. I worked up to forty-five-minute sessions, starting slowly and gradually picking up the pace. Today I can go five miles a day in under forty minutes. I no longer get angina with heavy exertion—that is, heart rates as high as 190. I used nitroglycerin at first, but don't need it any more."

Few cardiologists would recommend emulating Maule and Martin. One reason is that with the proliferation of medically sound rehabilitation programs, it's not difficult for most people to find one nearby. When qualified supervision is close at hand and reasonably priced,* it hardly makes sense to take needless risks.

* The program at the West Side YMCA in New York City, for example, cost $490 a year in early 1977. This fee includes membership in the Y, an exercise stress test, and an electrocardiogram three months after starting the class.

A growing realization of the influence of exercise on health is currently prompting large numbers of business firms to establish running programs of their own in an effort to keep valued employees from developing heart attacks. (One can view such programs cynically; the company will, after all, save money in the long run if key people can be kept on the job instead of winding up in hospital beds. But if the results are good, what do the motives matter?) At the Bonne Belle cosmetics company outside Cleveland, Ohio, practically all of the two hundred employees participate in a company-sponsored physical fitness program. (Those who do are given an extra thirty minutes for lunch.) When I asked Jess Bell, the president of the company and an indefatigable champion of running, about how he planned to measure results, he replied: "We do not intend to evaluate the program. . . . I think the results will be obvious. We intend to hire a nurse part time, who will help to administer the program, and we will suggest that people have their doctors' approval before getting into any strenuous participation. Previously we had paid a dollar a mile for anyone who pledged to run at least five times a week. This was unsuccessful and we would not do it again. We paid out too much money for very little benefit. I consider it a waste." Bell makes it clear that he doesn't consider the running itself a waste—only paying people to do it. He described his own entirely unpaid program: "I run a minimum of five miles a day or farther. I try to run approximately fifty miles a week. I've run in several marathons. . . . After three years of continuous running and very little dieting my weight is down to what it was when I was a paratrooper in 1951. In a stress physical given in Dallas I was considered to be in superior condition for under thirty years of age. I am fifty-one."

Not every business executive is as enlightened as Bell. However, more and more of them are these days, perhaps because they know that it costs business some $700 million a year to recruit replacements for employees disabled by heart attacks. The New York Life Insurance Company has an exercise program for workers who score poorly on their annual physical examinations. When I talked with Dr. Denis O'Leary, the company's vice-president for employee health, he explained that exercise is just part of an overall program of sensible living. "I'm in favor of operating within a parameter of social daily living," he said. "I'm against being an oddball. For me the joy of life is a good meal, but if you're eating two desserts a day it's bad news." I asked O'Leary if he had any studies showing what New York Life's program was accomplishing, but he brushed the question aside. "These guys *feel* so damned good," he said. "Just seeing how much energy they've got is enough for me."

O'Leary's rough-and-ready appraisal, accurate as it probably is, isn't enough for some managements. William M. Horne, a physical fitness specialist at the Mobil Oil Corporation, recently reported on a two-year study of Mobil executives who participated in a regular exercise program that included treadmill running. The results were everything the most fiscally conservative corporate manager could ask for: lower heart rate, blood pressure and cholesterol—virtually sure signs that the group would have fewer heart attacks than their sedentary colleagues.

But in the end it may be that running's most important changes are not in such physiological measurements but in styles of living. It has been established that the most likely victim of heart disease is a person with a so-called Type A personality—hard-driving, competitive, irritable and impatient. As mentioned in Chapter 2, the tranquillity gained by running has a radiating power that irresistibly affects other parts of our lives. If this tranquillity transforms a Type A person into a less competitive Type B, the chances of avoiding a heart attack and of leading a happier life are substantially increased.

Trust no thought arrived at sitting down.
—George A. Sheehan, Red Bank, New Jersey

Part III
THE WORLD of RUNNING

Joe Henderson

21

Spreading the Word

The Runner's Own Cult Magazine

It occasionally reads as if it were published by people too exhausted by running to put their minds on what they're doing. It contradicts and repeats itself, is uneven in quality and tone, and prints humor that would embarrass a reader of *Mad.* (*Question:* "What is the most important thing that could encourage a runner to attempt his first marathon?" *Answer:* "The fact that he hasn't run one yet.") And if its entire staff were locked in its editor's minuscule office there would still be plenty of room for all of them to do their warm-ups on the floor.

This unlikely magazine is a monthly called *Runner's World,* and though it is little more than a decade old it is already, deficiencies and all, the best and most influential running publication ever devised by the mind of man. Practically everyone who cares at all about running reads it, studies it as if it were the Rosetta stone and then preserves it along with *National Geographic* and other such journalistic treasures. To recycle it would be unthinkable. Many runners have lifetime subscriptions.

I remember my introduction to *Runner's World.* A few months after I had started running, a friend loaned me a stack of back issues. In those days it was an anemic little black-and-white thing and was about as inviting as a newspaper's classified-ad section. (Today, although there still isn't a great deal of color on the inside pages, it always uses four-color covers.) Yet as I began reading, I felt I had found the runner's grail. There were articles on how to train, what to eat, how to race, how to lose weight—everything a fledgling plodder needed. I went through the whole stack in a single voracious sitting.

All magazines like to think they occupy an important place in their readers' lives, but *Runner's World* really does. It is every bit as important as running shoes or winter running gloves. The reason is reducible to a single axiom: *Runner's World understands what runners go through, and it cares.* Listen to its editor, a shaggy-headed, perpetually smiling gnome in his mid-thirties named Joe Henderson: "What we've done is to promote the idea that your own performances not only have meaning but are actually more important than what somebody does in the Olympics. We'd much prefer to see ten thousand people down on the track running a mile in seven minutes than ten thousand people up in the stands watching one person run three-fifty."

Nowadays, when every park and path has its runners, Henderson's views hardly sound startling, but as little as a decade ago they were revolutionary. Americans had long worshiped winners, scorning those who came in second. To Henderson this seemed silly. What counted wasn't winning but the fact that a person was running. "The challenge in running," he wrote not long ago, "is not to aim at doing the things no one else has done, but to keep doing things anyone could do—but most never will."

Henderson's office is in Mountain View, California, in a building of undistinguished beige cement that rises between Route 101 and the sandy flats of San Francisco Bay. Just down the road are some tarpaper shacks and an abandoned Victorian mansion, its paint chipping away, its windows boarded up. It's not much of a neighborhood. In the room Henderson occupies, a mountainous pile of running shoes was stacked against a wall when I was there—Tigers, Adidases, Pumas, Nikes, and others. (He was working on the annual running-shoe issue.) Nearby were a couple of tubes of a glop meant to be smeared on the soles of shoes to make them last longer. The manufacturer had sent them to Henderson in hope of getting some publicity—apparently unmindful, poor fellow, that everyone these days uses little electric gadgets that exude hot glue.

Henderson stands five foot six and weighs 130 pounds. Although he wears fashionable gold-rimmed eyeglasses, there is something about him that hints at a simpler era than our own. He has a wide-eyed guilelessness that suggests he may secretly slip off at night to Bible classes. (He does not. What he does slip off to, or at least did one night during my visit, are meetings of something called the Tax Reducers Athletic Club.) Henderson takes his running seriously, spending from daybreak, when he gets up to write in his journal, to the end of the day thinking and writing about the subject. But he also laughs about it, and sees a certain irony in what he is up to. "All my troubles come from running," he told me ruefully. "Then I use running to go out and get rid of them."

Henderson acknowledges that *Runner's World* isn't everything it ought to be. "I have no time to plan ahead," he says. "We're doing only one issue at a time. We have practically no staff. But we do the best we can with what we've got." There's no question that he does it conscientiously, given the magazine's short-handedness and the magnitude of the job. I glanced at a couple of manuscripts he had edited. They were carefully and skillfully done, the chaff neatly eliminated with heavy black-penciled Xs, bright new words and phrases neatly penciled in.

The relationship between running and writing fascinates Henderson. "There's something curious about running and writing," he said. "Kenny Moore—he's probably the best writer on running that there is—once wrote that you just *have* to write about long-distance running because it sometimes hurts so much and is such a profound physical and psychological experience. Or maybe—this is my own idea, not Kenny's—people write to give meaning to something that may not *have* much meaning. Maybe that's why most runners keep some sort of log; they're trying to hold onto it all. People start out just running. Then sooner or later they start analyzing their running."

Some years ago Henderson himself started keeping a simple journal—so many miles at such and such a speed. Gradually it changed, and he found himself keeping track of thoughts he had while he ran. Now the journal, neatly stored in a multitude of ring binders, occupies a whole shelf in his study, and much of it has found its way into his books: *Long Slow Distance: The Humane Way to Train; The Long Run Solution; Run Gently, Run Long;* and his most recent, *Jog, Run, Race.*

Henderson's books have carried the gospel to thousands of runners. When he found a few years ago that his legs had begun to act up when he ran fast—he had been a respectable 4:22 miler in high school—he started investigating the virtues of running slowly. Today, as a result, he rarely runs faster than an eight-minute mile, though in the interest of strict accuracy it should be noted that he likes to throw in an occasional brief burst at close to top speed—

"just to stretch my legs out"—and one Sunday morning not long ago he entered a half-mile race and came in second with a 2:16. That's not exactly poky. Still, Henderson has been the most articulate exponent of LSD and even takes credit, albeit modestly, for coining the acronym. "If you try to run like a college miler, especially as you get older," he told me, "you're going to have all kinds of trouble. You'll burn yourself out. But the way I do it, you can run forever."

So it seems. Every Saturday morning at eight, Henderson drives to Foothill College, a futuristic little junior college in Los Altos Hills, to rendezvous with a pack of like-minded runners. They are of all sorts and conditions—from young to middle-aged, and both men and women—but they have all been lured by Henderson's LSD siren song. One morning when I ran with them, they headed slowly up the brown, grassless slope that rises just west of Foothill College—the place is aptly named—and ran slowly along twisting mountain roads, past towering stands of eucalyptus, up, up, up above Stanford University's artificial-intelligence lab where all of San Francisco, 360 degrees of it, can be seen far below. Once or twice while going uphill Henderson pushed a bit, stretching his legs out, but otherwise it was an easy pace. We moved along behind him as lackadaisically as old milk-wagon horses, our running shoes clipclopping rhythmically on the humpbacked California hills. Once someone called, "How about picking up the pace a bit, Henderson?" Henderson just smiled and kept right on bobbing along, covering each mile in exactly 480 painless seconds. We went on like that for two hours, until finally we were running down one last brown, grassless slope and there again were Foothill College and our cars. Nobody looked the least bit tired. Henderson has been doing this for years and clearly expects to keep right on doing it until he's ninety.

By early 1977, *Runner's World* had reached a circulation of some 65,000. It covers its field so thoroughly that a couple of years ago when one New York author decided to write a book about running, she simply ordered a lot of back copies of the magazine and rewrote the relevant portions. One way and another, *Runner's World* attracts the best authorities on running: the running doctor George Sheehan, the physiology researcher David L. Costill, and such knowledgeable writers as Hal Higdon, who set a national 10,000-meter record (32:37.8) in his very first over-forty race, and Dr. Joan Ullyot, who knows more about women's running, including its scientific aspects, than anyone alive. Henderson can turn a moving paragraph as well. Reporting on the nationalism that soured the 1976 Olympic games, he wrote: "The individual athletes have lost their faces in sport, as individual soldiers do in war. And in modern sport, like modern warfare, national leaders make the moves. The individuals are their pawns. Nations win and lose. But among individuals, there are no winners and losers in these kinds of games—only survivors and victims."

Runner's World is as much a runners' bulletin board as a journalistic enterprise. It publishes letters from readers, has a department for short unsolicited contributions (for which it pays an unvarying twenty dollars each) and manages to find a place for a great variety of theories, hypotheses and meditations. Its readers bestow upon it a certain amount of good-natured joshing, amused by the fact that if you wait long enough you can find support for practically any theory you want. But the fickleness of *Runner's World* is part of its charm. "If they tell you this month that you've got to train hard all the time, just wait," one reader says. "Next month they'll be telling you that you should always be sure to train easy."

Henderson agrees that *Runner's World* is something of a grab bag, but he doesn't apologize for it. "I don't think we've done anything that would get in any anthologies of sports stories of the year," he says, "but on the other hand, I think our stories as a whole have done a lot of good for a lot of people."

They have done exactly that, and Henderson has had much to do with their far-reaching influence. He is one of those lucky people who seem to have been destined from the beginning for the very job they're doing. He grew up in a hamlet called Coin, in Iowa, where his father was a farmer. He went out for track in high school, and because he did well at it, decided to be a coach. After graduation he enrolled at Drake University, and to help pay his way got a summer job sweeping floors and reading proofs for a publication called *Track & Field News* in Los Altos, California. This brief venture into journalism gave Henderson some fresh ideas about his career. He changed his major from physical education to journalism, went to work for the university daily and finally landed a job writing sports fillers for the *Des Moines Register.* He hated it. "I didn't want to be a *sports* writer," he says. "I wanted to be a *running* writer."

In 1967 Henderson went back to *Track & Field News.* It wasn't a great job, but at least he was doing something he liked. Then one day in 1969 he got a note from a twenty-two-year-old Kansas publisher named Bob Anderson. For four years Anderson had been singlehandedly putting out a little magazine called *Distance Running News.* Now he hoped to expand it and was looking for an editor. Would Henderson be interested? "Sure," he told Anderson.

"But I won't leave California. I've got a couple of girl friends out here."

"Fine," Anderson said. "Maybe I'll come out there. I've been thinking of leaving Kansas anyway."

So Anderson came to California, looked around, liked what he saw, went home, loaded his possessions into a U-Haul truck and headed west. He hired Henderson at seventy-five dollars a week, exactly what he was paying himself. ("It wouldn't have mattered how much he paid me," says Henderson. "I had no expenses. I lived in a shack up in the hills and drove a '63 VW.")

Like Henderson, Anderson had practically no expenses, so until then he hadn't needed to make much money. Now, with a full-time employee, it was time to get moving. He wanted to reach more readers and try his hand at book publishing. Anderson, who has steady, dark-brown eyes, a mustache and a quietly confident manner, was used to getting things done. His chief business principle, already well solidified, was that if you saw something that needed doing, you didn't fiddle around for a year finding out what the obstacles were; you just went out and did it. This was exactly how he had started *Distance Running News.* Back in high school he had become interested in running in marathons. Finding nothing in the local library about how to train for a twenty-six-mile race, he wrote to some well-known marathoners asking how to proceed. "Practically all of them answered," Anderson told me. "So I said to myself: With all these good contacts, why not start a magazine? I spent a hundred dollars and put out the first issue in January of '66. I published two issues that year, a thousand copies of each. Sales totaled $513. Soon I went to four issues a year and then to six. By the time Henderson started working here, our circulation was up to two thousand."

Anderson took some business courses at Kansas State, but the magazine kept getting in the way. "I was spending so much time with the magazine—so much time actually *running* a business—that I didn't have any time to learn all that theoretical stuff," he says. What he most wanted to do was make *Runner's World*—he changed the name in 1970—the best running magazine to be found anywhere.

He has, of course, done just that, and probably the chief reason is that he is a publisher with a sure instinct for the uses of unorthodoxy. While the typical publisher concerns himself chiefly with financial matters, Anderson has from the beginning kept a watchful eye on what goes into *Runner's World.* "My viewpoint is a little different from that of most publishers," he says, "mainly because I'm a runner first and a publisher second. I've been running since 1962, and I've run eight marathons. I started *Runner's World* because I wanted information on running that no one was providing. In the early days I read every word that went into it, and I still make the final decision on controversial articles." It is Anderson who has lured many of the magazine's most important writers into the fold, and it was he who, years before women's running achieved its present popularity, foresaw what was bound to happen and began to publish articles on female marathoners.

Anderson's most pronounced heresy, however, is his professed disdain for money. "Sure," he told me, "I want enough money so I can do what I want to do. But money doesn't come first; running does. My feeling is that if I do a good job, the money will come."

One weekend a few years ago Anderson was musing about ways he might make his company, World Publications, grow. Idly, he jotted down a list of thirty-two other possible sports magazines—on everything from weightlifting to bobsledding. Eventually he winnowed the list down to seven and, characteristically, simply started them. They were *Aquatic World, Self-Defense World, Gymnastics World, Soccer World, Bike World, Nordic World* and *Downriver* (with no *World*). "At that time," Anderson says, "no one knew much about the long-term effects of running. If the Surgeon General came out and declared that running was bad for people, we wanted to have something to fall back on. So we started *Bike World* first, and then the others." In late 1976, when he decided the first three were not attracting enough advertising or subscription renewals, he unsentimentally folded them. The others, however, are still going strong, and World Publications, which less than a decade ago had only two employees, now has eighty or so and brings in close to $3,000,000 a year.

Anderson's book-publishing business is also flourishing. In 1970, when he started it, he put out mostly booklets of 100 pages or fewer. Soon, however, he began publishing full-scale books. The company now issues about fifteen a year, a half-dozen on running and the rest on other sports. Most sell well. *Dr. Sheehan on Running*, one of the most popular, sold 35,000 copies in its first year and a half, respectable even by big-time publishing standards.

The chief problem with a magazine like *Runner's World* is letting people know about it. It's not the sort of publication that usually sells well on newstands, and there are no mailing lists that are exactly right, so Anderson relies mainly on word of mouth. He also depends on an invention of his called the Fun Run. Fun Runs, which are often announced in local newspapers, are held in some seventy-five cities throughout the United States, and even in a few foreign cities where particularly dedicated runners are willing to be missionaries. The peculiar virtues of a Fun Run are that there are no numbers, no fees, no registration and no long wait afterward for the results—the factors that clutter most races. All you find at a Fun Run is a lot of people in shorts, a person with a starting gun, someone else at the finish line reading out the times in a voice loud enough to be heard over the sound of hard breathing, and inevitably, a table piled high with copies of *Runner's World* and books from World Publications. The first Fun Run was held, naturally enough, in California, not far from the *Runner's World* office. Now they are staged all the way from Walla Walla, Washington, to Inverness, Florida, and Anderson has even prepared a special kit he sends to people who want to start a Fun Run of their own (see Appendix A).

Plainly *Runner's World* is not just a lark but a real business, with the same anxieties and concerns that bedevil businesses everywhere. Yet it is also subject to odd, unpredictable intrusions from a more carefree world. One lunch hour Joe Henderson went for a half-hour run with a colleague named Eric Evans, a former Olympian who edits *Downriver.* They changed clothes in their offices, then headed toward San Francisco Bay, moving along at an easy pace and talking about the problems of their magazines. It was both work and play. Suddenly a brown jackrabbit as big as a house cat popped out of a bush and bounded down the dirt path ahead of them. Henderson lit out after it, his arms working like a sprinter's, his toes kicking up puffs of dust, until the jackrabbit found a bush to disappear into. When he rejoined Evans, he was grinning. "If we'd been in an open field I could have taken him," he said. "Jackrabbits are fast, but they have no endurance."

22

The Runner's Philosopher

George A. Sheehan Isn't Like Any Doctor You've Ever Met

If a runner were to find himself on a desert island where he was allowed only one companion, who would it be? By all odds, the likeliest candidate would be a cardiologist from rural Red Bank, New Jersey, named George A. Sheehan. In the whole world of running, there is no one quite like Sheehan, and certainly no one whose knowledge of running and influence on it is as great. When he is not actually out running he writes and lectures on it, appears at meetings and symposiums concerned with it and goes on television to talk about it. In addition, he cheerfully conducts locker-room medical consultations with runners, maintains an enormous correspondence with lame and aching athletes the world over, and has devised the widely used set of runners' exercises described in Chapter 15. Some people say that he spreads himself too thin and is, on occasion anyway, embarrassingly self-revealing; yet the good he has done is undeniable.

Sheehan stands five foot ten inches tall, weighs a scrawny 136

pounds and is in his late fifties. He has a soft-spoken, halting manner, a lined, weary-looking face and the body of a thirty-year-old. A few years ago he set a mile record for competitors over fifty (4:47.6) and a two-mile record for fifty-four-year-olds (10:53), but what is most distinctive about him is his attitudes toward both medicine and running.

In a clannish profession, Sheehan is distinctly unclannish. He is outspoken in his criticism of doctors who say that running jars the spine, shakes vital organs loose and scrambles the brains. "These fellows ought to go out and run and find out for themselves what happens instead of presuming," he says. He is even outspokenly critical of well-meaning doctors who just don't know any better. ("The general physician is not interested in sportsmedicine. It's simple enough to treat sports injuries by telling people not to do it. Then if the patients don't get well, doctors send them to the orthopedic surgeon.") But what particularly endears Sheehan to runners is his contagious insistence that running is something more than just a sport—that it is an activity that offers glimpses of values that are profound and eternal.

In truth, Sheehan is not just running's doctor but its reigning philosopher. Not long ago, in a column he writes for *The Physician and Sportsmedicine* (it is called, and the self-depreciation is characteristic, "Running Wild"), he stated:

> Sport is where an entire life can be compressed into a few hours, where the emotions of a lifetime can be felt on an acre or two of ground, where a person can suffer and die and rise again on six miles of trails through a New York City park. Sport is a theater where sinner can turn saint and a common man become an uncommon hero, where the past and future can fuse with the present. Sport is singularly able to give us peak experiences where we feel completely one with the world and transcend all conflicts as we finally become our own potential.

Runners appreciate this sort of thinking because it bestows on a sweaty, exhausting sport a significance that does not readily attach to such pursuits. To read Sheehan rejuvenates one's faith that running really is as important as it seems. After all, if he can so consistently express such certainty, who are the rest of us to be doubters?

Sheehan would not enjoy such unassailable credentials as a philosopher of running if he were not the kind of doctor he is. Runners often express astonishment that he so willingly dispenses so much free medical information. A middle-aged marathoner told me what happened after he wrote a letter to Sheehan: "I had run the Boston and Yonkers marathons hurting a little. Then things got so bad that my hip locked. My knee hurt, too. I was in real trouble, so I wrote to Sheehan. As soon as he got the letter he called me up. He told me it sounded like some kind of imbalance and gave me the name of a podiatrist. I went to see him and he brought me right out of it." Another runner asked Sheehan why he was troubled by gas whenever he ran. "I was blowing up a storm," he said. "Sheehan told me to cut down on fresh fruit and raw vegetables. The problem was gone the next day."

Sheehan first ran competitively from 1936 to 1940, during high school and college, and raced the mile in 4:17 and the half-mile in 1:55, fine times for that period, and respectable by any standards. Then he abandoned the sport while he went to medical school, married, established a practice, became the father of twelve children and saw his weight rise to a puffy 160 pounds. One day in 1962, when he was forty-four, he broke his hand playing tennis and decided to see if he could still run. He could. He got the idea of trying to run a mile in five minutes, and in pursuit of this goal entered a hilly cross-country race in New York's Van Cortlandt Park. "I was hooked," he says. "That race was obviously where I wanted to be. You could really push yourself if you wanted to, yet there was nobody yelling at you to go faster. You were running through the woods and hurting at your own pace."

One day in 1968 the sports editor of Red Bank's local weekly, the *Register,* asked Sheehan to write an article about the Olympics then being held in Mexico City. Sheehan, who had written little for the public press, discovered that he not only had an aptitude for it but also enjoyed it. Before long he was writing a regular column for the *Register,* another for *The Physician and Sportsmedicine,* a third for a now-defunct magazine called *Fitness for Living* and a fourth for *World Tennis*—not to mention a regular column of medical advice for *Runner's World* (of which he is currently medical editor), occasional pieces for the *New York Times,* and books for publication by *Runner's World (Encyclopedia of Athletic Medicine* and his enormously successful *Dr. Sheehan on Running).*

Sheehan first met his future *Runner's World* boss, Joe Henderson, at the Mexico City Olympics, and they liked each other immediately. Henderson says, "At that time it was rare to find anyone who looked at running the way I did, who saw that you didn't have to be competitive but could do it just for fun. So when I began working at the magazine two years later one of the first people I got in touch with was George. For a long time he wrote for us without pay."

Today Henderson acknowledges that Sheehan has become one of the magazine's greatest assets. "One of the key points he's made," Henderson says, "is that each of us is an experiment of one, that what works fine for one person may not work at all for another. He's also written a lot about preventive medicine. As a result there's been some resistance among doctors. They say, 'What he's telling people isn't proven.' They also claim that diagnosing over the phone and through the mail is unethical."

There's no question that Henderson accurately reads the medical reaction to Sheehan—at least some of it. One doctor told me, "Sheehan is a pain. He's set himself up as someone who knows everything there is to know about running. He doesn't. No one could." Nonetheless, more than a few of the inquiries he receives come from puzzled doctors who turn to him for help with their patients' and their own problems after everything else has failed.

A good part of the appeal of Sheehan's writing comes from its style. It is simple, but its simplicity is deceptive. Unlike most sports writing, his prose is filled with references to such figures as Jung, Teilhard de Chardin, Tolstoy, Cervantes, Bertrand Russell and Sheehan's favorite, the Spanish philosopher Ortega y Gasset. Over the years, this style has become more natural, more supple and more suited to the tricky task of marrying sport to philosophy. "If you are doing something you would do for nothing," he once wrote in a column on the concept of play, "then you are on your way to salvation. And if you could drop it in a minute and forget the outcome, you are even further along. And if while you are doing it you are transported into another existence, there is no need for you to worry about the future."

Perhaps in response to the widespread acceptance he and his work have met with, Sheehan's writing has become more personal over the years. Not long ago he wrote: "I am a nervous, shy noncombatant who has no feeling for people. I do not hunger and thirst after justice. I find no happiness in carnival, no joy in community. I am one with the writers in *The New Yorker* whom Brendan Gill described. They touched each other only by accident, were secretive about everything, and never introduced anyone properly. . . . Ideas are more important to me than people. My world lies inside of me."

Runners find such characteristics appealing because virtually every one of them feels—and in fact prides himself on it—that he and his fellows are fundamentally different from other people. Sheehan feeds this attitude, and in so doing eases the sting of running's loneliness. On another occasion he wrote: "That he is not made for the workaday world, that his essential nature and the law of his being are different from the ordinary and usual is difficult for everyone, including the runner, to comprehend. But once it is understood, the runner can surrender to this self, this law."

Sheehan is a quietly witty man whose good spirits continually bubble up in his writing. "The intellect must surely harden as fast as the arteries," he once wrote. "Trust no thought arrived at sitting down." On another occasion, while musing on his inability to resist a free meal, he came up with a cure for overeating at home: "Put everything on a pay-as-you-go basis. When I get home at night I should be faced with a menu with everything à la carte and quite expensive. . . . Once I start computing cost per calorie and watching the right-hand side of the bill of fare, I'll quickly get back to my normal penurious self."

Runners sense that Sheehan is one of them because he knows that most of them run not for fitness but for fun. While most other exercise advocates urge us to run out of a sense of duty—it's good for us—Sheehan wants us to do it because we'll enjoy it. "I have come to run because it is the right and true and just thing to do," he wrote recently. "In the process I may be helping my arteries and heart and circulation, but that is not my concern." Sheehan would agree with the cynic who said, "Physical fitness is just a brief stage we go through on the way to learning how to run well."

I had not been involved with running long before I learned who George Sheehan was and in what high regard he was held. When I started racing, I occasionally caught glimpses of him in Central Park, in Van Cortlandt Park, at various races in New Jersey and

Connecticut, and two or three times in Boston; he was a fragile-looking ragamuffin of a man who wore some of the most unprepossessing running clothes I had ever seen. On such occasions we would nod and say hello, but we barely knew each other. Finally, when I started work on this book, I decided it was time to make a pilgrimage to Red Bank and spend some time with him.

I met Sheehan at Riverview Hospital, where he is director of the ECG department. Wearing an old pair of Tiger running shoes, he led me to the cafeteria to have a look at the Navesink River flowing past the hospital's windows. Far out the water was blue, and sailboats skidded back and forth on their moorings. "There's a ten-foot tide out there," Sheehan said. "They have regattas and everything. Isn't it beautiful?" It was.

In the medical library we sat down to talk, but from time to time the phone rang and Sheehan would speak with a runner. One called from somewhere in the Midwest. After listening—the injury had something to do with hamstrings—Sheehan finally said, "How about when you drive a car? Does it bother you then? What kind of shoes are you running in? You need a pretty wide heel. I would think the SL-72s might be the answer."

Afterwards Sheehan pushed his chair back and put his feet up on a table. "I get three or four of those calls a day," he said. "Unfortunately, the people who know anything about treating runners are few and far between. It's all right if you live on the West Coast, and we also have some pretty good guys in the East. But in the middle of the country you run into all kinds of problems. The really urgent problem is when somebody passes blood in the urine.* When this happens, they usually get on the wire pretty fast. One fellow called me because he was looking for a psychiatrist who ran. Most people get so they don't want to see anybody in any specialty unless he's a runner."

Sheehan said he had once hoped to educate doctors about running, but has all but given up. "These days," he went on, "I try to publish pieces where they'll be seen by athletes. I've found that our success in getting treatment for runners is proportional to how well we reach *them,* not to how well we reach doctors." When he first mentioned the Morton's toe problem, Sheehan said, runners hobbled in droves into the offices of orthopedic surgeons, confidently telling them what was wrong and asking for treatment. Undoubtedly there was more than a little midnight oil burned as doctors the country over studied up on Morton's toe.

Whatever other doctors think of the Sheehan system of medical

* A normal, if relatively infrequent, reaction to hard running, as mentioned in Chapter 16.

Dr. Sheehan's leg-limbering exercise

education, runners clearly like it and feel flattered by it. "Until the Morton's toe thing," Sheehan said, "I had honestly been trying to educate the doctors. But it didn't make any impact, not until the athlete himself started demanding the right kind of cure. That was the breakthrough. Now I'm not writing for the doctor at all, but the patient, in the hope that he'll educate his doctor. Most runners know more about physiology, more about biomechanics and more about the foot than doctors do. If you read Ken Cooper's *Aerobics* you'll know more about exercise physiology than the average physician does. I've kind of given up on the medical profession."

Before setting out for Red Bank I had made a bargain with my wife. Though I felt fine, for some time she had been prodding me to have a physical examination. I had told her that I'd not only ask Sheehan's advice, but would dutifully abide by whatever he recommended. Now I asked him what he thought a ten-mile-a-day runner with no troubling symptoms should do.

Sheehan replied, "Annual physicals are a waste of time. For runners, they're even dangerous. You're likely to run into a doctor who doesn't like your electrocardiogram, and before you know it you'll be in the Mayo Clinic having coronary-artery studies. You've got to listen to your body, and it's not going to be replaced by machines. Stress tests, for example, are virtually useless in athletes—and they're not always very useful for other people. We do a stress test at a temperature of seventy degrees and forty percent humidity. You haven't eaten in two hours and there are a lot of nice people around. When you go out to run, it usually isn't anything like that. Maybe the doctor has told you it's all right to run ten-minute miles, but your body says, 'No, that's too fast today.' You could have discovered this for yourself. Still, if you can find a doctor who won't be stampeded, I do think it's valuable to have tests we can compare later if anything goes wrong. Otherwise, all you're going to find out in an annual physical are things that you already know, or that are of no consequence to you."

I asked Sheehan what he thought accounted for the appeal of his writing. "I don't understand it," he answered. "These little old ladies in Maintenance and Dietary are always coming up to me here at the hospital and saying, 'I love your book.' Once one of them stopped me in the corridor and said, 'Now how do you handle heat, Doctor?"

As he describes it, Sheehan's writing technique sounds as laborious and painstaking as cutting diamonds. "It takes me ten or twelve hours to write six or eight hundred words," he said, "and that doesn't include the time it takes to experience it. Often I'll write something and then won't be sure I have it right, so I'll go out to run and see if that's the way it really is. It's only once in a while that writing a piece is like pulling the handle on a slot machine. Then my words go zing, zing, zing, and the whole column will be there, even the first line. Then all you need to do is get offstage." Sometimes Sheehan manages this with enviable deftness:

> Where have all the heroes gone? They've gone with the simplicities and the pieties and the easy answers of another era. Our lack of heroes is an indication of the maturity of our age. A realization that every man has come into his own and has the capability of making a success out of his life. But also that this success rests with having the courage and endurance and, above all, the will to become the person

> you are, however peculiar that may be. Then you will be able to say, "I have found my hero and he is me."

Although Sheehan knows that his writing has a special appeal for runners, he doesn't dwell on his accomplishments. "It's funny about my writing," he said. "I never expect to write another decent column. I'm reaching over my head every time. I said to Joe Henderson once that I felt like a .230 hitter waiting for someone to come along and do it really well. It's just that no one else has come along yet."

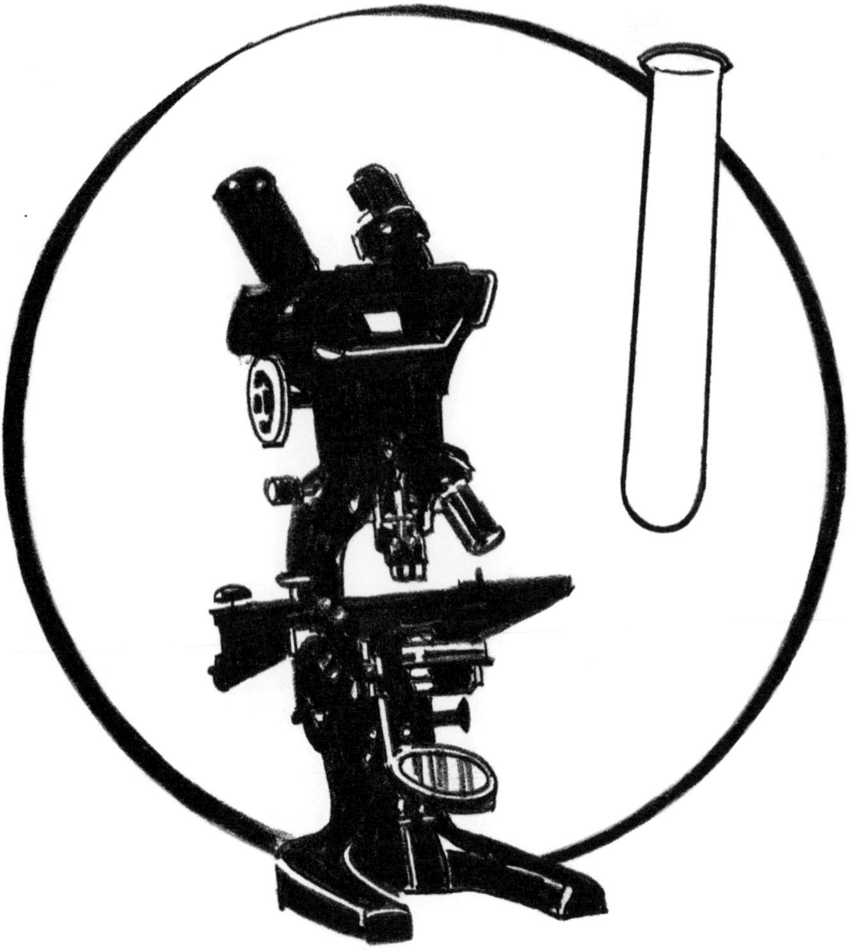

23

The Scientists of Sport

Laboratories That Search Out the Secrets of Running

At a laboratory in Dallas, a research scientist swabs Frank Shorter's slim, gristly calf with an antiseptic. As Shorter makes a sour face the researcher injects an anesthetic into the calf and, once it has taken effect, makes a deft quarter-inch incision with a scalpel. An assistant hands him a stainless-steel instrument, a hollow, needlelike apparatus six inches long and half as big around as a pencil. The scientist inserts its rounded end into the incision and presses until it is embedded in the fibers of Shorter's gastrocnemius muscle. Into the needle's hollow center he now slides a small cylinder with a sharpened end that is not unlike a miniature round cookie cutter. Within Shorter's calf the cylinder lops off a piece of tissue the size of an orange seed. Now both needles are withdrawn, the incision in Shorter's calf is closed with a Band-Aid, and the tiny sample of tissue from deep within his leg is frozen in liquid nitrogen.

The scientists of sport are at it again. Not too many years ago runners were largely on their own in figuring out how to train. Even if one of them was lucky enough to have a knowledgeable coach, so little was known about the ultimate sources of speed and endurance that any training method that worked was bound to be mostly the result of luck. All that—or much of it, anyway—has changed. In the past few years so much has been learned about the physiology of running, about nutrition, and even about that most elusive of all factors, motivation, that any athlete who wants to take the trouble can quickly soak up a whole lifetime of vicarious experience simply by reading. And not just top athletes—you and I can do it, too. Take, as an example, just one nutritional point. Until recently, many athletes, and even many coaches, assumed that if you wanted energy you had to eat protein. Eventually, however, researchers discovered to their astonishment that carbohydrate rather than protein is the main source of energy during hard exercise. If at some football training tables the pregame meal is still steak, it is only because common sense is too often no match for tradition.

The carbohydrate secret, along with many others, emerged from a phenomenon that began in the early years of this century: the exercise physiology laboratory. The first such laboratories were established in England and Germany. By the 1920's the idea had caught on in this country, and the Harvard Fatigue Laboratory—which owned, among other equipment, one of the first treadmills built for human beings—was in full cry in Cambridge. But the big growth period didn't come until the 1960's, when physiological curiosity and the availability of the right kinds of grants spawned laboratories all over the country.

Because there are now so many of them, they do diverse kinds of research. At the University of Illinois at Chicago Circle, Dr. Lawrence B. Oscai is trying to find out how exercise affects the size and quantity of fat cells; his study may one day be seen as a significant milestone in the fight against overweight. At Penn State's Noll Laboratory, Elsworth Buskirk has been investigating the effectiveness of portable defibrillators—devices designed to start a heart beating again after it has slipped into ineffectual spasms. And at Ball State University researchers have been looking into such subjects as the rehabilitation of patients after knee surgery and the role of exercise in helping diabetics lead more normal lives. Yet sooner or later most of the laboratories return to the first love of practically all exercise physiologists: running. The reason is that in running the human body is under such heavy stress that changes occur quickly and in easily measurable amounts. In the course of a year the body of a person who bowls one night a week may be slightly altered, but who could devise a way to measure the alteration? On the other hand, the change in the body of a person who runs five miles a day leaves no doubt that something significant is happening.

The work of the exercise physiology laboratories has had some impressive, if in some cases limited, practical effects. As I write this, New Zealand's John Walker is the world's fastest miler. He also receives more medical attention than perhaps any other runner in history. His physician, Dr. Lloyd Drake, keeps close watch on his pulse rate, his blood count, his aerobic capacity. If his hemoglobin level falls—and with it his blood's oxygen-carrying ability—Drake gives it a boost with an injection of vitamin B_{12}, intended to stimulate the bone marrow to produce more hemoglobin. If Walker suffers a slight injury, Drake takes care of it before it can turn into a serious one. He even specifies how fast Walker should run when he's training. (It's often at a five-minute-per-mile pace.) But the work of the physiologists is nowhere held in higher repute than in East Germany, where every world-class athlete is backed up by a whole team of specialists—in the words of one doctor, "just like mission control when an astronaut is sent up into space." Given the athletic success of the East Germans in recent years, it will be surprising if our own exercise physiology laboratories do not soon start to play an increasingly important role.

Not everyone thinks this would be a good idea. At a symposium on exercise and heart disease, Roger Bannister said he thought scientific research hadn't helped athletes much because each athlete is different from all others. "He has to try running fast and slow," said Bannister, "learn from his own mistakes and then figure out his own magic training formula." Furthermore, he said, physical factors are only part of what makes a successful runner: "I think the final quality that makes a runner better is his own drive and mental toughness. That's as important as any physical quality." Some critics also fear that we will end up creating a breed of mindless *1984*-style superstars, athletically perfected bodies manipulated by Machiavellian squads of researchers and technicians.

This seems unlikely. For one thing, as Bannister points out, mental qualities are important in running. For another, so many variables contribute to athletic success that it would be all but impossible to have each of them precisely tuned at any given moment. But who knows? After all, there *is* the example of East Germany, whose ability to win Olympic medals has climbed markedly since doctors got into the act.

To find out exactly what an exercise physiology laboratory does, I paid a call on one of the best-known and most highly regarded of them: the Human Performance Laboratory at Ball State University in Muncie, Indiana, presided over by an articulate, quick-thinking physiologist named David L. Costill.

The Human Performance Laboratory is an inconspicuous metal structure of no discernible architectural style, and is among the smallest and least impressive buildings on the entire Ball State campus. Nonetheless, these are boom times for it. Established in the mix-Sixties with nothing but a bicycle, a step bench and a

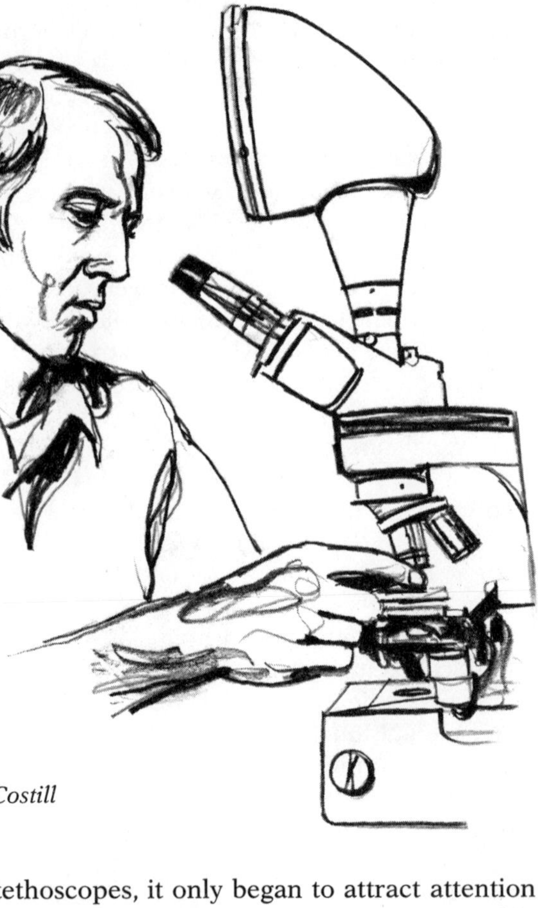

David Costill

drawerful of stethoscopes, it only began to attract attention after Costill's arrival in 1966. Costill is a lean, graying man in his early forties who, practicing what he preaches, runs five miles a day. Although he had been interested in athletics since childhood, exercise physiology didn't occur to him as a career until fairly late. "After I got out of college," he told me, "I was a high school swimming coach for a while. I quickly realized I didn't want to be a coach the rest of my life—there wasn't much satisfaction beyond my enjoyment of the kids. What I did like was doing studies on athletes. I'd spend hundreds of my free hours on those studies just because they were fun. Finally I went to Ohio State for a doctorate, but even then I didn't know what I wanted to do. Then I started hanging around the research lab. I'd go in and stay all day and just play. I suddenly realized that this was what I enjoyed most." With a Ph.D. in physiology, Costill started looking for work. Chance came to the rescue when someone mailed him an ad from Ball State, which was looking for a director for its lab. Costill answered it and was hired.

Along his laboratory's north wall are five or six ordinary-looking offices, including Costill's own, but the rest of the laboratory is crammed with up-to-the-minute scientific equipment: a computer; a centrifuge; devices for measuring oxygen, carbon dioxide and other gases as they go into and out of runners on treadmills; a ten-by-ten-foot heat chamber that is used to find out how people react to extreme temperatures; and in a central place of honor, the treadmill on which some of the nation's best runners have given their all for science.

Out of these rooms have come a number of significant discoveries, some of which have forever changed the sport of running. A few years ago, for example, while doing research with Bengt Saltin, a physician at the University of Copenhagen, Costill noticed that the muscles of world-class runners seemed somehow to be different from those of less accomplished athletes. Pursuing elusive clues, the researchers were led finally to the muscle fibers themselves. When they looked closely at these hairlike filaments, they noticed something interesting. After staining, two distinct types could be identified. Furthermore, the top runners all had a preponderance of the same type of fiber. What did this mean? Using complex analytical techniques, they began examining muscle fibers for such factors as enzyme activity and contractile characteristics. Out of this research eventually emerged a discovery of considerable significance: some muscle fibers, designated ST, contract slowly; others, designated FT, contract quickly. Virtually every top distance runner, they found, has more ST than FT fibers. When, for example, fourteen of them, including Frank Shorter and the late Steve Prefontaine, were examined, it was found that the average percentage of slow-twitch fibers was 79.* Since middle-distance runners (half-milers to two-milers) were found to have only 62 percent slow-twitch fibers, there was clearly a difference between the two groups. But was it the crucial difference, the one that makes one runner a good marathoner and another a good half-miler? Further research has indicated that it probably is.

* In a random sample of people, the average was only 57.

To some this might seem to suggest that top runners are born, not made. To Costill it implies nothing of the kind. What it does suggest is that someday athletes may be able to stay out of fruitless dead ends where the possibility for improvement is markedly limited, and to concentrate instead on what they're best at. Of course that won't guarantee that a given athlete will become a champion, but it will at least spare him or her a foreordained mediocrity. "We've shown that you're never going to be a long-distance champion unless you've got a lot of slow-twitch muscle fibers," Costill says.

Costill has also made some important discoveries about what happens to the body's fluids during intense exercise like marathon running. In the process he has probably saved more than a few lives. A few years ago he grew curious about whether the hoary old prohibition against drinking fluids during exercise made sense. Investigation, both by him and by other researchers, showed that it did not, and that in fact a failure to ingest fluids, especially in hot, humid weather, could contribute to heat stroke. Further experiments revealed that far from reducing efficiency, drinking during exercise increases it. One result was a landmark position statement issued in 1975 by the American College of Sports Medicine calling for an end to limitations on drinking fluids. It has already had a widespread effect.

Another practice Costill is currently changing involves mileage. Runners traditionally add up their mileage a week at a time. When I talked with Bill Rodgers, for example, he said, "I've put in a hundred and forty miles a week for the past three years." Weekly rather than daily mileage has become the accepted measure because that way a runner can more easily compensate for day-to-day fluctuations. Costill argues that even this isn't going far enough. He has the figures to back up his argument, derived from an experimental subject he knows better than any other: himself. The energy for running comes from a sugarlike substance called glycogen. Glycogen is stored in muscle tissue, and during exercise the supply is gradually used up. When it is gone, no matter how much will power you have, work must stop. Checking his own glycogen level in the days following three consecutive ten-mile runs, Costill found that it took as much as two weeks for the supply to return to normal. Plainly he could not possibly put in a full-scale training week and have enough muscle glycogen to get him through an important race. "My glycogen is very slow in coming back," he told me. "It's an individual thing. There's nothing I can do about it except eat lots of carbohydrates."

Costill's recommendation is that runners start keeping track of monthly rather than weekly mileage, thereby making it easier to permit themselves an occasional light week. He has included this recommendation, along with many others, in a remarkable unpublished book-length manuscript he calls *A Scientific Approach to Distance Running.* The manuscript, which he let me read, is probably the most comprehensive collection of training information ever assembled. On the week-vs.-month question he writes:

> The purpose of training is to tax and often tear down the biological systems essential for prolonged high rates of energy production in the runner. Such training is of no value unless the organism is per-

mitted sufficient rest to rebuild and supercompensate for the stresses of training. . . . Thus, rest is an equally important part of the training program, for without it the system will certainly fail. . . . In light of the fact that most physiological systems (i.e., muscle enzymes) require three to four weeks to respond to a given training stress, it seems the runner's training stress should be judged on the basis of total distance covered in a four-week period. This system offers the advantage of varying the weekly running effort, while permitting longer periods of light training to allow full recovery.

The scientific way to increase mileage

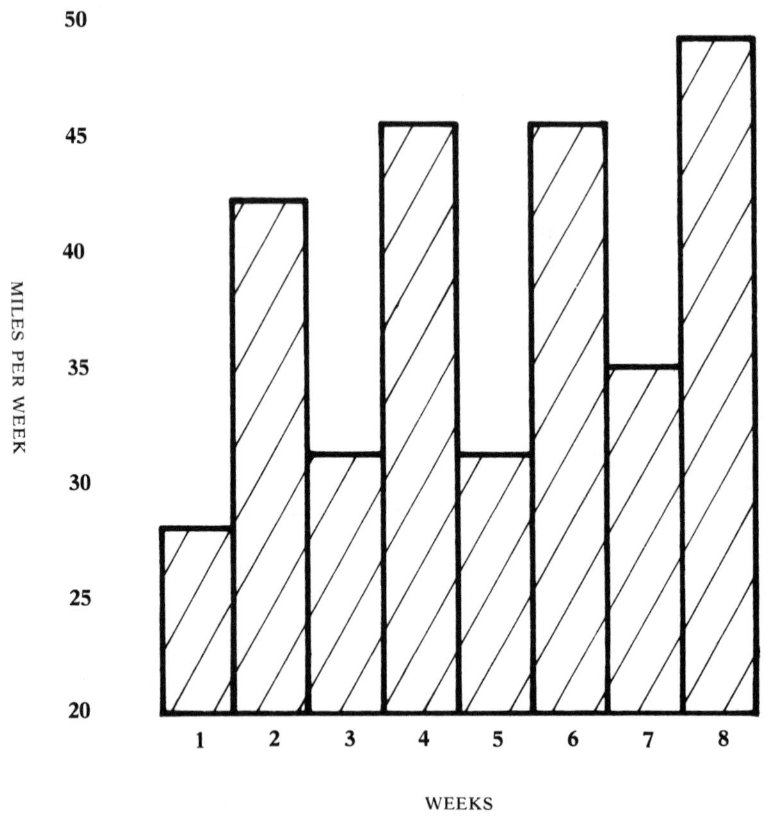

Adapted from A Scientific Approach to Distance Running.

Costill's discovery that he has a sluggish glycogen system has led him to still another conclusion: that no matter how scientifically valid a training principle is, it may have little application to some runners. "Each of us is different," he says. "If you want to find out what you're capable of, try different things, even things that seem extreme and totally unreasonable."

Among Costill's other findings:

1. Even distance runners need speed work. Some coaches deny this, but Costill's research shows that only during fast running are all the muscle fibers used in competition brought into play. Running fast also enhances biomechanical efficiency.

2. Heavy training depletes the glycogen supply for about three days. Thus more than just a single day of light training should precede a race. Costill recommends three light days. He has found, incidentally, that it is not necessary to avoid running on the day before a race, so long as the workout is not more than four to six miles and is done at a slow pace.

The week I visited Costill was a busy one. As we talked, just outside his window a backhoe growled and bit into the earth to start digging the foundation for an addition to the laboratory. A salesman for a scientific instrument manufacturer arrived to give a demonstration. In the laboratory itself technicians peered through microscopes and with needlelike instruments sorted individual muscle fibers for chemical analysis later on. Before I left I asked Costill one more question: What did he see as the next frontier in human physiology?

"Things are happening fast in this kind of work," he replied. "Only a few years ago we were using rats. The problem was you can't make a rat run hard, no matter how much you shock him. He'll just sit on his butt. Then we learned how to do muscle studies on living people, and that was a breakthrough. Now biochemistry is the frontier. We have to find out what happens in the muscle. I'm convinced that's where the action is. The stuff we've been doing up until now is like opening a door and kind of peeking in. We know there's a lot in there. Now we've got to get busy and find out what it is."

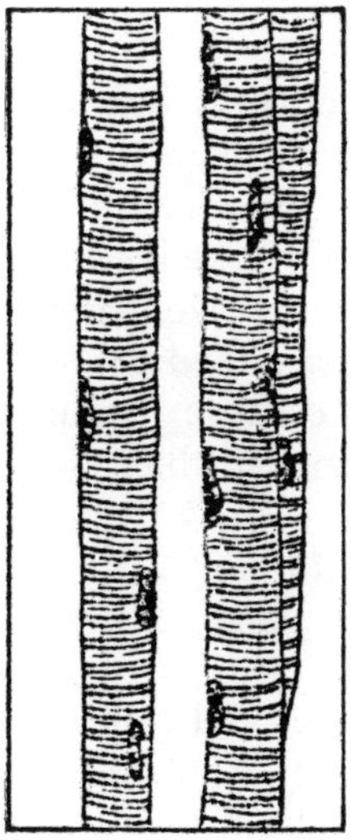

Muscle tissue

24

And Something More

Just in Case 26.2 Miles Isn't Enough

What does it feel like to run not just twenty-six but fifty miles? Bob Glover had just finished doing so when I interviewed him. What he had done was to run two hundred times around a quarter-mile track, for the simple reason that he is one of those runners for whom ordinary races are not enough. Now he sat in his office ruminating about the experience. As we talked he used a penknife to cut slits into the toes of a pair of blue running shoes—an attempt to relieve pressure on his toenails, which hurt because of bloodblisters.

Glover is tall, hollow-cheeked and fit. The day after his fifty-mile race he ran five miles. Now, two days later, he planned to run twenty. He did not look tired.

"If you have a good base of cardiovascular fitness and your legs are strong from a lot of running," he said, "the main problems in a fifty-mile race are only in your head. Between about thirty and thirty-eight miles was where the struggle was for me. After forty miles, it almost seemed as if I was surging on a new source of energy. First of all, there's an emotional high. I'd decided before the race that if I got to forty I was going to finish one way or another."

Glover's plans were changed a little by the August weather. "The temperature out there was ninety-some degrees," he said, "so my goal became not so much to race as simply to survive. How can I explain what I felt like between thirty and thirty-eight miles? My bad knee was hurting. I'm not supposed to run at all. I was feeling tired, as if I just wanted to lie down and go to sleep. And my back ached. But the race was starting to affect me more psychologically than physically. I had to start playing games in my head to keep going."

As he ran, Glover munched M&M's, drank tomato juice and water, and tried eating baby food—carrots, custard and a mixture of beef and vegetables. "I thought it would be good because it digests easily," he said. "The trouble was, it had been out in the sun and was miserably hot. I had to force it down. I almost threw up."

Glover finished in fifth place, in 7:45:30. It was 7:45 at night. "The first thing I did," he said, "was have a beer. It tasted good. Then I went home, sat in the bathtub for half an hour, and finally took a shower. I stretched for about fifteen or twenty minutes, then ate. Then I took another bath and stretched again. Then I put my feet up and watched television for a while. When I started to doze off, I went to bed."

What is it that prompts a person like Glover—a sane, industrious, productive citizen of the workaday world—to undertake such an ordeal? Not fitness. He is already superbly fit. Perhaps all that can be said is that Glover ran the fifty miles because they were there. He had already entered a number of marathons and one fifty-kilometer race—a trifle more than thirty-one miles—so this somehow was the logical next step. Or perhaps it was an antidote to boredom with ordinary races.

Whatever the reason, such a race demonstrates that in running there is always something else to do. If you are content with your customary pace or races, you can spend a lifetime running in a park or entering races of five or ten miles, perhaps occasionally trying a marathon to test yourself. But if you want more, the possibilities are there.

There's no reason, in fact, to stop at fifty miles. Ted Corbitt likes hundred-mile races. "To race a hundred miles was a natural extension of having run for as many years as I have," he said. "It's exactly the same impetus that causes you to run a marathon. Many marathoners finish a race and have too much left, so they speculate about how much farther they could have run."

Corbitt knows as much about long races—ultramarathons, runners call them—as anyone alive, and he discussed their subtleties like a horticulturalist describing prize roses. "When you go up to a hundred miles," he said, "you're in a different category. There are fatigue zones. At eighteen miles or so you hit the first one. You've got to run through it and come out on the other side. If you go farther, there are other zones waiting for you. You never know about these until you run a race of fifty or a hundred miles. For instance, it's very hard to get past eighty-five miles. You have to be determined; otherwise you just won't make it. It seems it takes forever to push through it and get to ninety miles. It's different from the marathon fatigue zone because your energy level has changed several times."

I ask Corbitt whether he had ever lost his will to continue. "Oh, yes," he replied. "You think, *Why didn't I stay home? What am I doing here?*"

Nonetheless, for people like Corbitt and Glover there remains something magnetically appealing about exploring the limits of endurance. Nor are they the only people who relish the idea of looking into the more remote—and in some cases more bizarre—byways of the running experience.

Tony Rafferty of Belfast, Ireland, for example, once ran for fifty hours, just to prove it could be done.

A runner named Park Barner ran a fifty-mile race in Central Park one day in 1976, then traveled to Pennsylvania and the next day ran a full twenty-six-mile marathon.

To call attention to the problems of black Americans, Dick Gregory, the comedian, ran from Los Angeles to New York in two and a half months on a diet of fruit juice, sunflower seeds and assorted health foods.

Richard Innamorato, a twenty-seven-year-old auditor, set out in October 1976 on a 2,400-mile run from Fort Kent, Maine, to Key West, Florida. (Anyone who would attempt such a stunt, he declared with unassailable logic, "has to enjoy it or is an eccentric moron.")

Dick Traum, a personnel consultant, runs races—including marathons—despite the loss of his right leg in an automobile accident. (He wears an artificial one.)

Joe Pardo of Flushing, New York, is regularly seen at races in New York and Connecticut. He is blind. So is Harry Cordellos of San Francisco, a 2:59 marathoner.

In Death Valley—a surprisingly popular place for running—two runners named Pax Beale and Ken Crutchlow, accompanied by a doctor who was curious about what would happen to them, ran 145 miles in two days, finishing on Mt. Whitney, 14,495 feet above sea level. In Death Valley the temperature hit 135 degrees. Beale lost fifty-five pounds in the two days but replaced all but eleven pounds of it by drinking a special fluid.

Every year in London, some one hundred runners gather in the shadow of Big Ben for the start of the 52½-mile London-to-Brighton race. Rod MacNicholl, one of the recent contestants, described his experience to his fellow members of the New York Road Runners Club: "At the end of the race I was bleeding from my nipples, feet, crotch, and a few other places. My legs were extremely painful, especially my thighs. Other than that, I felt terrific." At least two women have also run the London-to-Brighton course.

A New Zealander named Don Cameron ran nearly sixty miles a day to cover the length of his country, from Stirling Point on the southern coast to Cape Reinga lighthouse on the northernmost tip.

It took him twenty-three days, and he celebrated by having a beer with the lighthouse keeper.

A group called the Liberty Torch, which combines religion and running, recently ran 8,800 miles in all fifty states to demonstrate "faith in America."

Each year an uphill race is held in New Hampshire. It starts at the base of Mount Washington, snakes its way up an eight-mile-long road, and ends at the 6,288-foot summit. A friend of mine named Al Meehan has run in it several times, placing well up in the pack each time. Says Meehan: "You hurt all the way. A marathon is nothing compared to that race. People think that because they've done a little mountain climbing they can handle it. They're in for some surprises."

The rewards of the Mount Washington race

My own idea of fun is none of the above. I'm happiest taking a pleasant ten-mile run on a cool autumn day when the leaves are bright and the air is crisp; only occasionally do I go in search of agony. But who is to say that I'm right and the people I've just described are wrong? Endless possibilities await you.

Afterword: The Miracle of Running

Throughout these pages the question of why running is such an extraordinarily satisfying avocation has been explored time and again. Once you have been running for a few months, you invariably notice some remarkable psychological dividends—a feeling of calmness and power, of being in control of your life. Runners also speak of having an "addiction" (an entire book has been written on this subject), and in a sense they unquestionably do. It is rare to meet a runner, no matter how busy, who considers giving up his sport. More often, the contrary is true; someone who runs three or four miles a day—plenty for fitness alone—will in time inexplicably double or even triple his mileage.

Hence the search for health hardly explains the phenomenon. Mere good health can easily be earned without major dislocation of one's life; twenty or thirty minutes a day four days a week would do it. So why do people run eight, ten or more miles every day, in summer's swelter and winter's blasts, particularly when they know that they will never become especially distinguished at it?

Many theories have been suggested. Roger Bannister has compared running with music. Both stimulate our nervous systems in ways the human organism finds pleasurable. An hour's run massages the nerves with infinitesimal electrical impulses in much the same way that Handel's *Messiah* does.

Closely related to this theory is one recently offered by Thaddeus Kostrubala, the psychiatrist. Addressing a conference of doctors and researchers, Kostrubala wondered aloud whether a runner might, after forty minutes or so of running, somehow "obliterate" the influence of the right cortex (the logical part of the brain), allowing the left cortex (the intuitive, artistic part) to gain temporary dominance.

In his perceptive book *Gods and Games,* David L. Miller offers a third explanation. As young children, he writes, we play games in innocent purity, for the pleasure they afford rather than with any thought of winning. In infancy we make no such artificial distinctions. A child tosses a toy, laughingly searches for it, exults in finding it—and then joyously does it all over again. Our adult games, Miller holds, are an attempt to recapture the innocent play of youth. What we want is not to play games at all but to play *play.* Because competitiveness in running is so infinitely variable and so controllable, we are able to do exactly that in our sport.

Perhaps there is something to all these theories. Still, I have a different one. Most people who have considered the matter have, I believe, posed the wrong question. They have asked why running produces such extraordinary effects. Putting the question that way elicits a certain kind of answer, and I think it is the wrong one. My suspicion is that the effects of running are not extraordinary at all, but quite ordinary. It is the *other* states, all *other* feelings, that are peculiar, for they are an abnegation of the way you and I are intended to feel. As runners, I think we reach directly back along the endless chain of history. We experience what we would have felt had we lived ten thousand years ago, eating fruits, nuts and vegetables, and keeping our hearts and lungs and muscles fit by constant movement. We are reasserting, as modern man seldom does, our kinship with ancient man, and even with the wild beasts that preceded him. This, I think, is our remarkable secret, one we share every time we go running.

APPENDIX A
The Runner's Address Book
A Guide to Finding What You Need

SHOES

In case you can't find the kind you want, write the manufacturer for information:

ADIDAS. Libco, 1 Silver Court, Springfield, N.J. 07081; Clossco, Inc., 2200 Martin Avenue, Box 299, Santa Clara, Calif. 95050; Vanco, 5133 West Grand River Avenue, Box 870, Lansing, Mich. 48901; Hughesco, Inc., 2830 Merrell Road, Dallas, Tex. 75229. In Canada: Adidas (Canada) Ltd., 550 Oakdale Road, Downsview, Ontario M3N 1W6.

BROOKS. Brooks Shoe Manufacturing Co., Factory Street, Hanover, Pa. 17331.

CONVERSE. Converse Rubber Co., 55 Fordham Road, Wilmington, Mass. 01887.

EATON. Charles A. Eaton Co., 147 Centre Street, Brockton, Mass. 02403.

E.B. SPORT INTERNATIONAL. (For Lydiard shoes.) Sport International, 6117 Reseda Boulevard, Reseda, Calif. 91335.

ECONO-JET. Econo-Jet Sport Shoe Co., 1501 College Avenue, S.E., Grand Rapids, Mich. 49502.

KARHU. Carlsen Imports, 524 Broadway, New York, N.Y. 10012.

MITRE. Mitre Sports, Inc. 3042 Miller Road, Lithonia, Ga. 30058

NEW BALANCE. New Balance Athletic Shoes U.S.A., 38–42 Everett Street, Boston, Mass. 02135.

NIKE. 8285 Southwest Nimbus Avenue, Suite 115, Beaverton, Ore. 97005.

OSAGA. Osaga, 2620 West 10th Place, Eugene, Ore. 97402.

PATRICK. Action and Leisure, Inc., 45 East 30th Street, New York, N.Y. 10016.

PONY. Pony Sports & Leisure, Inc., 251 Park Avenue South, New York, N.Y. 10010.

PUMA. Beconta, Inc., 50 Executive Boulevard, Elmsford, N.Y. 10523; Beconta, Inc., 340 Oyster Point Boulevard, South San Francisco, Calif. 94080; Beconta, Inc., 6759 East 50th Avenue, Commerce City, Calif. 90022.

REEBOK. Bradford Distributors Corp., Box 356, Huntingdon Valley, Pa. 19006.

SAUCONY. Saucony Shoe Manufacturing Company, Inc., 12 Peach Street, Kutztown, Pa. 19530. Praise be! Shoes especially for women runners!

SPOT-BILT. 432 Columbia Street, Cambridge, Mass. 02141.

TIGER. Pete Buckley & Co., 650 Great Southwest Parkway, Atlanta, Ga. 30336; Curley-Bates Co., 860 Stanton Road, Burlingame, Calif. 94010; George A. Davis, Inc., 7205 Hibbs Lane, Levittown, Pa. 19057; General Sports Corp., c/o Demco, 5121 North Ravenswood Avenue, Chicago, Ill. 60640; Olympic Sports, 2607 National Circle, Garland, Tex. 75041. In Canada: Vikski Canada Ltd., 2058 Trans Canada Highway, Dorval, Quebec H9P 2N4.

SHOE REPAIR BY MAIL

FLEET FEET CO., 612 Emery, Longmont, Colo. 80501. $8.00 per pair includes resoling, repair of small tears, new laces and return postage.

FRESH TRACKS, 27 West Rayburn Road, Millington, N.J. 07946. $11.95 per pair includes new soles, repair of tears, replacement of missing eyelets, new insoles and arches if needed, and return postage. (Add $1.25 if you live outside the continental U.S.)

POWER-SOLER, 1065 West Broad Street, Falls Church, Va. 22046, and Power-Soler West, 4330 West Desert Inn Road, Las Vegas, Nev. 89102. $11.50 per pair for resoling. Recommended by the National Jogging Association.

TRED 2, 2510 Channing Avenue, San Jose, Calif. 95131. $11.95 (plus $1.50 for postage and handling) includes new soles, repair of outside tears, reinforcement of weak or worn stitching, and new laces.

MAIL-ORDER RUNNING GEAR

THE ATHLETIC DEPARTMENT, Box 743, Beaverton, Ore. 97005.

MOVING COMFORT, 1111 Army-Navy Drive, Arlington, Va. 22202. Specialists in running gear for women.

STARTING LINE SPORTS, Box 8, Mountain View, Calif. 94042. A *Runner's World* subsidiary. For Master Charge or Visa orders, phone 415-965-3240. A large illustrated catalogue is available on request.

ORGANIZATIONS THAT ENCOURAGE RUNNING

AMERICAN MEDICAL JOGGERS ASSOCIATION, Box 4704, North Hollywood, Calif. 91607. Although the AMJA's membership consists mostly of physicians, it also includes some lay members, chiefly heart patients. By special dispensation, AMJA members are permitted to run in the Boston Marathon without meeting its normal qualifying standards.

NATIONAL JOGGING ASSOCIATION, 1910 K Street N.W., Washington, D.C. 20006. $15.00 a year includes a subscription to the NJA's cheerful and informative newspaper, a discount on books and participation in a motivation-bolstering awards program. For $11.50 extra the NJA will throw in a pair of $26.00 Brooks running shoes.

NATIONAL TRACK AND FIELD HALL OF FAME, 1524 Kanawha Boulevard, Charleston, W. Va. 25311. Headed by Olympic gold medalist Jesse Owens, the Hall of Fame honors past and present heroes and publishes the bimonthly *Hall of Fame News.* Subscription: $5.00 a year.

PRESIDENT'S COUNCIL ON PHYSICAL FITNESS AND SPORTS, Washington, D.C. 20201. For a free log book and procedures for qualifying for a presidential physical fitness award (for boys and girls ages ten to seventeen) or a presidential sports award (for athletes fifteen and over), write Box 129, Radio City Station, New York, N.Y. 10019.

ROAD RUNNERS CLUB OF AMERICA. Jeff Darman, 2737 Devonshire Place N.W., Washington, D.C. 20008. The RRC, the country's leading running organization, has some 125 chapters. To find out about one in your area, send Darman an inquiry, with a self-addressed stamped envelope.

SENIOR SPORTS INTERNATIONAL, 5225 Wilshire Boulevard, Suite 302, Los Angeles, Calif. 90036. Sponsors the annual Senior Olympics for athletes twenty-five and over.

RUNNING PERIODICALS

Cardio-Gram, La Crosse Cardiac Rehabilitation Program, Mitchell Hall, University of Wisconsin, La Crosse, Wis. 54601. Bimonthly; $5.00 a year. The most informative and wide-ranging publication of its kind; of interest chiefly to those who have had heart attacks.

The Harrier, Box 188, Eltingville Station, Staten Island, N.Y. 10312. Weekly, September–December; $8.00 a year, $15.00 for two years. National cross-country coverage.

The Jogger. Newsletter of the National Jogging Association, 1910 K Street N.W., Washington, D.C. 20006. Bimonthly; NJA membership fee (see above) includes subscription.

The Physician and Sportsmedicine, 4530 West 77th Street, Minneapolis,

Minn. 55435. Monthly; $24.00 a year. Edited for doctors who treat athletes, including the casual, weekend variety. An indispensable, technically uncomplicated guide to the prevention and treatment of athletic injuries, among them those common to runners.

Road Runners Club New York Association Newsletter, 226 East 53rd Street, New York, N.Y. 10022. Quarterly; $4.00 a year, $2.00 for students. Not really a newsletter at all but a full-scale newspaper edited by former Olympic marathoner Ted Corbitt.

Runner's World, Box 366, Mountain View, Calif. 94042. Monthly; $9.50 a year, $18.00 for two years. The biggest and best of the running magazines.

Running, Box 350, Salem, Ore. 97308. Quarterly; $5.00 a year. Until recently *Running* concentrated on the scientific aspects of running. It has now broadened its scope, describing itself as "The Thinking Runner's Magazine."

Running Times, 12808 Occoquan Road, Woodbridge, Va. 22192. Monthly: $10.00 a year. Among the newest of the growing list of running magazines, edited especially for athletes in the eastern U.S.

Track & Field News, Box 296, Los Altos, Calif. 94022. Monthly; $11.00 a year.

Veteris. Published by England's Association of Veteran Athletes. For subscription rates write Clive Shippen, editor, 24 Fryston Avenue, Coulsdon, Surrey, England.

Yankee Runner, Box 237, Merrimac, Mass. 01860. Published eighteen times annually; $5.00 a year, $7.00 in Canada, $8.00 by first-class mail. Devoted to New England running.

MISCELLANEOUS

FUN RUNS. To organize a Fun Run in your area, write Bob Anderson, *Runner's World,* Box 366, Mountain View, Calif. 94042. To find out where Fun Runs are now being held, consult a current issue of the magazine.

BOOKS ON RUNNING. *The Sports Book Catalog,* available from *Runner's World,* lists more than 2,000 titles, a great many of them on running. $1.95 brings the catalogue and a coupon good for a $1.95 discount on your first purchase. Order from *Runner's World,* Box 366, Mountain View, Calif. 94042.

FREE FITNESS DIARY. Upon request to Pennsylvania Blue Shield, Camp Hill, Pa. 17011.

MORE INFORMATION ON FITNESS. American Alliance for Health, Physical Education and Recreation, 1201 16th Street N.W., Washington, D.C. 20037; National Jogging Association, 1910 K Street N.W., Washington, D.C. 20006; President's Council on Physical Fitness and Sports, Washington, D.C. 20201; Young Men's Christian Associations of the U.S.A., 291 Broadway, New York, N.Y. 10007, Young Women's Christian Associations of the U.S.A., 600 Lexington Avenue, New York, N.Y. 10022.

HEARTBEAT COUNTER. Time Computer, Inc., 901 Columbia Avenue, Lancaster, Pa. 17604, sells a solid-state Pulsar watch that gives a digital readout of your pulse rate at the touch of a fingertip. It's the first of its kind but has two drawbacks: You need to stop running to get an accurate reading; and you need to pay either $500 or $2,500, depending on whether you choose the stainless-steel or the fourteen-carat-gold model.

MAPS. Motion Sports Products, Box 821, Bozeman, Mont. 59715, sells a map of the Boston Marathon as well as one of the U.S. called the "Jog-Log U.S.A." The latter shows the interstate highway system divided into twenty-five-mile segments so you can calculate how far you've run. The price for each is $1.75 plus 75¢ postage; both together are $3.50 postpaid.

COURSE-MEASURING DEVICE. A good one, designed to be mounted on a bicycle, is available for $12.00 from Clain Jones, 3717 Wildwood Drive, Endwell, N.Y. 13760. It comes with its own instructions, but if you want to be really accurate order the set of instructions supplied by Ted Corbitt, chairman of the Amateur Athletic Union's Standards Committee. Send 80 cents to Corbitt at Apartment 8H, Section 4, 150 West 225th Street, New York, N.Y. 10463.

STOPWATCHES AND CHRONOGRAPHS. Wakmann Watch Company, 597 Fifth Avenue, New York, N.Y. 10017. Phone 212-751-2926. The best I've found anywhere, and at reasonable prices. Ask for the general manager, Hyman Kopf; if you identify yourself as a runner, he'll give you a 25 percent discount.

For subsequent editions, the author welcomes more suggestions for this listing. Please write him, with full details, c/o Random House, 201 East 50th Street, New York, N.Y. 10022.

APPENDIX B
The Physiology of Running

Running begins with the mind. As soon as you decide to run, your brain's cerebral cortex, its gray and wrinkled outer layer, emits a burst of electrochemical signals. Like telephone calls, each flickering signal has only one destination. Imagine that one of them is intended for a calf muscle. Setting forth from your brain, it travels down your spine and leg, leaping from nerve to nerve by instantaneously altering the balance of sodium and potassium in successive cells. As the signal arrives at junctions—the synapses—it vaults across, setting up a ripple of identical chemical shifts as it goes. In practically no time, for nerve impulses travel with almost unmeasurable swiftness, it reaches a so-called end plate, the place where nerve and muscle fiber finally meet. Additional chemical shifts occur as the muscle fiber contracts and relaxes.

A single fiber of muscle is so small you need to squint to see it. After it is freeze-dried, as it sometimes is in exercise physiology laboratories like David Costill's, a careless breath will blow it away like a dust mote. Yet within this infinitesimal scrap of tissue some of the body's most complex biochemical processes take place. Oversimplified, they involve the reaction of glucose with oxygen to form carbon dioxide, water and mechanical energy. When oxygen is in short supply, as it is to some degree in all running, part of the reaction is anaerobic (without oxygen). Incompletely oxidized compounds, such as lactic acid, therefore accumulate and an oxygen debt is incurred. In order to complete the breakdown of these compounds, your body must "pay back" the necessary oxygen. The function of the lungs, heart, blood vessels and blood is simply to get oxygen from the air to your 600-odd muscles so this can happen.

Muscles are not, of course, single fibers but vast bundles of fibers, packed together like parallel strands of spaghetti. The strands contract because of stringlike protein molecules called actin and myosin. Facing each other, actin and myosin behave as if they were two combs facing each other with their teeth meshed. The more closely meshed they are, the more tightly a muscle is contracted.

As no runner needs to be told, the effort of running produces enormous quantities of heat. Even at rest, Dr. Ethan R. Nadel of the Yale University School of Medicine recently reported to a gathering of scientists, metabolism's cellular furnaces generate enough heat to raise body temperature a full degree in only five minutes. When we run, the furnaces roar with infinitesimal metabolic fires, producing far more heat than the body needs. If we are not simply to burn up, we must somehow get rid of the heat. This is why we have a regulating mechanism.

The body's thermostat is far more intricate than most. Although it monitors both skin and internal temperature, it pays far more attention to the latter. As soon as it senses a rise, signals are sent to the hypothalamus, deep within the brain. On orders from the hypothalamus, the blood vessels in the skin enlarge in order to dissipate heat. Furthermore, sweat glands secrete their mixture of fluids and electrolytes if necessary, in order to induce evaporation and cooling.

If, on the other hand, the hypothalamus learns of a drop in temperature, it orders less blood sent to the skin and temporarily closes the sweat glands. If cooling continues, it increases heat production by causing the skeletal muscles to shiver. Even in winter, however, the problem in running is usually not excessive cooling but excessive heating.

The foregoing, in brief outline, is what happens when we take a single run. But what happens with repeated running? It is plain that while we train, profound and fundamental adaptations occur. How else can one account for the fact that when we first try running we are breathless within a block, while a year later we can be breathing easily and feeling fresh midway through the Boston Marathon? To see what happens, let's examine each physiological stage of the running process. Notice, as we do so, that what is called "training" is not just one effect but a multitude of interrelated effects.

THE MIND

Running, as we have seen, begins with the mind. Except in the case of involuntary muscles, the body will not do what the mind does not will it to do. As we train, therefore, one of the things we do is toughen our minds. When we run day after day, in good weather and bad, we learn self-discipline. Emil Zatopek once wrote, "Is it raining? It doesn't matter. Am I tired? That doesn't matter either. . . . I practiced regardless, until will power was no longer a problem." To an outsider, his behavior might sound indefensibly compulsive. Any serious runner knows, however, that sticking with a training plan is one of the best ways of insuring improvement—and, as mentioned earlier, of enjoying the psychological benefits of accomplishing exactly what you set out to do.

THE NERVES

Even the nerves, those hairlike tendrils that wind their way like vines into every cranny of our bodies, benefit from training. They become more efficient at transmitting electrochemical impulses and activate more muscle fibers, thus increasing strength. Furthermore, as reflexes replace voluntary actions, movement becomes more efficient. Wasteful muscular contractions become fewer, unneeded muscles relax more fully and movement is simplified. Dr. Lucien Brouha, an authority on the physiology of athletics, writes: "The final result is that for a given performance a decrease in energy expenditure occurs which can reach one-quarter of the total energy needed before training." A decrease of such magnitude is no small saving.

THE MUSCLES

With training, muscles become stronger. Until fairly recently, however, no one knew precisely why. Now, as a result of sophisticated analytical techniques, the mystery of strength has begun to be unraveled—and with it the related mystery of speed. It is known, for example, that changes occur within the cells of our muscles when we run repeatedly. The number of mitochondria, the microscopic factories in cells where energy is produced, increases, thereby providing more sites for production of an energy-rich compound called adenosine triphosphate (usually referred to simply as ATP). The quantities of mitochrondrial enzymes also increase and are synthesized faster. (One of them, succinic dehydrogenase, is as much as three and a half times more abundant in trained runners than in sedentary people.)

Nor are those the only changes that occur. Not long ago Dr. Kenneth M. Baldwin of the University of California at Irvine and Dr. Will W. Winder of the Washington University School of Medicine, experimenting on trained and untrained rats, found that glycogen, the storage form of glucose, remained higher both in the muscles and the liver after a twelve-week training program. (Presumably much the same thing occurs in human beings.) It is clear that even within the microscopic chambers and waterways of the cells themselves, important adaptations take place.

As cells change, so do muscle fibers. After training, contraction is both faster and stronger. Furthermore, because the fibers don't tire as quickly, work can continue longer. To make possible the greater efficiency of trained muscle, adjacent arteries sprout new branches and capillaries become more dense. The capillary density of one of the calf muscles, for example, almost doubles. In order to use the increased oxygen provided in this way, the muscle's supply of myoglobin—a hemoglobinlike substance that attracts oxygen—is also increased, in some cases even doubled. To the nonprofessional eye, these adaptations appear to be an essentially simple process: the muscle merely becomes harder, tougher and able to keep going longer. In fact the process is considerably more complicated than this.

THE BLOOD

Oxygen, the substance without which practically no human activity can occur, is carried to the muscles in the bright red rivers of the bloodstream. Embraced by hemoglobin, it is borne within only a few seconds from the heart to wherever it is needed. To increase the blood's efficiency as exercise begins, fluid leaves the bloodstream and seeps like a vast tide into the spaces between muscle cells. This movement serves two main purposes. First, the muscles work more easily when they are bathed in fluid; second, the blood's hemoglobin concentration rises, allowing a given volume of blood to carry more oxygen than usual.*

With repeated training, an important change takes place in the blood: the body, in effect learning to expect its blood volume to be periodically lowered, increases its supply. Thus when fluid leaves the bloodstream at the onset of exercise, a larger quantity remains to carry out essential tasks.

With exercise the composition of the blood is changed in still other ways. For example, its clotting ability is enhanced—a mechanism that no doubt evolved to protect active people from injury. Furthermore, since clots, once formed, must eventually be dissolved, an enzyme called fibrinolysin appears in greater quantities. (It is theorized that fibrinolysin may also dissolve long-standing clots—including small ones in the coronary arteries that if allowed to enlarge could cause a heart attack.) At the same time, certain lipids—such as the types of cholesterol and triglycerides associated with heart disease—become less concentrated. A recent study by Dr. Peter D. Wood and his associates at the Stanford University School of Medicine showed that when middle-aged men and women ran fifteen miles a week the concentrations of these lipids were markedly lessened. "These very active middle-aged people form a group with remarkably low risk of cardiovascular disease," wrote Wood.

* The beneficial effect of an increase in hemoglobin is what lies behind the controversial practice known as blood doping. Since an inability to transport enough oxygen appears to be the chief limiting factor in distance running, some researchers reason that an increase in red cells—and consequently in hemoglobin—should produce a corresponding increase in performance. In blood doping, therefore, either whole blood or red cells are introduced into the bloodstream before competition. However, blood doping's value has not yet been conclusively demonstrated. Even if it were, some critics would continue to shun it as Orwellian.

THE HEART

Few effects of training have been more thoroughly documented than those that occur within the heart. Research has repeatedly shown that with such endurance training as running the heart becomes a distinctly more efficient instrument, capable of doing more while working less hard. One of the most fundamental changes is that the heart muscle's fibers lengthen, much as leg muscles lengthen when we do stretching exercises. Longer fibers allow the heart's chambers, especially the powerful left ventricle that squeezes blood into the aorta, to enlarge and pump more blood with each contraction.* Simultaneously, the arteries serving the heart itself enlarge—in some cases to as much as three times normal size—and increase in number. In Chapter 4 the remarkable Clarence DeMar, a marathoner who competed well into his sixth decade, was introduced. When Dr. Paul Dudley White studied DeMar's autopsy findings he found that although DeMar had enlarged coronary arteries they were not a symptom of ill health but simply a natural response to his half-century of training. Predictably, oversize arteries can carry more blood and thus can provide the heart with an exceptionally rich oxygen supply. Researchers at the University of Minnesota found not long ago that in endurance athletes the blood flow to the heart may increase to five times resting levels, and other researchers suspect that the levels may be even higher than that.

As noted earlier, these changes enable the heart to pump more blood with each beat—in many cases twice as much as an untrained person's heart is capable of. Someone who before training is able to pump less than half a cup with each beat may pump almost a whole cup after training. The increase takes place because during diastole—the phase in which blood enters the atria—the heart fills more completely. Consequently, during systole—the pumping phase—more blood is available to be squeezed out. Since both athletes and sedentary people need essentially the same blood supply at rest, the trained heart beats less often most of the time. Decreases of ten or twenty beats a minute in resting heart rate are common, and it is not unusual for a well-trained athlete to have a pulse rate in the forties or even the thirties. (My own is in the mid-forties.) This slowed heartbeat—bradycardia is the technical term for it—often alarms doctors who don't customarily treat athletes.

The degree of bradycardia a runner develops depends not only on his amount of exercise but also on genetic factors. Not long ago Dr. John Davis Cantwell, of the Emory University School of Medicine, examined a thirty-nine-year-old marathoner who had a pulse rate that sometimes fell

* This is an appropriate place to lay to rest the old wive's tale about athlete's heart. Admittedly the hearts of athletes do grow larger, and among distance runners, left ventricular hypertrophy—the scientific name for an enlarged left ventricle—is common. Research has convincingly shown, however, that this enlargement is not only harmless, but is in fact a desirable adaptation of exercise. Not long ago, for example, Drs. William V. Raskoff, Steven Goldman and Keith Cohn reported on a study of thirty marathoners. Twenty-four were found to have enlarged left ventricles, but none, the three physicians said, had any detectable problems even during hard treadmill workouts. Left ventricular hypertrophy, they concluded, "may enhance overall vascular function."

as low as twenty-eight. On the other hand, at the peak of his running career the record-setting miler Jim Ryun had a pulse rate in the seventies. The implication is clear: as you run repeatedly, your heart will almost certainly slow down. But if it doesn't slow as much as a fellow runner's—or if, for that matter, it slows *more*—it's nothing to worry about.*

If running can cause a normal heart to mimic a diseased one, it can also correct some abnormalities. Dr. Elsworth Buskirk and some of his associates reported recently in the *American Journal of Cardiology* that when 196 middle-aged men, all of them judged likely candidates for heart disease, were given treadmill tests, fully half were found to have what cardiologists call premature ventricular complexes, a symptom linked with increased risk of sudden death. After an eighteen-month conditioning program, the PVC's declined markedly. Dr. W. Channing Nicholas, who worked with Buskirk on the study, summed it up in layman's language: "As people get in shape, the frequency of abnormal heartbeats appears to decrease."

Training has still another effect on the heart: it produces lower blood pressure during the resting phase. Since high blood pressure is known to contribute to heart attacks, a lowering of the blood pressure is a welcome side effect of running. When Dr. Fred Kasch studied sixteen men during a ten-year period of regular exercise, he found, as mentioned in Chapter 4, that blood pressure stayed below average for age and sex. Lowered blood pressure, he reported, "may act as a protective or physiological advantage, particularly in view of the propensity for hypertension in the middle-aged population."

Some medical authorities are less tentative in their judgments. As already discussed, Dr. Bassler, the California pathologist, insists that marathon training confers virtual immunity to heart attack. When marathoners do die, he says, it is from exactly the same causes that kill teenagers—infections, accidents and so forth.

A trained heart is more efficient not just at rest and during exercise but also after exercise, when it returns more quickly to normal (see the graph on page 286). Furthermore, since a trained heart beats more slowly than an untrained one, there is a longer resting period between each contraction—often a full second or more. At those times when an untrained person's heart would be working hard, the runner's is idling.

THE LUNGS

Of all the physical equipment a runner uses, the lungs, with their 300,000,000 moist, foamlike bubbles of tissue known as alveoli, are among the most efficient and trouble-free. Analysis of the various substances the running body relies upon—everything from oxygen to hemoglobin to

* Nor, usually, are a number of other irregularities. Medical literature is filled with reports of top athletes who, on the basis of electrocardiographic studies, should be flat on their backs in hospitals. Confronted with Wilt Chamberlain's ECG, with its alarming deviations from normal, most cardiologists would confidently diagnose acute myocardial infarction—damage to the heart muscle following a failure of its blood supply.

How the heart returns to normal after running

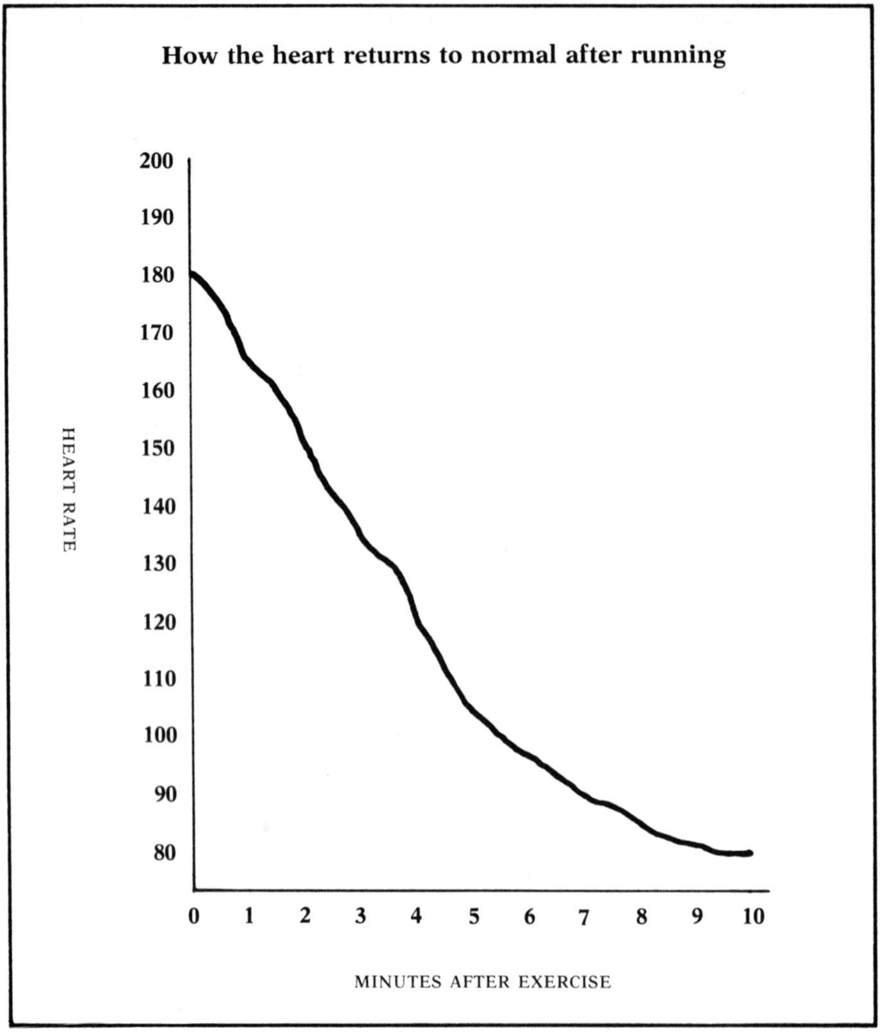

ATP—shows that the lungs usually offer plenty of oxygen to the blood passing through them. Furthermore, they are impressively adaptable organs, changing quickly in response both to a single period of exercise and to long-term training. As exercise begins, the lungs' blood vessels dilate, expanding the area through which oxygen passes into the bloodstream.* If it is continued day after day, the breathing muscles—those in the abdomen, diaphragm and thorax—become stronger and more efficient. Less oxygen is needed for the breathing process itself. At the same time, the amount of air a trained runner's lungs can take in at a single

* And, though it is not central to our discussion, through which carbon dioxide, the end product of the aerobic breakdown of glucose, is removed.

breath increases from less than five quarts to about six, and the volume per minute is tripled. Since more air means more oxygen, the advantages are plain.

HEAT CONTROLS

Earlier it was shown how the body efficiently resists both excessive heating and excessive cooling. With training, all its heat-related responses become more efficient. Dr. Carl V. Gisolfi of the University of Iowa's Stress Physiology Laboratory recently described a study in which college students, after an eight-week training program, were compared with runners who had trained for years and who worked out for an hour or two every day. Although both groups had the same oxygen intake and sweating rate, the distance runners maintained lower body temperatures and heart rates during treadmill runs. The difference, Gisolfi reported, was due entirely to training.

Training in hot weather brings still other adaptations, among them the ability to start sweating earlier and to cool more as a result of a given amount of evaporation.

It would be a mistake to assume that the adaptations discussed above occur only in champion runners; they happen to everyone who runs, regardless of age or sex. The degree of adaptation is, of course, affected by many factors—including some we can do nothing about, such as heredity—but you'll get fitter even if you're one hundred and six years old (as the well-known San Francisco runner Larry Lewis was when he died). Dr. John Naughton, dean of the medical school at the State University of New York at Buffalo, recently sent me a report of a program in which eighteen middle-aged and distinctly sedentary men were subjected to a seven-month period of calisthenics and running. At the end of this period, they had: 1) increased oxygen-processing capacity, 2) lower blood pressure, 3) lower pulse rate and 4) increased breathing efficiency.

Lest anyone with a chauvinistic bent suppose that these changes occurred only because the subjects were men, Drs. Leroy Getchell and J. C. Moore of Ball State University's Human Performance Laboratory reported in the *Archives of Physical Medicine and Rehabilitation* on a comparative study designed to confirm or refute exactly this supposition. For ten weeks, eleven middle-aged women and twelve middle-aged men participated in a program of walking and running. At the end of the ten weeks they were tested. The researchers reported that the women responded in exactly the same way the men did.

APPENDIX C The Harvard Step Test

The Harvard Step Test is one of the simplest ways to evaluate cardiovascular fitness. It requires you to step up and down on a bench for a few minutes, then see how quickly your heart recovers from the effort. The version of the test described here was devised by the American Medical Association's Committee on Exercise and Physical Fitness.

1. Get a sturdy bench 12 inches high if you're under 5 feet tall, 14 inches high if you're from 5 feet to 5 feet 3 inches, 16 inches high if you're from 5 feet 3 to 5 feet 9, 18 inches high if you're from 5 feet 9 to 6 feet, and 20 inches high if you're over 6 feet tall. Step from the floor onto the bench and down again thirty times a minute for four minutes, using a metronome or having someone time you with the second hand of a watch. (If you get too tired to go on, you can stop earlier, but it will lower your score.)

2. As soon as you finish, sit quietly and take your pulse, or have someone else take it, for 30 seconds one minute after you finish, another 30 seconds two minutes after you finish, and another 30 seconds three minutes after you finish.

3. Compute your Recovery Index (RI) by using this formula:

$$RI = \frac{\text{Duration of exercise in seconds x 100}}{\text{Sum of pulse counts x 2}}$$

If your RI is 60 or less, your rating is poor; between 61 and 70, fair; between 71 and 80, good; between 81 and 90, very good; 91 or more, excellent. The test itself is quite strenuous if you're badly out of shape, so use caution and stop if you have any adverse symptoms such as chest pain or extreme difficulty in breathing.

Reading About Running
A Selected Bibliography

Abbreviations: *TJ* = *The Jogger. JAMA* = *Journal of the American Medical Association. P&SM* = *The Physician and Sportsmedicine. RW* = *Runner's World.*

ADAMS, GENE M., and DE VRIES, HERBERT A. "Physiological Effects of an Exercise Training Regimen Upon Women Aged 52 to 79." *Journal of Gerontology,* Vol. 28, No. 1, 1973.

ALBOHM, MARGE. "Does Menstruation Affect Performance in Sports?" *P&SM,* March 1976.

———. "How Injuries Occur in Girls' Sports." *P&SM,* February 1976.

American Association for Health, Physical Education, and Recreation. *Nutrition for Athletes: A Handbook for Coaches.* AAHPER, 1971.

American Heart Association, Committee on Exercise. *Exercise Testing and Training of Apparently Healthy Individuals: A Handbook for Physicians.* New York: American Heart Association, 1972.

American Medical Association. *Basic Bodywork . . . for Fitness and Health.* Undated booklet.

———, Committee on Exercise and Physical Fitness. "Effortless Exercisers." Unpublished statement, December 5, 1969.

———. "Exercise Stress Testing of the Apparently Healthy Individual by Allied Health Personnel." Unpublished statement, November 1974.

———. *Guide to Prescribing Exercise Programs.* Chicago: American Medical Association, 1976.

———. "Lifetime Sports." Unpublished statement, October 14, 1971.

———. "Physical Fitness: A Definition." Unpublished statement, April 23, 1968.

ANDERSON, BOB, and HENDERSON, JOE, eds. *Guide to Distance Running.* Mountain View, Calif.: World Publications, 1971. A varied collection of useful articles, most of them reprinted from *Runner's World.*

ANONYMOUS. "Heart Claims Questioned." Letter to *Santa Barbara* [California] *News-Press,* March 26, 1976. An unidentified physician raises skeptical questions about the Longevity Research Institute. Accompanied by a reply from Nathan Pritikin, the LRI's director.

ÅSTRAND, PER-OLAF, and RODAHL, KAARE. *Textbook of Work Physiology.* New York: McGraw-Hill, 1970. The standard authority.

BAHR, ROBERT. "Channeling Our Meanness." *RW,* June 1976. On running as an antidote for aggressive behavior.

BANNISTER, ROGER. *The Four-Minute Mile.* New York: Dodd, Mead, 1955. A moving account of how he cracked the long-standing "barrier."

BARNARD, R. JAMES. "The Heart Needs Warm-Up Time." *P&SM,* January 1976.

BAR-OR, ODED. "Predicting Athletic Performance." *P&SM,* February 1975.

BASSLER, THOMAS J. "Athletes and Beer." Letter to *P&SM,* March 1976. The controversial pathologist argues that athletes should increase their beer intake during heavy training.

———. "Marathon Running and Immunity to Heart Disease." *P&SM,* April 1975.

———. "Quality of Life." Letter to *The Western Journal of Medicine,* April 1976.

BATTEN, JACK. *The Complete Jogger.* New York: Harcourt Brace Jovanovich, 1977.

BEISSER, ARNOLD R. *The Madness in Sports.* New York: Appleton-Century-Crofts, 1967. An examination of the sinister side of play.

BELLOC, NEDRA B. "Relationship of Health Practices and Mortality." *Preventive Medicine* 2, 1973.

———, and BRESLOW, LESTER. "Relationship of Physical Health Status and Health Practices." *Preventive Medicine,* August 1972.

BENSON, HERBERT. *The Relaxation Response.* New York, William Morrow, 1975.

Bike World, editors of. *Food for Fitness.* Mountain View, Calif.: World Publications, 1975.

BLACKBURN, HENRY, *et al.* "Premature Ventricular Complexes Induced by Stress Testing." *American Journal of Cardiology,* April 1973.

BLUMENTHAL, JACK. "Losing and Gaining." *RW,* September 1976.

BOGERT, L. JEAN, *et al. Nutrition and Physical Fitness.* Philadelphia: W. B. Saunders, 1973. A sound if somewhat conservative classic.

BONNER, MICHAEL. "Sit Down and Relax." *RW,* June 1976. Transcendental meditation for runners.

BOWERMAN, WILLIAM J., and BROWN, GWILYM S. "The Secrets of Speed." *Sports Illustrated,* August 2, 1971.

BOWERMAN, WILLIAM J., and HARRIS, W. E. *Jogging.* New York: Grosset & Dunlap, 1967. A small (127 pages) classic by a coach regarded by many as the best in the world.

BOYLE, ROBERT H. *Sport: Mirror of American Life.* New York: Little, Brown, 1963. An examination, now slightly dated but nonetheless revealing, of the role of a sport in our lives.

BRADLEY, DAVID. "The Happiness of the Long-Distance Runner." *Village Voice,* August 23, 1976.

BRADLEY, MICHAEL. "Automatic Psyching." *RW,* October 1976. Autosuggestion for runners.

BRESLOW, LESTER. "A Quantitative Approach to the World Health Organization Definition of Health: Physical, Mental and Social Well-being." *International Journal of Epidemiology,* Vol. 1, No. 4, 1972.

BRODY, JANE E. "Jogging Is Like a Drug: Watch the Dosage, Beware the Problems." *New York Times,* November 10, 1976.

BROWN, JAMES W. " 'Pure' Streams May Cause 'Backpacker's Diarrhea.' " *P&SM,* May 1976.

BROWN, WILLIAM. Untitled letter to *TJ,* June 1976. A seventy-two-year-old runner describes his first marathon.

BROWNE, NATALIE. "Jogging, the Mockingbird, and More." *TJ,* March–April 1976. Article on the benefits of running.

BUCKLEY, WILLIAM F., JR. "The Pains of Health." *New York Post,* July 29, 1976.

BUSKIRK, ELSWORTH R. "Cardiovascular Adaptation to Physical Effort in Healthy Men." Chapter 2 in *Exercise Testing and Exercise Training in Coronary Heart Disease,* J. P. Naughton and H. K. Hellerstein, eds. New York: Academic Press. 1973.

BUTWIN, DAVID. "Running." *Travel & Leisure,* May 1976.

CADY, STEVE. "Olympic Diet: Hold the Steak, Vitamins." *New York Times,* June 11, 1976.

CALDWELL, FRANCES. "You Can Run Down Running, But Bikers Are Hit by Cars and Swimmers Drown." *P&SM,* April 1975.

CANTWELL, JOHN DAVIS. "Athletes' Hearts: Disease and Nondisease." *P&SM,* September 1973.

———. "The Exercised Heart." *RW,* July 1976.

———. "Extreme Bradycardia in Middle-Aged Runners." *P&SM,* July 1976.

———. "Heredity: Just Part of the Story." Letter to *P&SM,* January 1976. A comment on heart-attack risk factors.

CHASE, DENNIS. "John Walker—World's Most Watched-Over Athlete?" *P&SM,* February 1976.

CLAREMONT, ALAN, and BOSTIAN, LLOYD. "Where Do You Begin?" *RW,* September 1976.

CLARK, TRUMAN R. "Active Alcoholics." *RW,* July 1976. Description of the Alcohlics Olympics.

COHN, VICTOR. "Genes Stunting U.S. Growth." *New York Post,* June 10, 1976.

CONCANNON, JOE. "He Runs to Glory—Alone." *Boston Sunday Globe,* February 29, 1976. An interview with Bill Rodgers.

———. "Marathon Man." *Boston Sunday Globe,* October 31, 1976. Bill

Rodgers after winning the New York Marathon.

COOPER, KENNETH H. *Aerobics.* New York: Bantam Books, 1968. The book that put running on the map.

———. "A Means of Assessing Maximal Oxygen Uptake." *JAMA,* January 15, 1968.

———. *The New Aerobics.* New York: Bantam Books, 1970. A revised and refined *Aerobics.*

———, *et al.* "Physical Fitness Levels vs. Selected Coronary Risk Factors." *JAMA,* July 12, 1976.

———, and COOPER, MILDRED. *Aerobics for Women.* New York: Bantam Books, 1972.

COOTER, G. RANKIN, *et al.* "Do Long Hair and Football Uniforms Impair Heat Loss?" *P&SM,* February 1975.

CORBITT, TED. "Frances Sheriden Goulart." *Road Runners Club New York Association Newsletter,* Fall 1974. Article about a vegetarian athlete.

———. "John Duncan Semple." *Road Runners Club New York Association Newsletter,* Winter–Spring 1975. Article about Boston Marathon official Jock Semple.

———. "Ultra-Marathon Scene." *Road Runners Club New York Association Newsletter,* Spring 1976.

COSTILL, DAVID L. "Muscular Exhaustion During Distance Running," *P&SM,* October 1974.

———, *et al.* "Muscle Fiber Composition and Enzyme Activities of Elite Distance Runners." *Medicine in Science and Sports,* Vol. 8, No. 2, 1976.

———. *A Scientific Approach to Distance Running.* Unpublished manuscript. Undated.

CRAIG, ROBERT L. "The Athlete's Pregame Meal." Letter to *P&SM,* August 1976.

CULLEN, MARK. "The Talk of Eugene." *RW,* July 1976. Conversations with Olympic Trials participants.

DANIELL, HARRY. "Try Not to Exhaust Yourself." *RW,* September 1976. The effects of carbon monoxide.

DANIELS, JACK T. "Running with Jim Ryun: A Five-Year Study." *P&SM,* September 1974.

DE SHAZO, RICHARD D., *et al.* "When an Insect Sting Can Mean Death." *P&SM,* June 1976.

DE VINE, SHERMAN S. "Longevity Center's Job." *Santa Barbara* [California] *News-Press,* May 1, 1976. A physician-patient gives support to the work of the Longevity Research Institute.

DE VRIES, HERBERT A. "Exercise Intensity Threshold for Improvement of Cardiovascular-Respiratory Function in Older Men." *Geriatrics,* April 1971.

———. "Prescription of Exercise for Older Men from Telemetered Exercise Heart Rate Data." Unpublished, undated paper.

———, and ADAMS, GENE M. "Comparison of Exercise Responses in Old and Young Men: I. The Cardiac Effort/Total Body Effort Relationship." *Journal of Gerontology,* Vol. 27, No. 3, 1972.

———. "Electromyographic Comparison of Single Doses of Exercise and Meprobamate as to Effects on Muscular Relaxation." *American Journal of Physical Medicine,* Vol. 51, No. 3, 1972.

DILFER, CAROL. "Jogging Through Pregnancy." *TJ,* March–April 1976.

DOHERTY, J. KENNETH. *Modern Track and Field.* Englewood Cliffs, N.J.: Prentice-Hall, 1963. A respected coach's sound, lucid and comprehensive survey of training methods in everything from dashes to distance runs.

DOLSON, FRANK. "An Athlete's Wife Copes With and Conquers the Interminable Track Season." *New York Times,* June 27, 1976. (Excerpted from *Always Young,* World Publications, 1975)

DONALDSON, RORY. "Dick Gregory Jogs Across Country." *TJ,* June 1976.

———. "Will Sports Make Us Free?" Letter to *P&SM,* May 1975.

DUNKLE, MARY. "Franklin's Club Fosters Fitness." Department of Public Information, the Pennsylvania State University, March 1976. Report on a women's physical fitness program.

EDIGER, DON. "Charting Body Heat—in Color." *P&SM,* January 1975.

ELRICK, HAROLD, *et al.* "Indians Who Run 100 Miles on 1,500 Calories a Day." *P&SM,* February 1976. A report on Mexico's Tarahumara Indians.

ERDELYI, G. J. "Effects of Exercise on the Menstrual Cycle." *P&SM,* March 1976.

FALLS, JOE. *The Boston Marathon.* New York: Macmillan, 1977. A sportswriter's lively history of one of the greatest races of them all.

FARDY, PAUL S., *et al.* "A Comparison of Myocardial Function in Former Athletes and Non-athletes." *Medicine and Science in Sports,* Vol. 8, No. 1, 1976.

FIXX, JAMES F. "The Devil Made Me Do It." *Oberlin College Alumni Magazine,* July–August 1972. Report on competing in the Boston Marathon.

———. "You Hurt More But You Feel Better." *Sky,* March 1977.

———. "Runaway Jogging." *On the Sound,* August 1973.

FLORIANI, LAWRENCE P. "Ankle Injury Mechanism and Treatment Guides." *P&SM,* September 1976.

Fortune, editors of. "Keeping Fit in the Company Gym." *Fortune,* October 1975.

FOSS, MERLE L., *et al.* "Initial Work Tolerance of Extremely Obese Patients." *Archives of Physical Medicine and Rehabilitation,* February 1975.

FRANKLIN, BARRY, and BUSKIRK, ELSWORTH R. "Effects of a Physical Conditioning Regimen on Middle-Aged Women Who Varied in Body Composition." Unpublished paper, September 28, 1976.

FREDERICK, E. C. *The Running Body.* Mountain View, Calif.: World Publications, 1973. A basic guide to running physiology.

FRIEDMAN, MEYER, and ROSENMAN, RAY H. *Type A Behavior and Your Heart.* New York: Alfred A. Knopf, 1974.

FURLONG, WILLIAM BARRY. "The Fun in Fun." *Psychology Today,* June 1976.

GARDNER, JAMES B., and PURDY, J. GERRY. *Computerized Running Training Programs.* Los Altos, Calif.: Tafnews Press, 1970.

GENDEL, EVALYN S. "Psychological Factors and Menstrual Extraction." *P&SM,* March 1976.

GETCHELL, LEROY H. "Energy Cost of Playing Golf." *Archives of Physical Medicine and Rehabilitation,* January 1968.

GETCHELL, LEROY H. *Physical Fitness: A Way to Life.* New York: Wiley, 1976.

______. "Physical Training: Comparative Responses of Middle-Aged Adults." *Archives of Physical Medicine and Rehabilitation,* June 1975.

GETTMAN, LARRY, and POLLOCK, MICHAEL. "The Amazing Blind Marathoner." *RW,* August 1976. An article on Harry Cordellos of San Francisco.

GIGUERE, PAUL. "Boston Marathon—Beating the Heat with Common Sense and Water." *P&SM,* June 1976.

GILMORE, C. P. "Taking Exercise to Heart." *The New York Times Magazine,* March 27, 1977. An examination of the evidence that running prevents heart attacks and promotes longevity.

GLASSER, WILLIAM. *Positive Addiction.* New York: Harper & Row, 1976. A physician demonstrates that good habits, running among them, drive out bad.

GLICK, JAMES M. "The Female Knee in Athletics." *P&SM,* September 1973.

GLOVER, BOB. "Fitness Fever," December 1975 and July 1976. Newsletters of the West Side YMCA, 5 West 63rd Street, New York, N.Y. 10023. The July 1976 issue includes expert advice on selecting running shoes.

______. "Flexibility—Why and How." Unpublished paper, November 1975.

GOODWIN, MICHAEL. "The Fastest Diet?" *New York Times Magazine,* August 15, 1976. A report on fasting as a way to lose weight.

GORMAN, JAMES. "A Running Argument." *The Sciences,* January-February 1977. A discussion of running as a preventative for heart attacks, based on lectures at the October 1976 New York Academy of Sciences conference on long-distance running.

GOULART, FRANCES SHERIDAN. *Bum Steers: How and Why to Make Your Own Delicious High Protein Meats, Fake Fish and Dairyless Desserts and Avoid Useless Calories, Cholesterol, Sodium Nitrite, Salmonella, Trichinosis and High Prices.* Old Greenwich, Conn.: Chatham Press, 1975. Recipes and an argument for vegetarianism by a long-distance runner.

______. "Sweat-Debt Solutions." *RW,* April 1976. Three home-made drinks for restoring fluid balance.

GRAHAM, GORDON L. "Reconditioning Following Athletic Injuries." *P&SM,* September 1976.

GREEN, LAURENCE H., *et al.* "Fatal Myocardial Infarction in Marathon Racing." *Annals of Internal Medicine* 84, 1976.

GREENBERG, ALICE S. "Women Joggers Turn to Racing." *TJ,* March–April 1976.

GREER, BILL. "How to Perform a Proper Sit-Up." Letter to *P&SM,* June 1976.

GWINUP, GRANT. "Effect of Exercise Alone on the Weight of Obese Women." *Archives of Internal Medicine,* May 1975. A reference to this study appears in the September 1975 *P&SM.*

HANLEY, DANIEL F. "Medical Care of the U.S. Olympic Team." *JAMA,* July 12, 1976.

HANRAHAN, PETE. "Beginner and Vet." *RW,* August 1976. A humorous comparison of experienced runners and novices.

______. "Smile and Drive Them Crazy." *RW,* October 1976. Iconoclastic advice on dealing with hecklers.

HARGER, BRUCE S., *et al.* "The Caloric Cost of Running." *JAMA,* April 22, 1974.

HARPER, FREDERICK D. "Jogging Research at Howard University." *TJ,* June 1976.

HAYCOCK, CHRISTINE E., and GILLETTE, JOAN V. "Susceptibility of Women Athletes to Injury." *JAMA,* July 12, 1976.

HELLERSTEIN, HERMAN K. "Exercise Tests Inadequate for Cardiac Patients." *P&SM,* August 1976.

HENDERSON, JOE. *Jog, Run, Race.* Mountain View, Calif.: World Publications, 1977.

______. *The Long Run Solution.* Mountain View, Calif.: World Publications, 1976. Meditations, invariably articulate, on how running helps the mind.

______. *Long Slow Distance: The Humane Way to Train.* Mountain View, Calif.: World Publications, 1969. The book that introduced LSD training.

______. "New Beginnings in Running." *RW,* April 1976.

______. *Run Gently, Run Long.* Mountain View, Calif.: World Publications, 1974. Henderson's eloquent argument that "running . . . can be as lasting as anything in this life."

______. "The Six in Ten Who Break Down." *RW,* December 1975.

HENN, BILL. "George Sheehan." *Road Runners Club New York Association Newsletter,* Spring 1974. Chiefly biographical.

HERMAN, ROBIN. "New Soviet 'Weapon' Puts Muscle in Athletic Affairs." *New York Times,* June 20, 1976. Description of a method for strengthening muscles electrically.

HIGDON, HAL. *Fitness After Forty.* Mountain View, Calif.: World Publications, 1977.

______. *On the Run from Dogs and People.* Chicago: Henry Regnery, 1971.

______. "Taking the Fall Sport Seriously." *RW,* September 1976. Cross-country techniques.

HOFFER, ERIC. *The True Believer.* New York: Harper & Row, 1951.

HOGE, WARREN. "Marathon Devotees Find Happiness in the Long Run." *New York Times,* October 25, 1976.

HOPKINS, BILL, and EDWARDS, DOUG. "Where Does the Time Go?" *RW,* July 1976. The authors argue that record times in racing invariably decrease at constant rates.

HORN, JACK. "Physical Fitness, Ten Years Later." *Psychology Today,* July 1976.

HORNE, WILLIAM M. "Effects of a Physical Activity Program on Middle-aged, Sedentary Corporation Executives." *American Industrial Hygiene Association Journal,* March 1975.

HOYT, CREIG, *et al. Food for Fitness.* Mountain View, Calif.: World Publications, 1975.

HUIZINGA, JOHAN. *Homo Ludens: A Study of the Play Element in Culture,* translated by R. F. C. Hill. London: Routledge and Kegan Paul, 1949. Also (paperback) Boston: Beacon Press, 1955. An indispensable classic.

HUMPHREY, NYLES R., and RUHLING, ROBERT O. "Second Wind—Trying to Catch It in the Lab." *P&SM,* May 1975.

ILLICH, IVAN, and KEEN, SAM. "Medicine Is a Major Threat to Health." *Psychology Today,* May 1976.

Intercollege Research, editors of. "Exercise: A Heartening Life-Lengthener?" *Intercollege Research,* the Pennsylvania State University, January 1976.

JACKSON, DOUGLAS W., and BAILEY, DANIEL. "Shin Splints in the Young Athlete: A Nonspecific Diagnosis." *P&SM,* March 1975.

JAMES, WILLIAM. *The Varieties of Religious Experience.* New York: Collier Books, 1961.

JEANSONNE, JOHN. "Frank Shorter, Finding Happiness in Long Distance." *Newsday,* April 18, 1976.

JESSE, JOHN. "Exercises in Futility." *RW,* August 1976. An article on the abuse of exercise.

The Jogger, editors of. "Harry Hlavac, Jogging Podiatrist." *TJ,* July–August 1976. An interview.

______. "Heart Rate Table." *TJ,* March–April 1976.

JOHNSON, BROOKS. "Sprint Myths and Methods." *RW,* June 1976.

JOHNSON, WARREN R., ed. *Science and Medicine of Exercise and Sports.* New York: Harper & Row, 1960. Everything from the function of the cell to the psychology of sport. Probably more than you really want to know, but skipping around is easy and almost always rewarding.

JONES, DEAN C. "Social Runners." *RW,* July 1976.

JONES, ROBERT. "Exercise Training and Risk Factors." In Zohman, Lenore R., and Phillips, Raymond E., eds., *Progress in Cardiac Rehabilitation: Medical Aspects of Exercise Testing and Training.* New York: Stratton Intercontinental Medical Book Corporation, 1973.

Journal of the American Medical Association, editors of. "Group Solicits Members for Diabetic Diet Study." *JAMA,* September 2, 1974. Description of the diabetes research of the Longevity Research Institute, Santa Barbara, California, with a brief report on Eula Weaver, who won two gold medals in the Senior Olympics at the age of eighty-five (accompanied by a photograph of Mrs. Weaver running).

______. "Is Your Patient Fit?" *JAMA,* July 10, 1967. A modification of the Harvard Step Test is described.

KERGES, DAVID E. "Forget Morton's Foot." Letter to *P&SM,* May 1974.

KASCH, FRED W. "The Effects of Exercise on the Aging Process." *P&SM,* June 1976. An earlier and much briefer report on the same subject appears in the July 1975 *P&SM* under the title "Stopping the Clock with Exercise."

______. "The Energy Cost of Walking and Hiking." *P&SM,* July 1976.

______. "Physiological Variables During Ten Years of Endurance Exercise." *Medicine and Science in Sports,* Vol. 8, No. 1, 1976.

______, *et al.* "Cardiovascular Changes in Middle-Aged Men During Two Years of Training." *Journal of Applied Physiology,* January 1973.

KAUNDER, ARNOLD. "Arm Action." *RW,* April 1976.

KAVANAGH, TERENCE. "A Conditioning Programme for the Elderly." *Canadian Family Physician,* July 1971.

______. *Heart Attack? Counterattack!* Toronto: Van Nostrand Reinhold, 1976. A physician's prescription for rehabilitating cardiac patients with running.

KIELL, PAUL J., and FRELINGHUYSEN, JOSEPH S. *Keep Your Heart Running.* New York: Winchester Press, 1976. A graduated health program written by two runners, one of whom (Kiell) is a physician.

KONECKE, SHELDON P. "Joggers' Foot and Leg Problems Can Be Helped." *TJ,* July–August 1976.

KORNHEISER, TONY. "Marathon Woman: She Runs with Pride and Pain." *New York Times,* April 16, 1976. Article on Kathy Switzer.

KOSTRUBALA, THADDEUS. *The Joy of Running.* Philadelphia and New York: J. B. Lippincott, 1976. A psychiatrist tells how running changed his patients' lives—and his own.

KRAMER, BARRY. "The Key to Health." *Reader's Digest,* July 1976.

KUSCSIK, NINA, and BLACKSTONE, LYNN. "The Women's 'Mini' Gets Big." *RW,* July 1976.

LAMB, LAWRENCE E. "Unrecognized Heart Attacks in Apparently Healthy Men." *Executive Health,* Vol. VII, No. 10, 1973.

LANCE, KATHRYN. *Running for Health and Beauty: A Complete Guide for Women.* New York: Bobbs-Merrill, 1977. A gifted writer's introduction to the sport.

LAWSON, JANE. "Can Athletes be Vegetarians?" *Vegetarian Health Review and Digest,* Vol. I, No. 1, undated.

LEE, SAM. "Norm Bright." *Veteris,* January 1975. Article on a champion runner in his sixties.

LEONARD, GEORGE. *The Ultimate Athlete.* New York: Viking, 1975. A provocative and sometimes poetic look at things to come.

LERNER, MAX. "The Old Ones." *New York Post,* November 19, 1976. A column on the problems and prospects of longevity.

LIKOFF, WILLIAM; SEGAL, BERNARD; and GALTON, LAWRENCE. *Your Heart: Complete Information for the Family.* Philadelphia and New York: J. B. Lippincott, 1972. A lucid, comprehensive primer, with chapters on preventive maintenance and getting back into the swing of life after a heart attack.

LILLIEFORS, JIM. "The Need to Fail." *RW,* April 1976.

———. "Training the Head." *RW,* May, 1976.

LOESCHHORN, JOHN. "Running Shoes." *womenSports,* February 1976.

LONGORIA, E., JR. "Spot Reducing." Letter to *TJ,* June 1976. (With editor's reply.)

LUDINGTON, SYL. "Joint Agreement." Letter to *RW,* July 1976.

LYDIARD, ARTHUR, and GILMOUR, GARTH. *Run to the Top.* London: Herbert Jenkins, 1962. Lydiard, a vastly influential coach, tells the training secrets that earned his athletes Olympic medals, world records, and probably the most relaxed and economical running style to be found anywhere.

MACAULEY, IAN T. "Marathon Men and Women on Their Marks." *New York Times,* October 22, 1976. Preview of the first five-borough New York Marathon.

MC CAFFERTY, WILLIAM B., *et al.* "Does a 'Threshold Age' Cancel Longevity Hopes of Exercisers?" *P&SM,* June 1975.

MC DANIELS, ANNETTE. Letter to *TJ,* March–April 1976.

MC KEAN, MARGARET. "They Learn a New Way to Live." Ventura County,

California, *Star Free Press,* July 11, 1976. Report on the Longevity Research Institute, Santa Barbara, California.

MADDOX, DARRELL. "Jim Ryun: Stability and Discipline." *P&SM,* September 1974.

MAHONEY, MICHAEL J., and MAHONEY, KATHRYN. "Fight Fat with Behavior Control." *Psychology Today,* May 1976.

MANN, GEORGE V. "In Leningrad's White Nights—A Symposium." *P&SM,* January 1976. Report on the International Symposium on the Nutrition of Athletes.

MARTIN, JACK. "Exploring the Frontiers of Fitness Knowledge." *P&SM,* May 1976. An article on the leading exercise physiologists and their work.

MATTINGLY, THOMAS W. "Paul Dudley White: The Porpoise Heart vs. the Athletic Heart." *JAMA,* July 12, 1976.

MAULE, TEX. *Running Scarred.* New York: Saturday Review Press, 1972. The subtitle says it: "The odyssey of a heart-attack victim's jogging back to health." A moving and dramatic adventure, told by a former *Sports Illustrated* writer.

MAYER, JEAN. *A Diet for Living.* New York: David McKay, 1975. Plain talk for people who mistrust fad diets. Mayer, former professor of nutrition at Harvard, is a respected authority on the subject.

MAYES, DONALD S. "What's Round and Pounds the Ground? A Slogger!" *P&SM,* April 1976.

MICHENER, JAMES A. *Sports in America.* New York: Random House, 1976. The old master turns his practiced hand to the playing field.

MILLER, BENJAMIN F., and GALTON, LAWRENCE. *Freedom from Heart Attacks.* New York: Simon and Schuster, 1972. A common-sense primer on how to avoid heart attacks (a key recommendation: exercise), and what to do if you suffer one.

MILLER, DAVID L. *Gods and Games: Toward a Theology of Play.* New York and Cleveland: World, 1970. A professor of religion at Syracuse University argues persuasively that our games are more than they seem to be, and in the process offers some profound insights into the meaning of play.

MILVY, PAUL. "Runners Who Rationalize." *Road Runners Club New York Association Newsletter,* Spring 1976.

MIRKIN, GABE. "How Much Training Do You Need?" *Washington Post,* June 3, 1976.

______. "A Key to Bad Knee Is a Fault in the Foot." *Washington Post,* June 17, 1976.

______. "Why Every Athlete Needs Muscle-Stretching Exercises." *Washington Post,* April 1, 1976.

MOE, JOHN F. "Push Running!" Letter to *P&SM,* April 1976.

MOORE, KENNY. "Appointment at a Starting Line." *Sports Illustrated,* June 14, 1976. Article on milers Filbert Bayi and John Walker.

______. "Watching Their Steps." *Sports Illustrated,* May 3, 1976. Description of tests conducted on top athletes by the Institute for Aerobics Research.

______. "Women's Trials Enter a New Era." *Sports Illustrated,* July 1976.

MORELLA, JOSEPH J., and TURCHETTI, RICHARD J. *Nutrition and the Athlete.* New York: Mason/Charter, 1976. A complete guide, with an eighty-page appendix listing the nutritional composition of everything from abalone to yogurt.

MORRIS, ALFRED F. "Exercise Labs, Athletic Records." Letter to *P&SM,* May 1976.

MORTON, DUDLEY J. *The Human Foot: Its Evolution, Physiology, and Functional Disorders.* New York: Columbia University Press, 1935.

MURPHY, ROBERT J. "Salt Pills and Leg Cramps." Letter to *P&SM,* July 1975.

MYERS, CLAYTON R. *The Official YMCA Physical Fitness Handbook.* New York: Popular Library, 1975. Proven, practical counsel.

NAUGHTON, JOHN, and NAGLE, FRANCIS. "Peak Oxygen Intake During Physical Fitness Program for Middle-Aged Men." *JAMA,* March 15, 1965.

NELSON, CHARLES M. "Rehabilitation Emphasis Should Be on Exercise." *P&SM,* September, 1976.

NELSON, DALE O. "Fitness Tips." Logan, Utah, *Herald Journal,* August 4, 1976.

NELSON, RALPH A. "What Should Athletes Eat? Unmixing Folly and Facts." *P&SM,* November 1975.

NEVINS, MICHAEL A., *et al.* "When a Pro Athlete's ECG Mimics Heart Disease." *P&SM,* January 1974.

New York Times, editors of. "Olympic Village Food: Good, Plenty and Free." *New York Times,* July 11, 1976.

The New Yorker, editors of. "In Central Park." *The New Yorker,* June 7, 1976. A report, not notably sympathetic, on a five-mile race.

NIDEFFER, ROBERT M. *The Inner Athlete: Mind Plus Muscle for Winning.* New York: Thomas Y. Crowell, 1976. A clinical psychologist's exploration of the mental aspects of competition, with "mental rehearsal" exercises applicable to every sport, including running.

NORMAN, JAMES. "The Tarahumaras: Mexico's Long Distance Runners." *National Geographic,* May 1976.

NOVAK, MICHAEL. *The Joy of Sports.* New York: Basic Books, 1976. In Novak's theology the players are priests, the spectators worshipers, and the whole ecclesiastical edifice, despite its undeniable wonders, is much in need of reform. Novak, a Catholic theologian, writes chiefly of basketball, baseball and football, but there is much here to amaze, amuse, delight and confound runners, too.

O'SHEA, JOHN P. "Weighing Issues." *RW,* July 1976. A brief discussion—with an acompanying counterargument—of weight training for runners.

PARMLEY, LOREN F., JR., *et al.,* eds. *Exercise: Proceedings of the National Workshop on Exercise in the Prevention, in the Evaluation, in the Treatment of Heart Disease.* Supplement to the *Journal of the South Carolina Medical Association,* December 1969.

PATE, RUSSELL. "Conditioning Without Crashing." *RW,* July 1976.

PAUL, LOWELL. "Sport Is a Three-Letter Word." *Intellectual Digest,* June 1974. Sport as a way of having fun.

The Physician and Sportsmedicine, editors of. "Achilles Tendon Problems

Increase." *P&SM,* March 1976. A round-table discussion.
______. "Athletes and Sports—Bigger and Better in 2001?" *P&SM,* February 1976.
______. "Balancing Heat Stress, Fluids, and Electrolytes." *P&SM,* August 1975. A round-table discussion.
______. "[Roger] Bannister Doubts Lab Helps Athletes." *P&SM,* January 1976.
______. "Biking Equals Jogging for Endurance." *P&SM,* July 1975.
______. "Cold Toes Mean More Than Just Discomfort." *P&SM,* March 1976.
______. "Exercise and the Heart." *P&SM,* March 1974. A symposium.
______. "Exercise Increases Bone Mineral in Women." *P&SM,* July 1975.
______. "Exercise Prescription Guidelines Listed." *P&SM,* July 1975.
______. "Female Athletes Need Courage, Seminar Told." *P&SM,* May 1976.
______. "Foot Problems in Runners." *P&SM,* July 1976. A round-table discussion.
______. "Heat Peril in Distance Runs Spurs ACSM [American College of Sports Medicine] Guideline Alert." *P&SM,* July 1975.
______. "Olympic Race Time Altered After Protest." *P&SM,* March 1976. Report on rescheduling of the Olympic marathon to reduce the possibility of heat stroke.
______. "Overcoming Overprotection of the Elderly." *P&SM,* June 1976.
______. "Physically Fit Women Have Fewer Complaints." *P&SM,* December 1975.
______. "Roger Bannister: 'Human Beings Are Not the Same.'" *P&SM,* September 1974.
______. "Run Properly for Workout, Coach Says." *P&SM,* February 1976. UCLA track coach Jim Bush argues that short, fast runs are more beneficial than long, slow ones.
______. "Scanning Sports." *P&SM,* February 1976. Includes a brief report on Dr. Paul S. Fardy's comparison of continuous and intermittent exercises.
______. "Scanning Sports." *P&SM,* October, 1976. Includes a brief report on Dr. William Morgan's investigations of the effect of exercise on anxiety.
______. "Sport Held Vital in Obesity Prevention." *P&SM,* July 1976.
______. "Sports During Pregnancy, Other Questions Explored." *P&SM,* March 1976. A round-table discussion.
______. "Trying for the Tyler in Texas." *P&SM,* December 1974. Report on the Tyler Cup competition, a race for corporation executives.
______. "Upper Respiratory Infections in Sports." *P&SM,* October 1975. A round-table discussion.
______. "What to Cover in Office Evaluation for Exercise." *P&SM,* June 1976.
PIEPER, JOSEF. *Leisure: The Basis of Culture.* New York: Pantheon, 1963. A profound examination of the meaning of leisure. Though there is hardly a word about running in it, its wise and radiating power can transform every step we take.

PILEGGI, SARAH. "It Took Shorter a Little Longer." *Sports Illustrated,* May 31, 1976. Report on the Olympic marathon trials.

POWERS, PETER. "Distance for a Diabetic." *RW,* May 1976.

President's Council on Physical Fitness and Sports and the Administration on Aging. *The Fitness Challenge . . . in the Later Years.* A single copy is available free from the Administration on Aging, 400 Sixth Street S.W., Room 3757, Washington, D.C. 20201.

PRITIKIN, NATHAN, *et al.* "Diet and Exercise as a Total Therapeutic Regimen for the Rehabilitation of Patients with Severe Peripheral Vascular Disease." Paper presented November 19, 1975, at the American Congress of Rehabilitation Medicine and the American Academy of Physical Medicine and Rehabilitation, Atlanta.

PROKOP, DAVE. "Bob Anderson Ten Years Later." *RW,* December 1975. An interview with the publisher of *RW* on its tenth anniversary.

RASKOFF, WILLIAM J., *et al.* "The 'Athletic Heart.' " *JAMA,* July 12, 1976.

Reader's Digest, editors of. "How Good Is *Your* Game?" *Reader's Digest,* July 1976. Condensed from *Medical Times,* May 1976. A report on the same subject—a comparison of various sports, compiled by the President's Council on Physical Fitness and Sports—also appeared in the August 1976 *RW.*

RICHARDSON, BYRON. "A View from the Hill." *RW,* August 1976. Techniques and benefits of hill training.

ROHÉ, FRED. *The Zen of Running.* New York and Berkeley: Random House–Bookworks, 1974.

ROMANES, G. J., ed. *Cunningham's Textbook of Anatomy.* London: Oxford University Press, 1964. A hypochondriac's delight. Tells the reader more than any runner needs to know, but is nonetheless a useful and comprehensive guide to muscles, tendons, bones, nerves and much else.

ROSE, CHARLES L., and COHEN, MICHEL L. "Relative Importance of Physical Activity for Longevity." Unpublished report of a study conducted at the Veterans Administration Outpatient Clinic, Boston.

ROSE, KENNETH D. "Warning for Millions: Intense Exercise Can Deplete Potassium." *P&SM,* May 1975.

ROTKIS, TOM. "A Strange Madness." Letter to *P&SM,* June 1975.

Runner's World, editors of. *The Complete Runner.* Mountain View, Calif.: World Publications, 1974. Covers everything from philosophy to staging a successful race.

———. "Looking at People." July 1976. A report on Jess A. Bell, the farsighted running president of Bonne Bell, the cosmetics firm.

———. "1977 Special Shoe Supplement." *RW,* October 1976.

———. *Runner's Training Guide.* Mountain View, Calif.: World Publications, 1973.

———. *Running After Forty.* Mountain View, Calif.: World Publications, 1971. A brief (36 pages) guide to running almost forever.

RYAN, ALLAN J. "The Aftermath of the Bunion Derby," *P&SM,* July 1976.

———. "Aging, Exercise, and Longevity." *P&SM,* June 1975.

———. "Carotid Palpation Practice Questioned." *P&SM,* September 1976.

———. "Conditioning the Deconditioned." *P&SM,* March 1974.

———. "Heat Stress and the Vulnerable Athlete." *P&SM,* June 1973.

———. "Running Into Trouble." *P&SM,* April 1975.

RYAN, ALLAN J., and ALLMAN, FRED L., JR. *Sports Medicine.* New York: Academic Press, 1974.

RYDER, HENRY W., *et al.* "Future Peformance in Footracing." *Scientific American,* June 1976.

SALTIN, BENGT. "Intermittent Exercise: Its Physiology and Practical Application." Lecture, Ball State University, February 20, 1975.

SCHAFER, WALT. "Stress and Distress." *RW,* August 1976.

SCHMIDT, J. E. "Jogging Can Kill You!" *Playboy,* March 1976.

SCHWARTZ, HARRY. "What Strategy for Health? *New York Times,* July 27, 1976.

SEDER, JOSEPH I. "Heel Injuries Incurred in Running and Jumping." *P&SM,* October 1976.

SELYE, HANS. "Stress." *Intellectual Digest,* June 1974. An excerpt from *Stress Without Distress.*

______. *The Stress of Life.* New York: McGraw-Hill, 1956. Seminal work by a pioneer investigator.

______. *Stress Without Distress.* New York: J. B. Lippincott, 1974. Selye's popular account of what stress—both mental and physical—is, how it hurts us and how to avoid it.

SHEEHAN, GEORGE A. "Bloody Urine: Don't Panic, Collect a Specimen." *P&SM,* May 1975.

______. "Carbohydrate Loading Doesn't Work for Everyone." *P&SM,* May 1976.

______. "Come and Play." *P&SM,* November 1974.

______. *Dr. Sheehan on Running.* Mountain View, Calif.: World Publications, 1975. The book that more than any other captures the magic and majesty of the sport.

______, ed. *Encyclopedia of Athletic Medicine.* Mountain View, Calif.: World Publications, 1972. The prevention and cure of runners' ailments.

______. "Exercise: The New Miracle Drug." *P&SM,* December 1974.

______. "Facing and Beating the Tragic Trio—With Sports." *P&SM,* February 1976. An essay on sport's ability to provide "peak experiences."

______. "Let Me Do My Thing—And You Can Do Yours." *P&SM,* June 1975.

______. "Let's Hear It for Morton's Foot." *P&SM,* March 1974.

______. "Measuring Maximums on a Merciless Machine." *P&SM,* September 1976. Description of a testing session at Ball State University's Human Performance Laboratory.

______. "Needed Diet Fad: Cash and Carry." *P&SM,* October 1976.

______. "A New Look at Heroes." *P&SM,* August 1974.

______. "In Preventive Conditioning, Consider Yoga." *P&SM,* November 1973.

______. "Six Steps Toward Painless Running." *RW,* December 1975. Exercises for strength and flexibility.

______. "Super Sugar Diet Solves Energy Crisis." *P&SM,* January 1974. One of the first reports on carbohydrate loading.

______. "That ECG is Loaded." *P&SM,* September 1973.

______. "Warning: Watching Can Be Hazardous to Your Health." *P&SM,* November 1975.

SHEPHARD, ROY J. "What Causes Second Wind?" *P&SM,* November 1974.

———, and KAVANAGH, TERENCE. "What Exercise to Prescribe for the Post-MI Patient." *P&SM,* August 1975.

SHIPPEN, CLIVE. "Roy Fowler—Supervet." *Veteris,* October 1974.

SILLITOE, ALAN. *The Loneliness of the Long-Distance Runner.* New York: Knopf, 1959. A classic fictional evocation of the myriad beauties of running.

SINGER, DALE. "Heart Attack Patients Jog Way to Health." *Sarasota* [Florida] *Herald-Tribune,* December 19, 1976.

SMITH, NATHAN J. *Food for Sport.* Palo Alto: Bull Publishing Company, 1976. Part of the common-sense Berkeley Series in Nutrition, this volume covers everything from losing weight to keeping in shape when you're old.

———. "Gaining and Losing Weight in Athletics." *JAMA,* July 12, 1976.

SOLOMON, NEIL. "The Bitter Truth." *New York Post,* December 8, 1976. Brief replies to readers' questions about sugar dangers and electrolyte balance.

———. "A Proper Diet." *New York Post,* July 28, 1976.

SPINO, MIKE. *Beyond Jogging.* Millbrae, Calif.: Celestial Arts, 1976. The Esalen view of philosophy, religion and running.

STAMPFL, FRANZ. *Franz Stampfl on Running.* London: Herbert Jenkins, 1955. A top Oxford University coach covers the sport from fundamentals to racing tactics.

STEINER, KURT. "2079 in National RRCA Age-Group Championship." *Road Runners Club New York Association Newsletter,* Fall 1974.

STILLER, RICHARD. *Pain: Why It Hurts, Where It Hurts, When It Hurts.* Nashville: Thomas Nelson, 1975. Though this is about pain in general, it sheds much light on the pain and pleasure of running.

SUBOTNICK, STEVEN I. "The Abuses of Orthotics in Sports Medicine." *P&SM,* July 1975.

———. "Orthotic Foot Control and the Overuse Syndrome." *P&SM,* January 1975.

SUINN, RICHARD M. "Psychology for Olympic Champs." *Psychology Today,* July 1976.

TALAMINI, JOHN T., and PAGE, CHARLES H., eds. *Sport and Society.* Boston: Little, Brown, 1973. A deftly orchestrated anthology on what sport does to us and we to it. The authors, a richly varied field, include Veblen, Mumford, Bannister and John F. Kennedy.

TAYLOR, H. L., *et al.* "Exercise in Controlled Trials of the Prevention of Coronary Heart Disease." *Federation Proceedings,* May 1973.

THOMAS, JOHN. "What Makes Eugene Run?" *P&SM,* October 1976. A report on Eugene, Oregon, the running capital of the U.S.

THOMAS, VAUGHAN. *Science and Sport: How to Measure and Improve Athletic Performance.* Boston: Little, Brown, 1970. A primer on the physiology of sport, with a lucid description of what happens to the body when it's working hard.

TOSSETTI, JO ANN. "Tips on Dealing with Lightning on the Links." *P&SM,* May 1976.

———. "U.S. Children's Fitness Unchanged in Decade." *P&SM,* June 1976.

TUTKO, THOMAS. "Trying Is the Only Thing." *RW,* May 1976.

______, and TOSI, UMBERTO. *Sports Psyching: Playing Your Best Game All of the Time.* Los Angeles: J. P. Tarcher, 1976. Tutko is as wily a gamesman as exists today. "Recall the best day you ever had," he and Tosi write, "the day you were 'hot,' the day your moves were flawless. . . . That's the day we're going to try to give back to you—again and again."

TYMM, MICHAEL. "Marathons and Manhood." *RW,* April 1976. They were, says the author, the ultimate virility test—until women came along to show that they are something else altogether.

ULLYOT, JOAN. *Women's Running.* Mountain View, Calif.: World Publications, 1976. A runner-physician's appealing introduction to the sport.

VAN AAKEN, ERNST. *The Van Aaken Method.* Mountain View, Calif.: World Publications, 1976. The training methods of one of the most influential coaches of our time.

VAN METER, DALE L. "In Defense of Jogging." Letter to the *Boston Sunday Globe,* August 29, 1976.

VEBLEN, THORSTEIN. *The Theory of the Leisure Class.* New York: New American Library, 1953. See, in particular, his chapter "Modern Survivals of Prowess."

WALLACE, STEPHEN. " 'Marathon Man' Alive in Melrose." *Boston Herald American,* November 28, 1976. A deftly written interview with Bill Rodgers.

WATT, EDWARD W., and GAHAGAN, H. E. "Coronary Risks for College Athletes."*P&SM,* February 1974.

______; PLOTNICKI, B. A.; and BUSKIRK, ELSWORTH R. "The Physiology of Single and Multiple Daily Training Programs." *Track Technique* 49, 1972.

WATTS, BARRIE. "World's Fastest Miler Says: My Psychic Powers Help Me to Win." *The Star,* August 31, 1976.

WATTS, DENNIS; WILSON, HARRY; and HORWILL, FRANK. *The Complete Middle Distance Runner.* London: Stanley Paul, 1972; revised edition, 1974. A wealth of training tips.

WEBSTER, BAYARD. "Running Is Debated as Benefit to Heart." *New York Times,* October 28, 1976.

WEISS, PAUL. *Sport: A Philosophic Inquiry.* Carbondale, Ill.: Southern Illinois University Press, 1969. A searching and provocative work.

WESTERMAN, RICHARD L., and MARTIN, CHARLES. "The Case Against Fluid Restrictions." *P&SM,* July 1974.

Westport News, editors of. "Local MD to Research Effects of TM on Area Long Distance Runners." *Westport* [Connecticut] *News,* December 4, 1974.

WHITE, JAMES R., and HUNT, HOWARD F. "When Doctors Test Themselves, the Prescription Is Exercise."*P&SM,* December 1975.

WHITE, PAUL D., and CURRENS, JAMES H. "Half a Century of Running." *New England Journal of Medicine,* November 16, 1961. Report on the autopsy of Clarence DeMar, who ran competitively from 1909 to 1957.

WHITNEY, CRAIG R. "Sports Medicine Shares in East German Success." *New York Times,* December 22, 1976.

WILL, GEORGE F. "Run for Your Life." *Newsweek,* April 19, 1976.

WILLIAMS, MARK. "Fighting Chondromalacia." *RW*, October 1976.

WILLIAMS, MELVIN H. "Blood Doping—Does It Really Help Athletes?" *P&SM*, January 1975.

WILMORE, JACK H. "Exploding the Myth of Female Inferiority." *P&SM*, May 1974.

———. "Adolescence: Training to Fit the Sport." *P&SM*, June 1974.

WILT, FRED. *How They Train*. Los Altos, Calif.: *Track and Field News*, 1959. The detailed workout schedules of 175 top runners.

WOLFSON, MARTY, and WEISBERG, DEBBIE. *The Athlete's Cookbook*. New York: Stadia Sports, 1975. What to eat and to avoid to perform at your best.

WOOD, PETER D. "Bos(huff)ton (puff) or (sigh) Bust." *New York Times*, April 21, 1975. A moving look at the greatest race of them all by a professor of medicine who is also an accomplished marathoner.

———. "Concentrations of Plasma Lipids and Lipoproteins in Male and Female Long-Distance Runners." Paper presented at the International Congress of Physical Activity Sciences, Quebec, 1976.

———. "Recent Physiological Studies of Male and Female Long-Distance Runners." Undated paper.

———, *et al.* "Effects of Physical Activity on Weight Reduction in Obese Middle-aged Women." *American Journal of Clinical Nutrition*, February 1976.

———, *et al.* "Prediction of Body Composition in Habitually Active Middle-aged Men." *Journal of Applied Physiology*, August 1975.

WOODSON, DORSEY. "Exercise for the Elderly the European Way." *P&SM*, February 1976.

———. "Jogging: An American Export." *P&SM*, April 1975.

WYNDHAM, CYRIL H. "The Physiology of Exercise Under Heat Stress." *Annual Review of Physiology*, 1973. A comprehensive report by a leading authority on physical activity in hot weather.

YALE, JEFFREY F. "Achilles Tendon Problems." Letter to *P&SM*, June 1976.

YOHALEM, STEPHEN B. "False Security." Letter to *New York Times Magazine*, August 15, 1976. A physician's criticism of annual physicals.

YOUNG, KEN. "The Best of Times." *RW*, May 1976.

YUDKIN, JOHN. *Sweet and Dangerous*. New York: Bantam, 1973. A professor of nutrition and dietetics at the University of London argues that refined sugar is responsible for numerous bodily ills.

ZEITLIN, MARILYN. "Meet Cindy Bremser, Madison's Running Nurse." *P&SM*, July 1976.

ZOHAR, JOSEPH. "Preventive Maintenance for Athletes." *P&SM*, January 1975.

ZOHMAN, LENORE R. *Exercise Your Way to Fitness and Heart Health*. Englewood Cliffs, N.J.: CPC International, 1974.

ZOLLER, GREGORY W. "Hazards in School Sports." *P&SM*, September 1973.

ZUTI, W. B., and GOLDING, L. A. "Comparing Diet and Exercise as Weight Reduction Tools." *P&SM*, January 1976.

Index

About the Author

When he started running several years ago, JIM FIXX weighed nearly 220 pounds and breathed hard just thinking about exercise. Today, at 159 pounds, he has been declared medically fitter than most college athletes, has competed in—and finished—six Boston Marathons, won the Connecticut 10,000-meter championship in his age category and run the equivalent of once around the equator.

A New Yorker and a graduate of Oberlin College, Fixx is a former managing editor of *Horizon,* senior editor of *Life,* and editor of *McCall's*. He now writes books—this is his third—and works as a freelance magazine editor. He is married, has four children, and lives in Riverside, Connecticut, where he runs ten miles every day.